SO MANY WORLDS

So Many Worlds

by

PATRICIA MADDOCKS

Patricia M.
December 2004

The Memoir Club

© Patricia Maddocks 2004

First published in 2004 by
The Memoir Club
Stanhope Old Hall
Stanhope
Weardale
County Durham

British Library Cataloguing in
Publication Data.
A catalogue record for this book
is available from the
British Library.

ISBN: 1 84104 113 0

Typeset by George Wishart & Associates, Whitley Bay.
Printed by CPI Bath.

*Dedicated to 'Satan' himself and to our
beloved children William and Julia*

Contents

Contents

Illustrations

Foreword

by
Anthony Kirk-Greene CMG MBE
Emeritus Fellow, St Antony's College Oxford

IF, AS Ralph Waldo Emerson once assured us, 'there is properly no history, only biography', surely autobiography too, especially when it is as informative as Patricia Maddocks' *So Many Worlds*, can lay claim to the same categorisation. This is all the more so when, as in this case, the narrative offers to post-colonial historians of the Commonwealth the opportunity to learn more about and to understand more intimately the expatriate experience of those who lived and worked in countries during the final decade or two before their independence.

Although *So Many Worlds* is essentially wide-screen autobiography, full of family and friends, it can also be read – especially in Chapters 3 and 4, the longest (over one third of the book) and in many ways the most valuable of them all – as a notable contribution to the relatively new genre of focused Colonial Service memoir. Out of the 500 or so Colonial Service memoirs appearing in the century since 1900, only seventy were published in the whole of the first sixty years. In the 1980s this figure rose to 100 new titles, and in the 1990s by a further 200 in that decade alone. Yet if the emergence of the Colonial Service memoir has become a conspicuous feature of autobiographical writing since c.1980, it has nevertheless remained primarily a male activity. Now and again in reading some of the memoirs, one begins to wonder whether colonial officials were ever allowed to have their wives with them! What has been far slower to emerge is the writing of memoirs by women who lived overseas, whether as wives of civil servants or as government officials in their own right – female educationists, nurses, doctors, legal assistants, even the occasional Woman Administrative Officer, and the popular post-war Secretariat phenomenon of PAs. *So Many Worlds* is a most welcome and major strengthening of the long-missing complementary autobiographical literature by the womenfolk of Her Majesty's Overseas Civil Service. At the same time, such is its sweep, with just twenty years of colonial experience out of the more than eighty years of an active and hugely travelled life described in detail, that it goes well beyond the typical career description, widening from focused memoir to all-inclusive autobiography.

Born just after the end of the Great War, Patricia Hare Duke cannot be said to have had a comfortable childhood – 'I never knew', she admits, 'what it was like to have enough money.' Her father went bankrupt and left for India when she was still a baby. For years her mother could not find even the £32 for the sea passage to India: strict economy had to be observed, notably, it seems, in the children's school fees. Despite taking rooms in Eastbourne, sensed by Patricia to be 'the cheapest form of rentable accommodation', the children somehow managed to live the sort of life their mother expected them to live. Above all, this was a nanny's world, in a way and intensity unknown after 1939. At Eastbourne, it was nanny and the sea that dominated their lives. Today medical scientists might attribute Patricia's subsequent pronounced wanderlust to her genes, with a mother and grandfather born and brought up in Persia in a Sicilian family resident in Malta.

India was the first of Patricia's many worlds – and what a start it was for any child brought up in rented accommodation in inter-war England, now with the average household counting at least ten servants. When her mother, who had eventually raised the fare to sail to join her husband in India, came home on leave, she took her children back with her. But before long the perennial problem of education raised its head. The answer was, to fourteen-year old Patricia's chagrin, a convent in Belgium. Worse was to come, for on a subsequent home leave her mother decided, at the very last moment, not to take Patricia, now 17, back to India with her. Her argument was that if she did, Patricia was bound promptly to get married in India. So, as Patricia tells it some seventy years later, her mother 'blithely asked a few people to "keep an eye" on me, and departed.' Patricia was now virtually on her own. The chapter on London in the war years constitutes a vivid replay of nostalgic history, with descriptions of rationing, queuing, the Blitz and fire-watching. Mother proved to be right – but on the wrong continent, for in 1943 Patricia married a young doctor in England. It lasted three years, ending in a divorce.

In claiming that Chapters 3 and 4, on her years spent in Africa, are outstanding and the most valuable part of the autobiography, I accept that my assessment may well be swayed by my own historian's interest in the men and women of Her Majesty's Overseas Civil Service (HMOCS). Patricia, single once again, accepted what turned out to be virtually a non-job in Lagos, to put into order a chaotic private library bequeathed to the Government by a Nigerian doctor. Enterprisingly, to equip herself for life in Lagos she enrolled in a Yoruba language course at the School of Oriental and African Studies (SOAS) in London. Soon after reaching Nigeria in 1946 she met an up-and-coming colonial administrator in the Secretariat, George Mooring, affectionately known throughout the Service as 'Satan'. They were married in 1947 and Patricia was quickly inducted into the art and anguishes of now being a 'colonial wife'. Six house moves in Lagos within twice that number of months; the adamant but in no way unusual refusal of Satan's houseboy (his batman during the war) 'to work for a missis'; and, of course, no longer having a paid job of her own. No wonder she felt she was 'a real townee among people who had lived tough lives in the bush'. Satan was transferred on promotion to headquarters in Ibadan, in the Western Region, where he later became deputy Governor. Patricia soon became fully involved in Red Cross work, and she describes at length her work as the Director of Red Cross in Western Nigeria. Shades of her own childhood returned when, with children now to care for, she found, like so many colonial wives, that for their sake she needed to spend longer in England rather than go back with Satan at the end of their leave. Yet of one thing she was now certain: at last she had found her own niche in life.

If her chapter on her fourteen years in Nigeria is excellent, her account of being Satan's wife when he was promoted British Resident, Zanzibar (a gubernatorial post) in 1960 is one of the best wives' vignettes of Government House life, responsibilities as well as relaxations, I have yet read and will rank as an extremely valuable source for colonial historians. It also shows how she managed to find time to develop her own interests, for instance her enviable personal relations with the royal Sultanas; her curiosity in the islands' old buildings, especially the mosques; her enthusiasm for collecting sea shells and building up an almost complete collection of the shells of Zanzibar, all found by herself and her daughter and none ever bought; and, need I say it, organizing a working Red Cross committee.

The Moorings retired just a month before the brutal Zanzibar revolution and settled in Suffolk. Following the death of Satan in 1969 (he had been unwell for a number of years, though still actively working), Patricia was ready to respond to the idea that she became a Red Cross Field Officer – an inspired suggestion, given her qualifications of such wide experience and a passion for travel. She spent 1971-72 in Mauritius, with a brief to separate the Red Cross there from the British Red Cross and effect its membership of the International Red Cross. Next she was sent to the Western Pacific (very much, as she found, another world), where she worked as a Field Officer in the Solomon Islands, the New Hebrides and the Gilbert and Ellice Islands. It was not until 1975 that she returned to England – typically, great traveller that she was, by bus from Katmandu to London. The journey took three months. Readers who rejoice in her meticulous 'naming of names' throughout her African chapters will miss this feature in her account of her five years of Red Cross work in the Indian and Pacific Oceans.

Back home in 1975, this time for good – apart, of course, from frequent holidays abroad! – Patricia Mooring settled in Aldeburgh. Her final chapter tells of her deep involvement (far from unexpected by the reader by now) in local affairs, including the Festival at several levels and later the Carnival. It was during this time that she met Sir Kenneth Maddocks, the retired Governor of Fiji, an old friend of Satan's from their days together in the Northern Provinces of Nigeria before the war and subsequently both as regional deputy Governors. 'Our lives', she reckoned, 'had been so similar, and we knew so many of the same people, that it was not difficult to conclude that we should go on together.' They married in 1980 and had over twenty happy years together before 'KP', as he was always known in the Nigerian Service, died in 2001.

In my interpretation of this highly attractive autobiography, Patricia Maddocks displays the rare quality of offering to her readers as much pleasure and satisfaction as she clearly derived herself from the recalling and recording of all her remarkable experiences in a score of countries across the world. *So Many Worlds* is at once a delight to read and a memoir to treasure.

CHAPTER 1

The Sickening Child
1918-1936

England

WHEN I WAS growing up my mother, who was always the life and soul of any gathering, to enliven an evening would produce a book which purported to tell you your character from the answers you gave to a set of questions, one of which was: 'Did you have a happy childhood?' Both my older sister Pam and I said no. Understandably our parent was astonished and upset, for she had done all she could think of to make us happy.

However, had I been asked while still a child whether I was having a happy time, the answer, if elicited at all, might not have been the same. Children seem to accept what is handed out to them as they do not compare themselves with anyone else. I enjoyed a lot of things, suffered others as a matter of course and reacted against anything I considered unfair with so much earnestness that I was known as the Sickening Child. In fact, I was a member of a loving family so probably came to no harm.

I was born, Patricia Josephine Hare Duke, a month after World War I ended, so was not subject to the privations other children suffered during the war. My father, Algernon, went bankrupt very shortly afterwards, so I never knew what it was like to have enough money, like the older members of the family had known. Algy and his very beautiful (and rather spoiled) wife Irma had had a trying war. They already had a son, Basil, and a daughter, Pam, born in 1908 and 1912 respectively, and Pam had suffered from rickets and had to have irons on her legs for a time. In 1916 they had another daughter, Ann, who shortly before my birth developed a brain tumour which was removed via an eye, leaving her with only one eye and an impaired brain. She was to be my constant companion until I was nearly fifteen. We had a nanny, who turned out to be the root of most of my troubles, who devoted herself to Ann from the time of the operation.

Algy had been experimenting with and producing margarine during the war, but then he went bankrupt. With his newly acquired knowledge of oils, he managed after several false starts to get a job in the United Provinces (now Uttar Pradesh) of India as Deputy Director of Industries, where he went when I was three, so I hardly knew him. He was a big Irishman, one of five handsome sons and two daughters of a Protestant canon in County Down. He

Canon John Hare Duke, DD, 1815-1900, my paternal grandfather.

was the only brother not to have gone to university: his extremely erudite father reckoned it would be a waste of money. He was a very good athlete and had such a well-made body that Sandow, the body-builder, took photographs of him for advertisements.

He became a stockbroker, and used to take part in their annual London to Brighton walk, toe and heel. One year, when he was the favourite, he was poisoned with croton oil by somebody else's trainer, and was left halfway, writhing in the gutter. The other competitors were so enraged that they clubbed together and gave him a huge silver urn as compensation, bigger than anything he ever won. He had a typical Irish sense of humour and fun, and was good at impersonations. He must have had to work very hard in the end to keep an extravagant wife, four children and a nanny in another country, so he paid dearly for his early insouciance.

My mother, Irma Stagno Navarra, was the most vivid and attractive character, for all her faults. She was born in Persia, where her father, who had also been born there, was in the Telegraph Company; his father was of a noble Sicilian family domiciled in Malta, who had been medical officer in the Shah's

Algernon Hare Duke, 1883-1938, my father.

army and to the Shah himself, and had married a Welsh girl in Malta. Two of their children married English, but William, my mother's father, married a Hungarian girl whose father was a general in the Shah's army. She died young after bearing six children, three boys and my mother surviving.

At eight, therefore, Irma was deprived of her mother; her older brothers were at school in Europe; within two years her father had collected everything together, made the harsh caravan journey from Teheran to the Black Sea with Irma, and settled himself as British vice-consul in Palermo; he then took Irma to England to be brought up by friends in the British way which was so important to him, to his father, and to his Welsh grandmother. It was the thing to be in the nineteenth century, if you had the slightest claim: British!

Irma's parents had spoken French as their common language and Irma arrived in England able to say in English 'You are very kind!' and nothing else. She was sent to Sutton High School and set herself to become more English than the English, with some success. A few years later when somebody told her she was the perfect English rose, she blushed not only from modesty but from achievement. All the same, French idioms littered her conversation and

Irma Hare Duke (née Stagno Navarra), 1888-1951,
my mother, with Basil, Pam, Ann and me, 1921.

she was a hopeless speller. Her guardians were William Timberlake and his sister, but the sister soon died, and Uncle Tim, as she called him, brought her up alone. Inevitably, the spoiling she had doubtless had as the only girl left in the family was continued by him, for she was the darling of his heart; but she grew up into such a beautiful girl, with such character and charm, with wickedness and humour, that most people seem to have loved her and spoiled her too. Her father had a large family of English cousins nearby, nine brothers and sisters, the children of his aunt Nina Zohrab and of General Percy Lee Holmes. Irma saw a great deal of them and they meant more to her in fact (though not in theory) than her own family whom she very seldom saw. Through these cousins she met Algy.

At the time that I was born, my brother Basil was eleven, a writer of poetry and stories, a dreamer of dreams, a useful rugger forward, and a good mixer with all classes of people. Pam was nearly seven, out of her irons, and resigned to the new baby, though when Ann had arrived she had wanted to throw her out of the window. Ann was still wearing a black patch over one eye; she had

General Johann von Nemiro, 1813-1868, my maternal great-grandfather.

altogether ceased to sing, which was sad as she had been wonderfully good at tunes even at eighteen months. Soon after my arrival she was fitted with her first glass eye, and the secrecy surrounding its removal and washing was always a part of my life, like going to the lavatory. When my son was five and we had a one-eyed friend of his to stay, I noticed the boy handling a bottle of Optrex in the bathroom, so I tactfully extracted William, telling him outside that we should allow Brian to be alone because he had to remove and wash his glass eye.

'I know!' exclaimed an exasperated William. 'He's going to show me!'

What a much healthier attitude than the one I was brought up in!

In spite of my being yet another mouth to feed (and not a male one as they had hoped) I was very welcome. I was fat and healthy and happy and my mother had great hopes that at last she might have produced a daughter who would be as lovely as herself. This hope died hard and even when I was grown up she seemed to be expecting that something would happen soon and I would shed my chrysalis and emerge.

It was Nanny's world, however, in which I lived. Nanny saw me as a threat

Basil Hare Duke, 1908-1982, my brother.

to Ann's position in the centre of the stage. She refused to look after me at first, and for some months, in spite of the state of the finances, another nurse was employed for me. Then it became impossible; almost all the servants were dismissed; only Nanny and the cook were retained. The cook was Old Florence, a sinister person who also had one eye but made no bones about it and did not even have a patch.

When I was three and my father went to India, Irma let 'The Dell', Uncle Tim's house which had been left to her, and we all moved to Eastbourne into 'rooms'. This was the cheapest form of respectable accommodation and highly unsatisfactory, as one was living in somebody else's house and sharing essentials like the bathroom; the landlady did the cooking. Life was very difficult and we often moved. In one place I met running hot water for the first time, and used to shut myself in to the downstairs cloakroom and soak my freezing hands in hot water till they were scarlet. I remember the iciness of the sheets if one dared to stretch a foot out to the end of one's bed, the pattern on the ceiling of the cut-out top of the oil stove left in the room when we were put to bed, and the wall gas lamps which had to be lit at dusk each day.

I caught chickenpox at this time and the landlady would not have me in the house, so I was sent to a sanitorium. It did not worry me being away from home but I was excessively embarrassed at being bathed by a very pretty nurse. Nanny's early teaching may have been responsible for my coyness, though I was surprised some thirty years later to find my four-year-old son instructing his little sister how to remove her knickers from under her dress on the beach, and then to draw on her bathing pants before removing her dress – certainly they had had no prudish training from me, and were used to seeing their parents nude at home. Another evidence of this prudishness was displayed by me at the age of about three when I was being photographed in a studio, and I absolutely refused to remove my woollen combinations; in the end they were pulled down below my shoulders, which were then smothered in tulle. It would be interesting to know whether this is a natural instinct or not.

In another of these boarding houses I saw a gnome. I really did. Nanny must have said that if we picked out noses a gnome would come and cut them off, because when one night our bedroom door opened to admit one, in full uniform of green with pointed hat and shoes, I knew exactly why he had come, and dived under the bedclothes. Luckily he seemed content only to remove Ann's nose, I thought, as the time went by and I was undisturbed. In the morning I was glad to find that he had not taken hers after all. So that was one lesson Nanny got across.

In that same boarding house I saw Pam cry, which I had never seen before. She was a good pianist and was proud of her success at examinations. One day I found her certificates in the wrong place and in all innocence, used them for scribbling on. When it was discovered, for once Nanny took my part and said that Pam should not have left them lying about. I can remember wishing I knew why it mattered but knowing it was something awful I had done because of Pam's anguish, and wishing I could undo the damage, but saying nothing in case the wrath should turn on me.

When I was six we returned briefly to 'The Dell', while Irma reluctantly put it on the market. She was for ever hoping to join Algy in India but never had the required £32 for her sea passage. Economies had to be effected, her main one seeming to have been on school fees. Basil was taken away from several schools because she could not manage the fees, and at one time went to Rockport in Northern Ireland, a school run by our father's sister's husband, Geoffrey Bing, Senior, no doubt without fees at all. After St Columba's public school near Dublin he did not go to university, as in those days one had to pay. When she sold 'The Dell' she felt temporarily well off but it did not last long and she did not immediately set off for India.

My memories of the house, though early, are very clear. The drawing room was out of bounds to me except when I went to be shown off to visitors. In the dining room at the back Basil used to choke down his breakfast, late again, before dashing down the garden path to catch a train for his London job with British Petroleum, leaving his spoon and eggcup by the gate for me to collect. The doorway to the kitchen, where Old Florence sometimes used to appear, was up two steps and hidden by a thick curtain. I remember especially the night nursery, where Ann and I slept with Nanny, she and I with rags knotted into our hair (what agony!) but Ann's hair was so curly she did not need them, and where Basil one night appeared climbing through the window, having been shut out, and was discovered by Nanny crouching by our door trying to find the key to let himself into the rest of the house. The day nursery was beyond our parents' room, where we did lessons, and Pam's and Basil's rooms were down a long passage past the bathroom; this had a large iron bath with legs, and the lavatory next door was one of those with a wall-to-wall wooden seat and a pull-up plug fitted into it.

The house was called 'The Dell' because it had one, with a tennis court in it, and three sides of the high bank all round were covered with trees and bushes with a secret path running through. The fourth bank was a rockery with a path winding up it. In front of the house was a lawn with a tall oak and a mulberry tree overlooking the tennis court, and on the drive alongside it Ann and I learned to ride bicycles. Years later I visited the house. It was then a Kodak processing establishment and the garden had been sold off and dotted with little houses.

When 'The Dell' sold, we returned to Eastbourne and Irma took rather a grand flat in one of the best roads in the town, Devonshire Place, leading from the bandstand on the front to the cenotaph. She also bought (or rented) a shop with her cousin Bertha, who was divorced and had a small daughter about my age, and they made dresses and hats and employed a small staff. Thus we saw very little of Irma. When she was not in the shop, she was shopping or going to tea dances or the cinema, and certainly had various interested beaux. On Sundays we used sometimes to have to parade with her on the lawns outside the Grand Hotel after church. I did not enjoy this, particularly as my plaits would be undone and my hair brushed out, and I was terrified of anyone from school seeing me thus, got up in my best.

In spite of the lack of money, we lived the sort of life my mother expected us to live. She did not raise the money for her fare to India for years, but we went to dancing classes in the ballroom of the Grand Hotel, dressed in whatever the teacher, Miss Ratcliffe, decreed, and wrapped in expensive gossamer Shetland shawls, carrying our dancing shoes and skipping ropes (for very fancy skipping) in little cloth bags. We were sent to the snob Dame School, Miss Cleather's, by the Town Hall, where all the 'best' people sent their boys and girls for a year or two. Here on Mondays we recited the collect we had had to learn on Sunday; we stood in rows to answer questions and if we got the answer right we went to the top of the row, if wrong to the bottom; we copied elaborate 'wrought iron' designs for drawing lessons. I was made very unhappy here by being accused of hiding books. There could have been no evidence against me as I did not do it, but because I would not confess, my desk was turned to the wall for the rest of that term and nobody was allowed to speak to me. During the holidays Nanny found out from another nanny that it was her charge, one Betty Hall, who had done it and at the beginning of the next term Miss Cleather had me and Betty into her room:

'Betty has something to tell you,' she said, and Betty did just that, without apology, 'and wasn't it a joke that everyone had thought it was you?' I had not expected an apology, but when Betty died the following year I felt that justice had been done.

My life was dominated by Nanny until I was twelve. She was the daughter of a gardener and a washerwoman and had eleven siblings; her name was Mabel Blanche Turner. She came to us as a housemaid at the same age as Irma, nineteen, (when we found out they were the same age, Irma forbade Nanny to say what that was) and when Basil was born she became under-nurse. She was so competent that she soon became the only nurse, assisted by a monthly nurse whenever a new baby arrived. When bankruptcy hit us, and all the servants had to be dismissed, Nanny would not go; she said she could do without her wages until my father got himself established. She just would not leave Ann, to whom she was devoted.

She was a remarkable woman and in the bad times not only ran the nursery but the whole household. She did the cleaning, the washing, the mending, at least half the cooking, knitted and sewed us clothes of all kinds, and she taught us. What Ann learned, she learned from her, as she was not quick enough to pick up much at the schools to which we were sent. Ann went to school with me for the first time when she was eleven, by which time she could read and write and do simple arithmetic, knew a great deal of history and more geography than most young people learn today, amongst many other things that Nanny saw fit to impart. Nanny herself had gone to the State 'board school' until she was fourteen. She had me reading by the time I was three, which got me out of the way satisfactorily while she concentrated on Ann. There was much exclaiming when I was found reading Lamb's *Tales from Shakespeare* at the age of six, and I clearly remember bursting into my mother's bedroom soon after dawn to enquire whether she could spell Nebuchadnezzar backwards (which I had been practising half the night). I had a shiny black notebook in which every day Nanny wrote a column of words in her bold round writing which I had to learn to spell, with the result that I have never had any trouble with spelling. We did copy-writing every day, that is, trying to reproduce exactly a line of writing printed in a copybook; there were three of these books, each depicting different styles: script, bold and copperplate, and one had to reproduce each line three times.

Nanny was so anxious to give Ann a good chance in life that she failed to notice that she was not being fair to me. Irma did notice but she could not contemplate life without Nanny, so that, although they often had rows over me, she never took it too far; instead Irma spoiled me, which made matters worse. The only contributions that she made to my education that I can remember were about behaviour: when one was shouting, the admonition 'Pretty voice! Pretty voice!' would be heard, and she used to say 'Touch everything once,' which enigmatic saying had come to her from her own mother (in what language I cannot imagine), meaning 'Don't just put it down, put it away in its proper place.' Once and only once I was beaten by her with a cane and I can understand now how her patience was exhausted. During a family meal I transgressed in some way and was ordered to leave the room. This I did, slapping each member of the family with my napkin as I circled the round table. I was pursued...

Ann had been there since I began, but by the time I was three it was clear to even a casual observer that I was normal and she was not. It is hard to say what was wrong but I came to think it was an incapacity for original thought, coupled with slowness, caused by brain damage. Fortunately she had an excellent memory. She responded well to Nanny's care and teaching and to my (normal) companionship, and even learned to ride a bicycle and to dive, which we felt was the ultimate! It was difficult to play improvised games with her, and card games that needed skill were out, though she was good at Pelmanism because of her memory. She took an extraordinary interest in cricket, extraordinary because nobody else in the family did. She loved music but only sang in church, when she could not keep up. I was unable to accept any invitation that did not include Ann, and friendships were difficult as I had to look after her so much, pair off with her on school walks and so on. She was always a very cheerful, sweet character which made it easier, and in any case I just accepted the situation without questioning. I was made responsible for her which used to annoy me sometimes as I knew she was not as helpless as they seemed to think, and she certainly played on their indulgence. I was incensed, for instance, when Nanny, having heard our affirmations that yes, we had cleaned our teeth, felt only my brush and not Ann's. She did not seem to realise that Ann was capable of lying too! One result of this turbulent upbringing was my being a persistent bed-wetter until I went to boarding school for a term at the age of nine. I can remember half-waking with an urge, getting out of bed, getting the pot from underneath and sitting on it, only to be completely woken by the awful hot wet feeling in the bed and the realisation that I had been dreaming. Boarding school cured me. I was also an inveterate thumb-sucker and even caught myself at it after I was married.

The most joyful time was when we acquired a fox terrier called Jane; I appropriated her for my own and she was my first real friend. We had a tabby cat later called Simon, who came for walks with us on the Downs; Nanny would carry him in a covered basket and let him loose when we left the roads, and if we took a picnic there would be a herring for him. They cost a penny each. The deaths and loss of both these are shrouded in my mind as they were probably kept from me at the time, but their successors, Percy, a near-Yorkshire and mine, and Sally, a rather stupid wirehaired fox terrier (Ann's), had to be given away when we all went to India, and that worried me dreadfully. Animals came to mean a great deal to me, and I studied the way their minds seemed to work, and often felt I preferred them to people. I have nearly always had an animal living with me since Jane came into my life.

The sea was very much a part of our lives and I loved it. In winter we walked beside it and knew its moods and found the things it threw up on the beach. In summer we learned to swim in it. I do not know how, as Nanny did not swim, but everyone else in the family did and Pam was very good. We spent a lot of time on the beach, Nanny somehow making herself comfortable and reading or knitting, and I improvising games for Ann and me; 'shops' was popular behind the cross beams of the high breakwaters, 'selling' stones of different colours labelled potatoes, or whatever they most looked like, or seaweed as laces and shells as buttons. We paddled with our dresses tucked inside our knickers, and shrimped, though I did not enjoy this much. We helped young men build mounds of stones from the top of which they preached rousing sermons; we looked for tracts, mostly religious, stuffed into drainage holes in the promenade wall. Once I fell off the totally unguarded edge of the Bricks, as the promenade was called, and was picked up unconscious. How many times had I been told not to go near the edge (as well as 'Mind where you are walking' and 'Pick up your feet')? I came round and walked home but was concussed and spent two days I knew nothing about. Swimming was the best part of the sea, though, and I loved diving through the breakers and riding about on their backs.

We bowled hoops, and on Saturdays had a sixpenny ride on the ponies on the front, which is the way I learned to ride. My pony was a grey called Beauty and her groom was known to us as the Beauty Man; Ann's pony unfortunately was called Monkey…In the spring we would go to the bluebell woods at Polegate by train, taking a picnic and sometimes accompanied by the cousins Diana and Penelope, daughters of two of the Holmes cousins; we would return laden with primroses and bluebells. In the autumn we went black-berrying.

Pam Turral (later Drake-Brockman), (1912-1996), my sister.

Every day we went for walks and Nanny patiently bore with my reading aloud every house name and every street name and every notice. She taught us the names of flowers in the gardens and on the hillsides and of many of the trees we saw. Some of her regular injunctions stick in my mind: 'Don't touch the banisters', 'No, you can't play on those swings, you don't know who's been on them!', 'Don't drag your hand along those railings' and even running one's hoop stick along them was not allowed – such a pity as it made a highly satisfactory noise, but it was 'common'. She taught us how to go up to people sitting on benches and very politely ask them the time; she never owned a watch. In the long winter evenings she would play card games with us, teach us to sew and knit, and play the gramophone for us to interpret the music into dance. Every year I was chosen among many others from our dancing class to dance in a charity show at Devonshire Park; the first one was distinguished by me as a fairy dancing off the stage altogether at the wrong time. The dresses were most elaborate and beautiful and I enjoyed this immensely.

Ann and I were usually dressed alike and beautifully dressed at that. We had covert coats (grown-ups had these short, light overcoats used for shooting and

Ann Hare Duke, 1916-1988, my sister.

riding) and leggings with buttons up the side which had to be done up with a buttonhook which often caught one's leg as well; we also had knitted leggings which were much easier and were for everyday wear. In summer we had straw hats with flowers round the crown. Our underclothes were ghastly: combinations which I loathed, with their vent that went through from front to back, very difficult not to soil when going to the lavatory so they became stained and repulsive, and if they were not folded over the behind properly one looked a real podge. One supposes they were invented in the early nineteenth century when knickers themselves began that shape, but I always thought them a disgusting idea. We wore knickers on top with elastic at waist and knee, made of thick cotton – socks left one's legs bare. We also wore liberty bodices for extra warmth and later on suspenders could be fixed to them for holding up stockings. They were rather like a boneless corset, with reinforced strips, sleeveless and coming down below the waist, buttoning up the front; they flattened an emerging bosom nicely but luckily for us we had a modern mother who put us into bust bodices (brassières, or bras, as they became known). Nanny's endless knitting provided us with tam o'shanters and Fair

Isle jerseys and gloves. Sometimes I inherited a garment of Pam's, which I longed to do. I particularly remember a fawn knitted dress I felt was like a monk's tunic, with a cord girdle, and I watched over it longingly while Pam had it, hoping she would not spoil it.

Pam, meanwhile, was having her 'unhappy childhood'. She was too fat, which was her greatest burden, I imagine, because Irma never hesitated to criticise her children and we all knew where we failed to come up to her expectations. She wanted at least one of us to be beautiful but we just could not manage it. I, too, was sturdily built, though after babyhood was not fat. She continued to hope that my legs were not as big as Pam's (which they were) and was always saying hopefully that she thought I took after herself, which must have dashed Pam considerably. I never forgot Pam telling me I was pyramid-shaped, with a pointed head, big hips, huge legs, and enormous feet! No doubt it made her feel better but it left a lasting scar on me. Being so much older than Ann and me, she inevitably had to take some responsibility for us and we were a great trial to her. She was intelligent and had an excellent sense of humour, and a lot of her good remarks stay with me.

Pam went away to boarding school in Seaford but at fifteen Irma decided to take her away because of lack of funds; the headmistress was horrified. Pam was in line to be head girl in this, her last, year and was doing well in the scholastic field. She offered to keep Pam without fees, providing she helped with the little ones, and she would have to share being head girl. This my happy-go-lucky mama agreed to, but when it came to School Certificate time, she said she did not believe in examinations for girls and did not allow Pam to sit for it. Poor Pam, and her last term was made ghastly by the arrival of one of our third cousins, Penelope (a very naughty one), and me, in the hope it would cure me of wetting my bed – it did and I was taken away at the end of the term. It was a fruitful term because I was introduced to Latin, and although I never again studied it, it gave me an idea of its influence on other languages and enabled me to understand a good bit of the Latin I came across in future. At sixteen Pam went to look after two cousins, and then after four little brothers who lived near Eastbourne.

Anna Stahlnacke came into the family when I was ten and became a great friend of Pam's. She was a Swede and came as a paying guest to practise her English, together with another Swede. Irma was trying hard to save up to go to India and managed it the following year, so this had helped with her passage and her 'trousseau'. Anna asked if she could travel and stay with Irma, as she had plenty of money but in those days a young woman found it difficult to travel alone. This was arranged and Anna stayed with my parents until she married a charming young policeman, Douglas Tidy, of a very good family, and utterly unsuited to her. I loved Douglas like a brother; he was a simple friendly person but probably never grew up enough for Anna. In any case the marriage foundered after a few years, but the links between his family, ours and Anna's were only ended by death.

It was 1929 when Irma managed to get to India. Basil had long flown the nest and was in Samoa, and now Pam was away in Hampshire looking after the cousins, and Nanny could well cope with the two little ones. We were sent to another school, Rippingale, as day girls, and life went on much as before. We probably did not miss Irma very much.

We were living in this rather grand flat in Devonshire Place, on the top floor. One day, Nanny locked me in my attic bedroom for some misdemeanour, and I climbed out of the dormer window, slid down the roof to the gutter, along which I edged till I got to an iron plank over the area round which the flats were built. I was thus able to get across into the flat opposite, where a bemused French maid let me out. I could think of nothing better to do than ring our front door bell and in fact there was probably nothing better I could have done; Nanny must have had a dreadful fright. After that she never locked me in that room but somewhere where I could not get out, so all I could do to annoy was to yell at the top of my voice. I was busy doing this one day when Uncle Jack, husband of one of the Holmes cousins, came round to see us, was unsatisfied with the reason for my being shut in, and insisted on taking me out to tea – me alone, without Ann! Once we were out, he said we were going to the cinema, which was the very height of wickedness, as he well knew, because Nanny did not allow it and I had never been before. We saw *White Cargo* which was about the white slave traffic and I was absolutely terrified and quite saw Nanny's point for once. Tea was better, as he said I could have as many cream cakes as I liked at Gunthers, but I was disappointed to find I felt sick after only two of these unaccustomed treats.

Nanny soon moved us out of that expensive flat and we found ourselves in a cosy semi-basement not far away from 'our' dress shop. Our lives became more restricted: no games or sewing on Sunday, but two church services helped to pass the time, and three during the week. Nanny had joined the Foursquare Gospellers and became more and more fanatically religious. Their services had their moments: when they sang hymns the tunes were catchy and we waved hymnsheets; after the emotional sermon we all bowed our heads and the preacher exhorted those who were not saved to come to the Lord. I put up my hand every time to boost the numbers and pass the time, until Nanny found out. The healing service was quite fun, too, and we always hoped Ann would be healed. I never actually saw anyone healed because I could never see properly, but you could sometimes hear them shaking and banging or shrieking as the devil left them. Sometimes people spoke with tongues and that was deliciously creepy.

Nanny now did not approve of dancing classes so no longer took me to them, though she had to allow me to go; every year I continued to get a part in the charity show at Devonshire Park but she would not make my costumes. Aunt Bertha came to the rescue but it was very disturbing to be living under such disapproval. Once Bertha's daughter Penelope invited me to a gymkhana she was performing in, but when I heard it was on a Sunday I said at once I could not go; I remember longing to go but knowing it was a fact of life that I could not; I do not remember raging against it. Eventually word got to our parents that if they did not want me to become peculiar they had better do something about Nanny. Typically they made a mad decision. They knew Nanny would never leave England, even if anyone could pay her fare, so they took us to India after two years of living alone with her.

India

Then began the happiest time of my life so far. Irma came home and stored the furniture, and scooped us off on to a ship. I said goodbye to poor Nanny, whose life was in ruins, without a pang, though I wept buckets when I parted with Percy, the near-Yorkshire terrier, and afterwards at the thought of his distress. Nanny got jobs as housekeeper and companion after that, and I never saw her again. She must have had a great deal to do with my make-up. Basil took Ann to see her once, years later when she was dying. I feel the family owes her a lot.

Now I was with my beloved mother, prepared to be as good as gold under her loose management. The voyage itself was magic. Ann helped somebody else with her children, I threw myself into deck games, discovered how to knit socks, and read, uninterrupted, in the ship's library. I had never been stopped reading anything I wanted, except once when rather a charming book, by Dodie Smith I think, was forbidden me and of course I read it under the bedclothes by the light of a torch as soon as possible, without finding out why I should not read it – it escaped me that the principal characters were living together unmarried.

At Marseilles we went ashore to see Irma's brother John, who had retired there, and I was amused to find that Irma, always boasting that she had been brought up speaking French, could only come out with Urdu in the Post Office. Uncle John was disappointing to me at the time; he had gone to seed and was very foreign-looking and fat, and spoke English with an accent. But he produced the Sicilian family tree, my first glimpse of it, and I never forgot it.

At Port Said we went to a wonderful emporium called Simon Artz where one could buy anything and at very good prices; we bought sun helmets. But it was the gully-gully man I most appreciated, on the quay with his vanishing chicks and other nonsense. Three weeks brought us to Bombay, where we embarked on a train; we had a large compartment with several bunks and its own lavatory and basin and electric fan. Pam was with us and during the night she turned in her upper bunk, flung out one arm and caught her fingers in the blades of the fan, with horrid results. The journey took several days and I think we had food brought to us by servants whenever the train stopped; there was no corridor.

Reunion with my father made no impression on my memory. I had not seen him for four years, when he had come home on leave. I may have been embarrassed to resume what childish relationship we might have had. He was full of jokes and play on words, but harassed as often as not, and out at work most of the time.

Irma and Pam had a gay social life with plenty of tennis and dancing, Pam slightly handicapped by her mother being so very beautiful and attractive; however, in time she held her own as she was good fun and amusing. I set up my own programme, to everyone's hilarity, having a timetable for a very full day. Horses were sent round every morning by Army officers for use by any of us and I always went, sometimes with Pam, very occasionally with Irma, who was a good horsewoman, sometimes just with the horseboy. A bath would be essential upon my return, the water being brought and poured into the tin bath by the sweeper, a man of low caste who also dealt with the latrines; these were known as thunder boxes, and one shovelled sand from a nearby box on to all contributions. There was a large opening in the wall behind, with doors through which the sweeper could remove the inner bucket for disposal, and he cultivated a discreet cough before doing so, which one hastily returned to deter him if one was there. After my bath, the ayah, or woman servant employed to look after the women's and children's needs (including the washing, poor thing, of linen sanitary towels), would come and empty the bath down the drain in the bathroom and clear up generally.

The average household would have at least ten servants. There were several gardeners and one of them was responsible for casting buckets of water at the *kus kus tatties*, or grass mats, which hung over outside doorways, thus keeping the interior cooler; there was no airconditioning in those days. The head man was the *khitmagar*, or butler, and under him would be several house men; the cook was a law unto himself and had his own assistant. There were no telephones, so every household had its own messenger who would take notes on his bicycle to other houses, to shops or offices. If one owned a horse, one also had a horseboy. A *derzi*, or tailor, was almost permanently employed though was not part of the household; he would sit on the floor stitching away on one of the verandas, making clothes for us all, uniforms for the servants, linen of all sorts, and even the aforesaid sanitary towels. Of all these people I only remember the name of the *khitmagar*, Nabi Ahmed, and I can remember his face; but we were not encouraged to think of them as human beings and the idea of any kind of relationship was unthinkable. I can to this day hear my father cursing about somebody in the office and calling him 'a bloody *babu*' which meant a low grade clerk. He was not exceptional, and I look back now in amazement that we were all so insensitive.

My morning would be divided between reading and writing (I did not bother myself with arithmetic), and with caring for and training the animals. My father had three dogs, a one-eyed fox terrier, John, and two Highland terriers, a brother and sister called Jack and Jill. They were fully grown and trained but they became my friends and I took them for walks. I soon acquired a monkey called Adam who needed all the training anyone could give; he was exceedingly wicked and the main thing he learned was not to get caught. He stole food at every opportunity and if he did not have time to eat it on the spot, he would stuff it through his mouth into pouches on each side, so one always knew by his extraordinary appearance that he had been at it again. He was fun but rather a worry as he had to be on a chain most of the time or he would have wrought too much damage, and I hated that. I also had a parrot, Theophilus, with whom I spent hours under a cloth, trying to teach him to speak, although everyone assured me he would never learn as he was the wrong kind, green. They were right, but I never gave up, and became very fond of him, so that when one day I forgot to move his cage into the shade and he died of heat, I was smitten with terrible remorse.

After lunch everyone retired to their bedrooms to rest, and after tea was exercise time. The grown-ups played tennis and golf, but nobody persevered with teaching either game to me. My father was so exasperated by my exploits on the first tee, driving several of his balls into a stream, that he never invited me to try again. I always hoped to be taken swimming, which did happen very often. I was good at swimming and diving, having learned to cope with water in the hard school of the English Channel. A young subaltern called Edward Palmer took me in hand and improved my style and taught me new tricks, like handstands under water and diving in fully clothed to a supposed rescue, and so on. I reminded him of his younger sister and whenever a group of officers came to the house, he would be among them and paid attention to me. It did not strike me that he was doing so, until when we were leaving he gave me a writing case and purse made of the skin of a crocodile he had shot, and began regularly to write to me all through my school days, giving me a terrific edge over the other girls. He also gave me a large book on dogs which taught me about the different breeds. Years later he happened to mention that he felt every man should have a good dog, a good horse, and a good woman. Observing the order in which he put them, I scratched him off my list.

One day Pam and I had an unpleasant adventure. We lived inside the

Agricultural Station and we had taken the dogs for a walk along the golf course and back through woods. We were followed by a strange dog and in the woods we realised it was mad, slavering and snarling. Jill was in season so I carried her but she was very fat and heavy. Our other two dogs were very much afraid and made no attempt to attack. Eventually we came to a standstill and thought out a plan, with the creature circling and trying to close in, and John and Jack sitting on my feet trembling. Not far from where we were was the house of the Allens (Charles was to write *Tales of the Raj* many years later), and we knew they had guns. Pam would go for help and I would stay with the dogs, as the mad dog seemed quieter when we were not moving, and the others would have followed me if I had gone to the house. To me it seemed she was gone hours, and I could not imagine what she was doing. I could hardly bear to go on holding Jill but was afraid of what might be precipitated if I put her down. Pam got to the house to find the whole family out and only the secretary there, who knew nothing about guns. However, he let Pam into the gunroom where to her dismay she found all the guns dismantled; she knew quite a bit on the subject and was able to put one together and load it, but it did take time. When she returned she had to avoid shooting me and our dogs, but she did eventually succeed in killing the poor mad one.

After a while the parents bestirred themselves and found us a governess. She was very old and old-fashioned, Miss Bonfellow, inevitably known as 'Bonnywot'. She rather took over my mornings and we sat at a table on a shady veranda and did a few desultory lessons about which my mind is blank. Adam got loose on one occasion and I watched him stalk her as she sat there expounding; then he leapt on to her hat (which I never saw her without, indoors or out), and sat there grinning and chattering and hanging on, while Bonnywot emitted the most ladylike, though agitated, remarks (you could not call them shrieks) of 'Oh! Oh! Oh! Oh! Oh!' Once a week she took us in a tonga, a two-wheeled horse-drawn vehicle, to the bazaar to shop, and we bought Nestlé's chocolate in large bars; it was the cards inside that I was particularly keen on as I had an album for them, covering all sorts of topics like butterflies, Wonders of the World, and such like. Poor Bonnywot – one wonders what happened to her in the end; she went to an Indian family after us, which my mother thought an absolute calamity, and probably Bonnywot did too, but what could she do? I can imagine now with what respect and eventually affection they would have treated her, and that when finally she was past dealing with the endless supply of small fry, they would have cared for her to the end, as they would any of their own people.

With the help of a boy of thirteen I built a tree-house in the garden and he fitted it up with electricity. Permission was sought for us to spend the night in it so as to appreciate the electricity, but the idea was vetoed with horror and the friendship severed (his mother was considered 'unsuitable' anyway! Oh, the snobbishness and narrowmindedness of those days.) This was particularly sad as there was literally nobody else of my age around. There was the daughter of, I believe, the Collector in Lucknow, Betty Clay, whom I was always hoping to meet, but she was fifty miles away from us in Cawnpore and I never did. Goodness knows what Ann did with herself, but probably lessons and reading were enough, and listening to grown-up conversation, and swimming in the Army pool.

Occasionally we went shooting and, although I hated the actual killing, it was an exciting expedition. We would be woken about 3 o'clock in the morning when it was very cold; we would dress very warmly, with trousers tucked into thick socks to defeat the creepy-crawlies, and with our sun helmets as well, we would pile into Algy's large touring car with canvas hood and open sides, the boot full of guns and food, and us covered with blankets, and thunder off along the dusty roads. The dust was unbelievable, lying inches deep, so that passing anything was torture and we were soon filthy. Algy got very angry about Indians asleep on their oxcarts, the oxen left to slog on all night and holding innocently to the middle of the road; no amount of hooting would waken the driver and on one occasion at least Algy, having to get out to move the oxen over, actually turned them round and set them off the way they had come. I felt this was a dreadful mistake as the driver would be so angry with the oxen when he woke up. At our destination we would be met by a party of *shikaris* or hunters, some of whom would shoulder our loads; they were fierce-looking, mainly handsome men, and were very kind to children. After this point, speaking out loud was forbidden and we would slog off through the jungle looking for whatever particular game we were after, often *nilgai* (blue buck), peafowl, pigeon, mallard, teal, widgeon and geese, all of which made very good eating. Once when Edward was with me, he allowed me to use his rifle and I shot a *nilgai*, but unhappily only wounded it; although he grabbed the rifle and pursued and killed it, I never wanted to shoot to kill ever again. Sometimes we went to the Ganges to shoot mugger, or crocodile, and had to lie quietly for a long time waiting for the sun to rise and the mugger with it. A *shikari* would be in charge of keeping me quiet and would amuse me by making things out of grass.

Our house was on the Ganges which was nice except for one thing. The garden stuck out into the river in a little point, and half-burnt corpses on little rafts would catch on this, so that a sweeper had to keep an eye out to push them off with a pole. It was the Hindu custom to burn the dead, after which they would set the remains off, smouldering on rafts on the holy river: if the family was poor, they could not afford enough wood to do the job properly.

In the hot weather we went up to Srinagar in Kashmir and took a houseboat on one of the lakes, Naghim Bagh. It was sheer bliss. One moved about between the three lakes in *shikars*, long canoes with men wielding heart-shaped paddles, and we had one of our own for getting out to a raft in the middle of our lake from which we swam. Irma, aged 42 at this time, to me as old as the hills, learned to dive here though she used to go very flat. Pam was a very good performer which spurred me on, and even Ann was quite good.

The Srinagar houses had carved fronts which distracted one's attention a little from the filth that lay in the surrounding lanes. Srinagar was a water city with bridges over the Jhelum River, and beyond the Dal Lake, which was being encroached on by the city, lay the Naghin and Naghim Baghs which were very beautiful. The Shalimar Gardens were here, as romantic as their name; they were made by a Mogul, with wide terraces and a central water channel of marble with pools and fountains and fretted marble slopes so that the water made a lovely sound as it poured over them. This is typical of an Eastern garden, having much stone instead of grass, and water, which is such a valuable commodity and is so refreshing to listen to when it is falling. These gardens did have lawns too, and roses, lilac and fruit trees.

The snow-covered mountains surrounded us and once we went on an expedition on *tats*, little hill ponies, to camp and fish in a stream of ice-cold water coming down from Nanga Parbat. It was wonderful to sit on the rocks and splash in this stream in the middle of the day. We were quite a large party: one man was too tall to ride the biggest pony and had to walk all the way or his feet would have trailed on the ground. Douglas and Anna Tidy, who had become part of the family, were with us too. We passed a flea-ridden puppy on the way, obviously abandoned and very pathetic. Anna did what nobody else could have done in that party, what was clearly the right thing to do – she took it by the hind legs and bashed its head against a rock. In revulsion she flung it into the river, where it caught against a sandbank and the water kept moving it – or was it alive? She went, and she did it again. I knew she was right and I respected her, but I hated her too. Yellow mustard and red tulips growing on rooftops in the next village we passed through helped to distract me from the horrid happening.

Basil was with us for six months of my time in India, and the Christmas of 1932 was the first for nine years, and the last that we all had together. Algy's brother Aubrey, who was in the Railway Department in Calcutta, joined us and it was a lovely family occasion. Basil had completed two years on a New Zealand farm, making life-long friends of the farmer and his family, and had then joined the Samoan Police during an emergency. He became more than interested in a Samoan girl and in order to extricate him our parents scraped up the fare for him to join them in India. He could never resist travel, so he went.

While he was with us there were riots in Cawnpore town; it was on the anniversary of the hanging of some national hero by the British, and began with marching students. Irma, driving home from the town, saw a militant crowd ahead of her and with much presence of mind kept driving, regardless. She did not hit anyone but they threw bricks and stones at her; she had several abrasions and a number of missiles were found in the car upon her somewhat hysterical return home. A man driving through the same mob a few minutes later, stopped and was lynched. The Army was called out and order was restored, but as so often happened, the thoroughly aroused people, made to return to their homes, broke out again to massacre their enemies, Hindu against Muslim, and terrible atrocities occurred. When it all began Algy and Basil went down after dark, to try to rescue clerks and other staff from Algy's office, and were appalled at the scenes. Families were burnt when their houses were fired, people were thrown into the flames from rooftops, people were killed in horrible ways with knives of all kinds. Basil, who had been in the police, had never seen such sights.

My father was good at impersonations, and his prowess was much discussed in Cawnpore; however, by the time I arrived he had promised my mother he would never do it again, as he had once gone too far. With his collar turned back to front, his hair powdered, and his face disguised by warts and cotton wool in the nostrils and cheeks to change the contours, with tin-rimmed spectacles and the assumption of a completely different character, as was his usual game, he had called on a not very popular couple who did not recognise him. He spun a tale about his wife having died, his being a missionary in a remote part, having been left with three little girls, whom he had come to the conclusion he must have adopted. He produced photographs and, rather to his dismay, this pair never recognised him and agreed to adopt one of us. He left without being detected and did not have the nerve to tell them, but sent a message. They were naturally very upset and he knew it was a shocking thing to have done. However, the Army officers who frequented the house said it was ridiculous of the couple not to have recognised him, and that they themselves would know him however much he disguised himself. Inevitably the temptation to hoodwink them was too great, and my mother agreed, provided it was done in the privacy of our house.

To my great joy, they were invited to dinner and I was allowed to sit up for it, with Ann and Bonnywot, who were not in the secret. The three men arrived and my mother apologised for Algy's absence, saying he had been called away on business; they did not mind as she and Pam were there! We were all sitting on the veranda before dinner when the wrong kind of horse-drawn vehicle drew up – it was used by Indians who naturally sat crosslegged, and it had no place to put one's feet, and was much cheaper. On it sat Algy, crosslegged.

'Oh dear!' said Irma, quite a good actress herself, 'here is that dreadful old friend of Algy's. I'm afraid I shall have to ask him to stay to dinner.'

This she did, and he sat on the veranda next to Bonnywot and managed to persuade her to give him 14 rupees for his mission! At dinner he was sitting next to Edward and produced a rat trap he said he had invented (and which I helped him make earlier in the day). It consisted of a tin for fifty cigarettes, empty save for a little liquid 'poison' and a cheese grater which had strands of wool knotted through the holes, the ends of which trailed in the 'poison'.

'In the hot weather,' said Algy with a perfectly straight face, 'the rats get prickly heat and come to scratch their backs on the cheese grater, when of course the poison rushes up through the wool into the rats and they die in their hundreds.'

Nobody believed this, but nobody thought he was Algy; they just thought he was mad. They were all laughing and trying not to show it, and in the end it was the way the family was laughing that gave him away. Even then they were not quite sure for another few minutes.

Eventually it occurred to my parents that I ought to be going to school. It was never even considered that I might do so in India because if I had, I would inevitably have acquired a 'chi-chi' accent. I must have been backward by then, but Basil took the view (and won the day with no trouble at all) that girls needed no education beyond French and beautiful embroidery. This touched a chord in Irma's mind and she decided that Ann and I should go to a Belgian convent that a much older cousin had gone to, where presumably I would study both these subjects. Arrangements were made and we all set off home about that time, except Algy. Basil was to get a job in the Shanghai Police and Pam was to take a secretarial course paid for by her godfather.

En route we stayed with a man friend (who died of smallpox shortly after we left), and I began my period for the first time when everyone was out except me and him. I did know about periods as Ann already had them, but I was rather frightened and went to bed till my mother returned. I had no idea why women had this manifestation, they just did. My education in the Facts of Life was quite neglected. I think Irma expected that because Pam knew them (and I wonder if she did, I have never checked and now it is too late) I must too, but I knew nothing; there was after all a big age gap between us. A foreign cousin left in charge of Ann and me when I was about four, attempted to rape me; he probably did not know how to, being only fourteen himself, and he certainly only succeeded in terrifying Ann and mystifying me. He was beaten by his father when I told Nanny about this extraordinary experience, and he grew up to be homosexual! At the Dame School another girl had told me babies came out of their mothers' tummies which I felt was manifestly absurd, because HOW? I stumped off home to ask Irma and was so confounded when she said it was true that I omitted to enquire further as to how they got there or how they emerged, and remained in profound uninquisitive ignorance until I was living alone in London.

Belgium

The Belgian interlude was a pretty miserable one. The contrast between the freedom and brightness of India and the restrictions and drabness of the Belgian convent was too great, and at first the responsibility of having Ann in this environment weighed heavily upon me. We started off in the pensionnat among six hundred girls getting a secondary education. There were two other English girls but in different forms so we hardly saw them and were not supposed to speak any English anyway. Poor Ann did not master the French language and just sat through everything, lessons, meals, church services. Even going to the lavatory was nerve-racking as there were no locks on the doors and when somebody banged, the occupant had to shout 'Occupé', and Ann could not say it quickly enough; I guarded the door whenever I could but it was not always possible. We were only allowed one bath a week but soon found we could get at least two more from the Belgians who did not believe in total immersion.

My first bath there was quite an experience. When I emerged a nun was waiting outside the door, and went in. She asked me if I had my own *chemise*, which I thought meant vest, so I said yes, and she asked to see it. It transpired that I should have worn the one which lay over the chair in the bathroom, like a tent with a hole in the top, when I was in the bath. I enquired why, as the room was very high up and there were no windows overlooking it.

'The angels of the Lord may see you' was the reply.

I earned my first bad mark by retorting crossly that if they were angels they ought to be able to see through a chemise. Three of these bad marks earned expulsion from the school, but I managed to stick at two. The other one I received when my friend and I were caught sucking gobstoppers in the cloakroom; these were enormous round sweets which changed colour as they grew smaller, so one had to keep taking them out to see. This was unbelievably unladylike behaviour, added to which we were quite unable to answer the nun politely in any language because of these obstructions.

The nuns on the whole were not lovable people: they mostly did not have vocations, as the youngest or the plainest in one of their huge families would be dedicated to God by her parents and literally sacrificed. This meant we had some pretty soured characters in charge, with one or two exceptions.

After the first term the school took it upon itself to put me into the Examination House, which was good from my point of view as I then studied for English School Certificate in English with ten other English girls and one

Me aged 14, off to the Belgian convent.

Belgian. However, Ann was left behind and my agony of mind over it must have equalled, if not exceeded, hers. Every morning after breakfast when there was a little spare time, I would belt down to the dividing fence to see her, and she was always there, holding onto it, and looking for me. Again at break time, after lunch and after tea, we would meet there. I was thankful when it was decided during the next holidays not to send her back as she had developed pneumonia on the boat going back to England. We spent the holidays with Aunt Bertha and she stayed there till Irma could fetch her.

I made an excellent friend called Betty Wansey Bayly, and we made life possible for one another with laughter and confidences. She was everything I abhorred: scruffy, opinionated, knew she was clever, and she was not at all attractive to me. We were thrown together as new girls, and I came to love her for characteristics which were not so obvious but much more important: humour, human understanding, loyalty, and in fact she was very intelligent. We became life-long friends. The work I *did* enjoy; it was meat and drink to me after the changes and the weaknesses of my education so far; I worked hard to catch up and eventually got seven credits in the examination, which exempted me from matriculation and meant I could have gone on to university, though of course such an idea never entered the heads of anyone in the family, including my own.

I was at the gawky stage and Irma had not helped by the way she had fitted me out. An edge-to-edge coat of her own was dyed navy-blue and was very draughty, and was not long enough to cover my skirt below. My feet were enormous, and she gave up trying to find me suitable shoes and bought me men's walking shoes, with the result that I wore my indoor ones whenever I could without being found out. The one thing she made me which I liked was a Russian tunic in tussore instead of one of the pleated uniform blouses, but I was not allowed to wear it because it showed the figure too much. Blouses always had to be buttoned to the neck even in the hottest weather, and sleeves could not be rolled up. Imagine how much we enjoyed rollerskating which, surprisingly, we were allowed to do on an uneven brick surround to the house. The great thing was to fall down as untidily as possible when nuns were near.

We were taken on excursions to see art galleries and battlefields but we were not educated to appreciate them. I have a photograph of myself in a trench aiming a rifle at the camera, which appals me now. At the time I had no idea of the agonies and the terror and squalor that had been experienced where I stood, but I suppose one would not wish young people to have to understand it so early. I was put off the art galleries of Bruges, Ghent and Amsterdam by the large number of Flemish classics portraying such horrors as a man being flayed alive. Perhaps the beauty of such cities seeped in unnoticed; certainly I much appreciated them later on. We were taken to the Brussels Exhibition, about which I remember singularly little, except the sister convent in which we spent the night, which happened to be a lunatic asylum. This did not really alarm us, even though every door we passed through was unlocked and locked again. Betty managed to infuse humour into the situation by hanging on the windowsill a pair of knickers she had washed, which blew away in the night. The strategies we employed to retrieve them without letting on what we were after are far too long to list. On another excursion, our train pulled up in open country next to another train carrying – oh horrors! – a boys' school also on an excursion. They sat there, drinking beer and smoking and looking as debauched as they could in the most extraordinary clothes, leering at us, until the desperate nuns managed to get round to all our windows and pull down the blinds. On one memorable day we went to Zuider Zee and did some paddling. These excursions were for the English girls only, when the Belgians went home for half-term.

Perhaps the most valuable thing I learned at the school was patience. Our form mistress, who was a real darling called Sister Marcia, was quite elderly. She often used to take 'prep' in the evening and she would sit at her desk above us unravelling the most ghastly mess of muddled silks. I wondered, so used was I to the idea of penance, whether they were deliberately muddled, or whether she was in fact doing something useful besides mortifying the soul. She never seemed to get to the end of her job, and the memory of it has helped me through many an unpicking or unravelling job.

They had told my mother that there would be no attempt to convert me to Catholicism, but in fact we had to attend chapel whenever everybody else did, and she was greatly worried when I won a rosary as a prize; it was so pretty that I certainly used it at school. But I did not at this stage of my life apply my mind to the mysteries of religion: I had had enough of it with Nanny. In fact whenever possible I tried to avoid religious ceremonies. For instance on Corpus Christi Day there was a ghastly slow procession through the grounds along dusty paths, and one year when it was particularly hot, Betty and I considered it worth while to try and make our noses bleed by punching each other. I did succeed in making Betty's bleed a little but it stopped before the procession began.

There was one house which was a finishing school and we were taken to some of the lessons there. A fascinating one was on social behaviour. We were taught to curtsy to our hostess upon arriving at a function in her house; she was curiously ensconced in a chair in the middle of the room so we were left to presume she was the queen or that their customs were very different from our own. We were taught to enquire, upon a young man proposing marriage, whether he had venereal disease or insanity in his family. We learned monotonously every term to dance the Boston Two Step, holding each other rather far apart, and that when we went to dances out in the 'World' we should always wear a flower in our bosom which we could, upon our return, show uncrushed to our mama – not as we thought, from not having been kissed in the conservatory, but from not having been held too close in the dance.

The girls in the finishing school learned cooking, and we in the examinations school benefited thereby and often had most delicious puddings. We had asparagus too, which is rather remarkable. I remember being rather superior about the Belgians eating it with knives and forks. Wine was served at the main meal, but one always added water, as was the custom for young people in their homes. *Tartines* were enormous thick slices of bread and margarine which we had daily for the last meal of the day, with our own jam added. One was allowed unlimited *tartines* and we made thorough pigs of ourselves, seeing how many we could consume in the allotted time.

The dormitories were divided into cubicles with wooden partitions, over which we were forbidden to peer. Needless to say a good deal of communication did go on over the top, and one of my jobs was to report to the other girls on the one Belgian, who happened to be in the next cubicle to me –

did she change her green knitted petticoat from one end of the term to another? No. Did she strip off to wash all over? No. And so on. How horrible the young can be. When washing was completed one had to carry the bowl of dirty water down the centre aisle and empty it in a sluice. One day I slipped on some spilt water when doing this, broke my basin and made a terrible mess. The nun on duty was one of the worst and gave me a dreadful verbal pasting, until she realised that I had a bad cut at the base of a thumb. The doctor who stitched the cut had the filthiest nails imaginable.

In 1934 Irma came home and took a flat belonging to Edward's parents for the Easter holidays in Westward Ho. Edward was on leave and after much heart-searching, Irma allowed him to take me to my first dance. She was reluctant because Ann was not invited and she had hoped to put off this moment for a year or two. I went with all Edward's family, and his sisters were horrified when I appeared wearing plaits, as usual, and whisked me off to the ladies' room where they coiled the plaits up into 'earphones'. When they had finished I retreated into one of the lavatories and took them down again. Edward did not care and I had a lovely time, duly completed by my first kiss – on the cheek. It lasted me for a couple of years.

That year was memorable for another reason. Long years before, my mother's brother Henry had married his headmaster's daughter, with whom he ran away from school. Her sister ran with them and had lived with them ever since. She had been a great support to them, for they lived in Persia where Henry was in the Telegraph Department, and they lived through many vicissitudes. On one dreadful occasion when the whole family were on tour, the wife May and the three children contracted cholera. The servants ran away in fear, so that Henry and his sister-in-law, Bunny, were left to cope in an isolated rest house with the nursing and care of the family. All the children died. Henry dug their graves and buried them himself, and the next morning found that they had been dug up and partially eaten by wild animals. The presence of Bunny must have been a great comfort to both parents. In due course four more children were born to May and her sister stayed on and helped her. From this distance it seems that Bunny herself probably loved Henry and that was why she never married, for she was an attractive woman. This summer of 1934 she came to stay with us in Devon, following a nervous breakdown. She had threatened to kill herself but Irma had a theory that 'they never do it if they say they are going to.' So when one day we were going to the market and Bunny did not want to come, Irma thought nothing of leaving her alone. When we got back to find her gone, though, Irma was uneasy and when she did not come in for lunch, we all went out to search for her. I knew what Irma feared but had no idea what method Bunny might have chosen or where to look. Ann and I together scoured one area, looking gingerly under every bush, but without result, and by nightfall the police were alerted. Three weeks later Bunny's body was washed up by the sea.

The following year Algy came home on what was to prove his last leave, after a five-year tour. It was the last time I saw him. We were then living in a house at Middleton-on-Sea near Bognor, and spent a lot of time on the beach. My memories of him are not sharp. I had left school at sixteen, and was entranced to be free and at home for what I thought was to be an indefinite period. The plan was that I should return to India with Irma and Ann at the end of the year.

In the meantime, Irma had a French girl called Régine Gautier de Bonneval to stay on an exchange visit. She was a very handsome aristocratic girl, and she wore a very smart red coat which she said she could not wear in Paris because of its communist implications. Douglas Tidy was with us for part of her visit and fell for her heavily. When she returned to France I went with her, in order to perfect my French, as Irma imagined. In fact my French was not nearly so good as it might have been, as I had been studying in English and had spoken English as much as I could get away with in my spare time at school; added to this I had learned to speak with a Belgian accent which did not commend me to this snobbish French family. They had an apartment in Paris of extraordinary grandeur: huge rooms with panelled walls and Louis XV furniture, all gilt and spindly legs and tapestry, not to my eyes at all homely. Régine marched me furiously but dutifully round Paris on foot, to see what I needed to see, and I rather hated it because I was so exhausted. Then we went to Mégève, where they had a chalet and in winter went there to ski. It was very beautiful and we walked in the mountains, where the snow lingered but the sun was hot. Her two brothers, who were at St Cyr, the equivalent of Sandhurst, joined us there and were glamour personified, one blond and the other very dark. I could not decide which one to be in love with, which was just as well as neither showed much interest in me. We all put up politely with my visit but never communicated again.

By this time I was seventeen and had put my hair up in a coil round my head. Upon returning to England I went for three months to an old lady who very successfully taught me shorthand and typing, in that short time getting me typing accurately at sixty words a minute, and although I did not finish the course, taking shorthand at very nearly 120 words a minute. Her awful nephew attempted to teach me bookkeeping but was not so successful.

This was the year George V died. Pam was sharing a flat with Anna and, as luck would have it, it was in Cambridge Gardens off the Edgware Road, on the route to Paddington Station which the funeral cortège took. We all went and had front row seats on her balcony, or when it was too crowded, on the roof. It was a wonderful sight with all the different contingents, military, naval and air force, in particular the Life Guards around the gun carriage glittering on their magnificent horses, and the Royal family in carriages or walking behind. It was a very emotional occasion when the nation mourned together.

The great excitement in the family was that Pam had become engaged and that summer was married, sadly without Algy. Her fiancé was Joe Turral, a China Consul, whom she had met through the Tidys. He was a great addition, a man with a wonderful sense of humour, and I loved him dearly. He spoke, besides the usual European languages, seven oriental languages, and wrote Russian and Chinese. He had a splendid bass singing voice and encouraged Pam with her singing. He told me, not at all in confidence, that if he had not met Pam he would have married me, and when they were abroad he often wrote me nonsense letters which cheered me up like nothing else did. Irma made all our dresses for the wedding, including the wedding dress, and it was a great family party. After the honeymoon they set off for Joe's Manchurian posting in Harbin.

It was a happy year, anticipating returning to India with Irma. She was busy buying materials to be made up into dresses for us all, and I was humming along in joyous freedom, unthinking and with no premonition of trouble ahead. At the last minute Irma decided to leave me behind. She convinced herself that if she took me to India I would get married at once, and at seventeen that was too young, though how she convinced herself that leaving me alone in London could be anything but a fiasco I cannot imagine. She blithely asked a few people to 'keep an eye' on me, and departed.

CHAPTER 2

London
1936-1946

THE NEXT TEN YEARS covered the Second World War, most of which I spent in London. That was dark enough, but personally I was fighting to keep my head above the jungle that was the London in which I found myself, and to find a way of life that would give me happiness. I was ill-equipped, being remarkably ignorant and insecure, all my bastions gone. I had been tossed from one authority to another: Nanny with her solid narrow discipline, Irma with her light, laughing presence and sudden snap, the Belgian convent with its alien rectitude. Now I was free to do as I liked, but I did not know what I wanted, or would not admit, even to myself, that all anyone had thought of in rearing me was marriage. I was not trained for a career, nor was it thought the thing, in our circles, for girls to want one, and the idea of university for me never entered anyone's head. So in fact I was husband-hunting, in very unpromising circumstances and however subconsciously.

Letters were the last tenuous ties with the family and they helped enormously. They flew round the world from India to Manchuria to Shanghai to London, and Irma made sure we all saw letters from each other even if they were to her. One from Basil in Shanghai to Brenda Monypenny, the wife of the farmer he had worked for in New Zealand, and who were then living in Surrey, said:

> If you ever feel like doing a charitable deed, what about dropping a line to my youngest sister Pat and asking her down one Sunday for a breath of fresh air? The remainder of the family having fled the country, she is alone at some gal's club in Princes Gate (I think No. 17). She was left quite jobless in that rather optimistic manner of my mama, but by her own efforts she managed to secure a typist's job in the 'French glove trade' somewhere in Regent Street. If the trade is confined to gloves I trust she remains there safe and sound! Having been brought up almost entirely in the country and seaside I think she would simply love to be asked down to your dear little place, since she is more or less confined to the metropolis. I think she's fairly happy in her job but she is rather a home-lover and only about 18 so I wouldn't be surprised if she is a bit homesick now and again with all the rest of the family abroad. I think you'd find her a very easy person so if you feel equal to it one day be a dear and ask her down.

I was furious with Irma for leaving me behind. The first thing I did was to change the digs she had found for me, in a depressing Bayswater hostel, sharing a room with a strange girl, with mean meals and awful rules and a martinet of a proprietress who called herself a warden. The hostel I found was quite indistinguishable from the first one but I found it myself.

My father was allowing me £10 a month which was quite a lot of money then, but I had to augment this with a job and this was soon achieved at the glove agency (actually Czech) in Regent Street, at a wage of thirty-five shillings a week. It did not last very long because, when the boss's son came over from Czechoslovakia, he expected me to sit on his knee, so I left.

I ricocheted from job to job. For a short time I worked as the junior in the Sesame Imperial Club in Grosvenor Street, a literary club for ladies. I worked with two superb old ladies: one was rather a roué in appearance, the other a spinster who wore very old-fashioned clothes. A sort of boned net tube encased her neck to the chin, her dark dresses were belted in a slope from back to front, and her deep full bosom loomed above; she wore long pointed shoes and a pompadour hair style, put on rather too much face powder and had a cackle of a laugh. She clearly disapproved of her companion in many ways, but found her amusing, and they were friends. One evening a week and every other weekend I had to take charge of the cash desk in the dining-room, to give the cashier time off. This was quite entertaining, apart from the horror of keeping the books, as I met some of the members. Edith Sitwell was one, and she would buy me a sherry and chat. She had a whispered reputation amongst the staff, who knew she drank in her room before ten in the morning and sent for untold numbers of bottles of gin. Her enormous jewellery fascinated me, colossal ivory beads and crucifixes, amber pieces and huge rings, but her long white face and half closed eyes were intimidating. Another member one had to recognise instantly, for the poor woman was incontinent, and one had to rush up with a basket chair. I left because they had to economise and I was the most expendable member of staff.

The next job was in the Records Library of John Lewis, which was very boring but the people I worked with were nice. The head of the department was a woman and one day she asked us all to look out for her for one of those new silk scarves with place names dotted about on them. I came bouncing in a few days later crying:

'Oh Miss Senter, I've found just the scarf for you, covered with French letters.' A slip of the tongue – I meant 'words' – but I had no idea what I had said, though by the silence, I knew something was wrong. A girl called Pamela put me wise later on.

By this time I had some idea what sex was all about. The first episode was in a Notting Hill Gate cinema where I sat in the sixpennies. A wandering hand set off up my leg and reached a suspender, where it paused. I was behaving like a rabbit in headlights, paralysed and perplexed. What was he doing? As the hand set off again, the penny dropped: Irma had said 'If anyone is a nuisance to you in the cinema, call the attendant.' Without further reflection I stood up and did so, and the man was duly ejected, no doubt very disgruntled that I had shown him no previous discouragement.

Pamela discovered how miserable my hostel was and asked if I would like a room in her lodgings in Oakley Street, Chelsea, and I accepted with alacrity. The occupants were quite fascinating to me and I learned about homosexuality. The two men running it were 'pansies', as they were then whispered. George was lame, a great dear, and did the cooking; the other one was a male model and had exquisitely mascaraed eyelashes. Upstairs lived Quentin Crisp, who in his old age was to acquire a certain fame. When homosexuality was made legal, a film was made of his life, he appeared in stage shows and wrote a book. At this time he was an elfish young man with rather long reddish hair and painted finger and toe nails, and when he went out he wore a cloak and sandals. He earned part of his living by a form of painting, spraying paint on to canvas by running a finger over a paint-laden toothbrush, with quite effective results. I felt it was safe to accept his invitation one day to go up and see his paintings, and he was most entertaining the way he leapt about the furniture to show me this and that, scaling the sofa and sitting on the sideboard for a drink.

I stayed here until my schoolfriend Betty left her secretarial college a year later. She had had time in a finishing school and then had had to do her secretarial course twice because hers were not the kind of brains that coped easily with typing and shorthand. She had wanted to be a doctor, like her father, but he said women did not have careers; however, they jolly well earned their livings. We took a first-floor drawing room in South Kensington; it had very little furniture beyond two beds and a grand piano which neither of us could play, but it had a parquet floor and two French windows on to a balcony and were delighted with it. Winter made us realise a smaller room would be wiser; also the occupant of the next room snored. We had a lovely big party before we left, and took a tiny room in Bute Street nearer to the station, for which we paid £1 a week each, including tea and toast for breakfast. We tried to cheer it up by painting things black and orange but it was not a great success. Food was quite a problem as we had no cooking facilities and eating out was expensive. Cold baked beans were popular, and bread and butter, and one hoped to be taken out to dinner several times a week. Lunch consisted of a glass of milk and two penny buns. We went to the cinema a great deal in those days before television, two or three times a week, and usually found the films uplifting in one way or another, unlike those of the present day.

In 1937 the coronation of King George VI was held. I had been lucky to see both the procession for the Jubilee of George V and his funeral in 1936. The sadness of that occasion was soon followed by the disillusionment of Edward VIII's abdication. When George VI was crowned it was a joyful occasion, with many of us rejoicing that we were not to be ruled by a man who had put his love life before his country, but by a man everyone liked, a shy retiring man with a stammer, whom we hoped would do well with his redoubtable little Queen, Elizabeth, by his side.

Betty and I and two other girls (Brenda Scott, a lifelong friend of mine, being one) planned our coronation with care. We went to bed at the other girl, Beryl's, flat at eight o'clock the night before and rested till eleven, when we sallied forth in a fog to Westminster Abbey. There were few people about and we propped ourselves up on doorsteps and dozed until around 2 a.m. when there was a sudden surge of people from the Underground. We hurried forward to get near the front and I got separated from the others, who had the food. However, I learned later that it was no good to them either because the bag it was in was on Betty's feet and the press of people was so great she was unable to pull it up. I was in the second row of people lining the barriers and could see well enough, but after an hour or two a woman in front of me fainted and was carried off, so I had a splendid position. A man beside me gave me a nip of brandy about dawn when I too felt faint because of the people behind pressing me against the barrier, and later I was given some cheese and chocolate by Douglas Tidy, who sauntered up and down grandly on a horse (in the Queen's Rifles) and eventually responded to my cries and waves.

Opposite us we saw the peers and peeresses alight from their cars and carriages. Lord Derby, apparently wrongly, had put his coronet on before the ceremony and stood bewildered on the pavement looking like Old King Cole. I recognised Prince Charles of Belgium, and King Michael of Rumania, who looked sturdy and brown and not like his photographs; Princess Juliana of Holland who looked charming and was greeted by rousing cheers, and her husband; Prince Chichibou and lots of Indian maharajas and other Eastern potentates all looking absolutely superb. We saw Signor Grandi with his funny little beard, and Lloyd George and the Aga Khan, and two Germans who looked very grim in their steel helmets; there was rather a sticky silence when they got out of their car but we soon remembered ourselves and cheered them! The colours of the procession against the grey day were so marvellous and all the uniforms made one feel it was centuries ago.

Everyone nearly burst over Queen Mary, who returned after the ceremony in an open carriage with the two little princesses, Elizabeth and Margaret, in their golden crowns. Margaret Rose suddenly waved to somebody who managed to get an arm free to wave – I imagined the person stuck with his arm up for hours! The Duchess of Kent looked lovely but not nearly as lovely as the Duchess of Gloucester. I thought Kent looked as though he had had a thick

night when he came by on his horse. The crowd nearly went mad when the
King and Queen came by and they did look nice, all made up, I think, but I
suppose they would have looked so pale from a distance otherwise. When they
had all come and gone, we crept away to baths and a couple of hours' sleep
before going to various parties. We had stood from 2a.m. till 4p.m. and I had
managed half an hour's sleep standing up against that rail. One's legs were all
right but one's back well nigh broke – but it was worth it.

John Lewis soon went out of my life: they moved me to a welfare job which
was beyond me at that age, and I again had to leave. I found another job in a
French insurance brokers in Aldgate, working under a very nice woman, Mrs
Partridge, who was Alec de Rougemont's secretary. I applied my Pitman's
shorthand to French with some success, though scared myself on occasions
after a late night by dropping off to sleep momentarily, to wake and wonder
how many words I had missed which I could not possibly improvise. Alec's
son was about my age and we went skating on the Serpentine once or twice,
and there was an amusing young man called Shelley on the staff who wrote the
following skit on life in that office, which is a better description than any I
could write:

A QUIET MORNING IN THE OFFICE

Scene: *An office, the desks of which are piled with papers, papers lying on floors and
windowsills. Seated at one desk the secretary Mrs Pheasant, facing five telephones, into three
of which she is speaking.*

MRS PHEASANT: He has not arrived – Il n'est pas encore arrivé – Er is noch
nicht eingekommen.

*At another desk Assistant Belly is pasting newspaper cuttings on to a piece of blotting paper.
Miss Grand-Duchess is taking dictation. The door opens and a head appears:*

HEAD AT THE DOOR: About that fire risk –

CHORUS: What fire risk?

Head disappears. Enter the Chief waving a bag. All rise and chant.

CHORUS: Good morning, dear Teacher, good morning to you.

CHIEF SINGS: We've got a lot of work to do, a lot to do today
               I know that you've been idle all the time I've been away
               But now that I am back again we're going to have some fun
               You think your work's half over – my dears, it's just begun.

Reaches desk by throwing papers right and left. All phones ring.

MRS PHEASANT: Yes, yes, yes, no, no, no – will you speak to the Lord Mayor,
the Fire Brigade, the…

CHIEF: I won't speak to anyone. I am expecting a call this morning. Ah, *(as door opens)* this will be it.

VOICE AT DOOR: About the fire risk…

CHIEF: <u>What</u> fire risk?

Enter boy with card.

BOY: Monsieur XYZ to see you sir.

CHIEF: Show him in. *(Kicks papers aside as visitor enters.)* Oh bonjour, cher monsieur, etc.etc.etc.

VISITOR: I have a very interesting proposition which I think might prove… *Telephone rings.*

MRS PHEASANT: Paris call, will you take it?

CHIEF: *(taking phone)* Oui, oui, oui, oui, oui. Mais non, mais non, mais non. Empoisonnant. Impossible. Mais oui. Mais oui. Certainement. Pas du tout. Quelle horreur. *(Turning to visitor)* I am so sorry. I am all attention.

MRS PHEASANT: *(dictating)* severe shock to the engine: after consultation with chief engineer and other members of the crew and after testing the supports of the bridge, she found the bracelet was missing. Thorough search in the neighbouring cafés having revealed that the boiler damage was caused by there not being sufficient air in the holds in which the maize was shipped and by the native craft being caught in the surf, it was decided to blow up the dam…

VISITOR: *(rather wearily)* …a very interesting proposition which I think…

VOICE AT THE DOOR: About that fire risk…

CHORUS: <u>What</u> fire risk?

Telephone rings.

CHIEF: Monsieur…Ah cher ami, enchanté d'entendre votre voix. Mais non, non, non, non. Ce soir, hélas, je ne serai pas libre. Demain, ah, les affaires, vous savez, les affaires…Je vous téléphonerai dans quinze jours… *(Puts down the phone.)* Ah, one moment, I forgot, Miss Grand-Duchess, take this schedule and make six thousand copies, at once if not sooner…Now, then, you said?

VISITOR: A very interesting proposition which… *Enter two brokers.* A slip has been traced to this room, last heard of October 9 1854.

CHORUS: We <u>have</u> no slip, we have <u>no</u> slip, we have no <u>slip</u>.

Telephone rings.

CHIEF: I have never heard of such infernal…the risk must be placed…

VISITOR *(faintly):* A proposition of great interest…

Tapping at the window, face of painter appears. Window opens, letting in traffic noises. Painter sings 'Farewell to the Isle of Capri'.

Telephone rings.

CHIEF: Paris call? Non, non, non. Mais oui, mais oui, mais oui…

VOICES AT DOOR: Can we allow 110 per cent discount on…? Has the vessel sailed from…? What is the cost of the fifth stone to the left in the diamond necklace belonging to the aunt of the last President but one?

Visitor faints away on floor.

CHIEF: Belly, remove this rubbish. How anyone expects to be able to do work with bodies lying around. Get me five calls to Paris. Thank goodness, we can do some work at last.

Mr de Rougemont was in fact a very kind man, and he was distraught when I was brought to the office by ambulance one day with a bandaged jaw. I had been knocked off my bicycle, on which I rode from Kensington to Aldgate every day, by a taxi turning right suddenly in front of me near Buckingham Palace. I came to in the Horseguards Barracks, lying on a bench being tended by these glamorous beings in tight white breeches and polished boots, gleaming helmets lying around. I was quite sorry to leave in the ambulance they had summoned, but enjoyed the siren rung specially for me.

I was going regularly to swimming baths, and also tried to keep up my riding, but it was very expensive for one of my means, and after taking rather a toss in Richmond Park, I gave it up. This toss left me with some sort of spinal defect which dogged me the rest of my life; I would be perfectly all right for a long time and then it would suddenly go. I went to art galleries, exhibitions and concerts with one girl friend, to the ballet and occasional theatre with another, to the cinema whenever I felt like it. I often went away for the weekend, to my father's brothers or to friends of Irma's who were all supposed to be 'keeping an eye' on me. Uncle Reggie and Aunt Lilla lived at Liss and had tennis parties and Lilla would try to teach me Edwardian etiquette; one of their daughters was at Dublin University, the other about this time caught polio and the invitations ceased. Another of my father's brothers, Uncle Cecil, who was Bursar of Balliol, used to have me to stay at his Oxford flat, when he would lecture me about getting a job with a pension, and walk me round the colleges. Eva Tate was a school friend of Irma's, and lived at Sutton with her son, who would take me for walks and drives, and to motor-racing and wrestling, neither of which activities attracted me any more than he did, but they were both very kind. Aunt Bertha at Eastbourne had me to stay occasionally but I was not keen; Penelope worked in a stables and I once or twice got some riding there.

Betty was working for the comedian Vic Oliver who was married to

Winston Churchill's daughter Sarah. As Betty worked in their flat she often met interesting people, including Winston, and brought home good stories and free tickets to shows. We decided we would go round the world together, an almost unheard-of adventure for girls at that time, and we saved every penny we could and plotted our route. We relied largely on relations and friends, mostly mine, dotted around the world, to give us accommodation, and the £100 each we reckoned we should need was for fares. We did realise that it would not be enough but planned to work when we reached America. It was a wonderful goal to keep our eyes raised to rather than looking at the depressing world in which we found ourselves, and we only relinquished it because of the war.

We needless to say fell prey to males, all of us, and to older males at that; we were doubtless subconsciously seeking security. At nineteen I became enamoured of a man who admitted to being forty-two but who I feel must have been more; he was a friend of a cousin's husband (also asked to keep their eyes on me as they were in London). Ronald Brodie, Cousin Nora's husband, of whom I was afraid, was a tall, lean, handsome man, cruel and fierce; he was in the Cameronians and had been involved in a brawl in Malta when he thought he had killed somebody. He escaped and joined the French Foreign Legion but eventually heard that the man had not died. It was some time, however, before he returned to his regiment when war broke out. He did me a great disservice by introducing me to his friend Brian, who had been in the Army, and who finally dispelled for me the mysteries of sex. He had attracted me in the first place more as a father figure, so it was a great shock. In an elementary way I clung to him for a long time as the man who 'possessed' me, but when I got over that stage I could see no way out: he was very possessive. He was a somewhat sinister character and violent, and we had a very stormy time, all very much in the background of what appeared to be my quite ordinary life. In the end I had literally to disappear, changing both job and address and swearing all my friends to secrecy. But this came some time later.

In the summer of 1938 Basil left the Shanghai Police. He was just off to a new world in his chequered career. After two years farming in New Zealand, a year as a policeman in Samoa, and a year in an advertising office in Bombay, he had completed five years in the Shanghai Police. The last had been a bad time in an organisation about which he told us very little. It was composed of a polyglot of men with all kinds of backgrounds and experiences; tough men who had fallen on bad times in most cases. Corruption was rife in the Force as well as among the people who were also of mixed races. Many Japanese lived there; White Russian refugees who could go no further and had to eke out a living as best they could; Sikhs, many of whom were in the Force; likewise Gurkhas, and of course there were Chinese of all kinds. Cruelty, fraud, murders, rapes, drug-running, gang warfare and the constant fear of being killed one way or another: one wonders how Basil managed to maintain his integrity and character. He loathed it and as soon as his contract was up, he left. He travelled up to Harbin in Manchuria where Pam and Joe were expecting their first baby, and hoped he would be there to see this first member of the next generation. He took Pam for bumpy droshky drives over cobbled streets, he made her run up the stairs to their flat over the British Consulate, but young Richard held on and was not born till shortly after the expiration of Basil's visa and his departure on the trans-Siberian railway.

From Warsaw, where it deposited him, he met me in Copenhagen, and we went to Sweden to have a wonderful holiday with Anna and another, older friend, Nina Lynch. She ran an hotel in Russell Square where the family always stayed when in London, where even my grandfather had stayed. She was of Irish descent but looked like an Italian madonna with her long face, huge eyes, long thin nose and black hair drawn back in a classical bun. She was a rounded, elegant woman with beautiful hands and clothes, fastidious and unusual, with a languid air and voice which belied her efficiency and humour. We went to a fishing village and lived in different fishermen's cottages round a pump, Basil and I in the same one. He fell in love with Anna who had, unknown to Douglas, just left him, but she was most dissuasive (after all he did not even have a job!), even throwing a jug of water, complete with the jug, at him one night when he tried to gain her room up a drainpipe. Otherwise we had a lovely time, swimming, often in the nude, as was the custom in Sweden, and eating crayfish and drinking schnapps and laughing.

I was so happy to be with my own people again, particularly Basil, whom I had always idolized. We hired a rowing boat and went off to other islands, rowing hard, with Basil mostly doing cox. One day I dropped a powder compact down a slit in the rock on one of these islands, and he made a great drama of rescuing it. It could not be reached by hand but he said he knew exactly the tool required. Next day he appeared in his bathing gown, got rather stiffly into the boat and remained standing up until we were well out to sea. Then he withdrew a mysterious weapon from under the gown, a long iron rod with a hook on the end; it was just the thing, but what it was for we never discovered. He had noticed it in the lavatory of the hotel and much enjoyed smuggling it out and in again.

Nina returned to England first, and when Basil and I arrived at Tilbury by ship, she was there to greet us. She brought us the sad news that our father was dead. As he was only fifty-seven, this was entirely unexpected. It must have affected Basil far more than me because he knew him so much better; for me it was simply the removal of the main prop in family life. Also, of course, as was borne in on me later, my allowance stopped; I was earning £2.15s.0d. a week then and until I earned £3 I could certainly not afford new clothes or even three meals a day.

Algy had died a violent death. He had had unpleasantness with the Army Saddle Factory in Cawnpore over deliveries of oil he made to them which they said were watered; he took every precaution and even accompanied one delivery personally, but still the accusations were made, and he maintained that the tampering must be occurring at their end. He, Irma and Ann were about to set off for a holiday in the hills when something went wrong with the car; he put his womenfolk on a train and said he would follow when the car was fixed. On the Saturday night he went, as Secretary, to the Club dance where two of the Saddle Factory employees picked a quarrel with him. After heated exchanges other people came between them and the evening progressed smoothly, but when Algy left to go home, locking up behind him, several of them were waiting for him outside and beat him up. When they left him he was able to crawl to a tonga which took him to the hospital; here he spent the next two days, but then he drove as planned to Naini Tal to join Irma. The following week was miserable and the rain fell heavily. He did not tell Irma what had happened but she realised he was ill and that they must go home. She drove the whole way and when they arrived he could not get out of the car, so she drove on to the hospital. His brother Aubrey was sent for from Calcutta, and decided he should escort him back there, where medical facilities were better. In the train he ran a high fever, no ice was available, and he died. He was taken off the train at Asansol, and Irma was sent for. There was a convent and the nuns were kindly but insisted on Irma paying her last respects to her lord and master; after three days in the Indian heat this was an ordeal indeed, and she became hysterical. Thereupon they locked her in a cell for the night. Algy was buried next day.

Irma was left destitute. Algy had no pension and, with all of us to provide for, had been unable to save. When he went bankrupt during the war, he was unable to pay his insurance premiums and the policy lapsed; when he got back on his feet he was not allowed to pay up the back premiums but had to start again. He was so enraged that he did not insure at all. The whole incident of his death was such a disgrace to the European community that it was hushed up, everyone rallied to help, and a whip-round raised the fares to get Irma and Ann to England.

Now trouble began for me. Irma wanted me to live with her but after two years on my own I no longer wanted to. I had made a sort of life for myself of which I was neither proud nor fond, but it was mine, and I had not yet forgiven her for having left me. So she returned to the rented house at Middleton-on-Sea where she had friends, Basil paid the rent and she earned a living by hemming the rolled edges of Jacqmar silk scarves. She insisted that I should come home once a month but this was difficult as the train fare was 13s.10d. return, which I just did not have. I had my bicycle, which I was buying in instalments from the insurance broker's office, so I took to cycling the sixty miles every month. I would leave work a little early and start from Aldgate at 5 p.m. on a Friday, reaching home as a rule around midnight. I would sleep till lunchtime on Saturday and set off back after lunch on Sunday, so she did not see much of me but she felt she was being a good mother.

The cycle rides became a bit tedious and I borrowed Brian's motor scooter once but it was not at all satisfactory so I bought a proper motor bike. It only cost £6, being made up of spare parts from all kinds of makes. I learned to ride it up and down wide Queen's Gate and it did me proud for several runs home; but when it broke down I never had any idea what to do and was reduced to pushing the great heavy thing. I went back to my bike and sometimes got a lift on a lorry. I could get helped up hills by getting into the slipstream of a lorry and occasionally grabbed hold of the odd dangling chain; once on doing that I found the lorry full of grinning soldiers.

Betty and I became more ambitious and just before the war broke out we took a four-roomed mews flat near South Kensington Station. Somehow we furnished it, and let one of the rooms to the girlfriend of an architect we knew, who said she was in dire distress; she had discovered the hard way that her two flatmates were lesbians and wanted desperately to move. It was difficult to hire a van then as there was a fuel shortage, so we conceived the brilliant plan of hiring a fruit barrow one evening, to move Kat's stuff from Theobald's Road, the other side of Holborn. We piled the barrow high but it was clear we could not get everything on, so the others decided that, as I was the biggest, they would push this one off and I should go and find another for the lesser residue. I was lucky and met a tired woman pushing her barrow home; yes, I could have it for half-a-crown but it must be back by 3 a.m. Then I realised I could not manage to get on to the barrow the items I had to push: a trunk, an armchair and a chest of drawers. They were in the hall and I did not dare go up to the flat and ask the lesbians: I had no clear idea what they were but they sounded rather fierce and I did not risk it. A kind policeman helped me, and off I set. It seemed a long way and the slope outside Selfridges was much steeper than I remembered. Stopping at traffic lights I was unable to get started again, slipping on metal studs in the road. An elderly man stepped off the pavement and gave me a hand to the next crossroads. A bus conductor hung off the back of his bus and shouted:

'All yer want now's a nice mantelpiece to put yer feet on, ducks!'

Going down Park Lane I began to think about the horrors and steepness of Hyde Park Corner, and thought it would be better to go into the park opposite the Dorchester Hotel. Two heads being better than one, the others had thought of this at Marble Arch, and met the policeman on point duty at the Dorchester entrance, who told them firmly that commercial vehicles were not allowed in the park; they, cross and tired, gave him lip. He could not believe his eyes when I appeared, in a balaclava helmet like Betty and Kat and to him seeming to be one of them, and I got very short shrift; like them I had to toil round Hyde Park Corner in the thickening snow. Once home we had to push the barrows back in the dark, with kerosene lamps tied on.

When war was declared we had no idea what to expect but we thrilled to the propaganda and became very patriotic. Not quite enough to join up though, the stockings in the women's Services were too awful. I did apply for a job at the War Office but was turned down without an interview because my mother's name had been Stagno Navarra. We were all called up but as long as one was in what was considered to be a 'reserved' job one did not have to join the Services, and of course there were many jobs that had to be done in war or peace. The first night Betty and I trailed along to the nearest air raid shelter, carrying a mattress on which we both attempted to sleep, but apart from the proximity of an unaccustomed body, we were surrounded by ladies who did not stop clacking all night. We agreed not to do that again, and the next night took the mattress down to the garage below, empty except for a large table under which we spent another horrid night. We decided that we preferred to risk death by bombing, and at least expected to be killed outright as there was nothing between us and a bomb but the roof. The bombing in fact did not begin for a year.

We had three white cats at this time; white was the theory, as of course in London they were always grey. They lived as far as we knew entirely on rooftops when they were out. They bred freely and we had a dreadful on-going problem looking for homes for the kittens. The war did not inhibit them at all.

Until the Blitz began, the war meant very little to me personally. I had seen a dogfight high in the sky when I was sunbathing at the Roehampton swimming pool. Douglas Tidy, who had become a solicitor and whom I saw frequently, joined up and so did Basil. The worst thing was clothes rationing, which allowed only so many points a year and you had to go without stockings if you needed a dress. We took to painting our legs in summer but it was a fag and did not always look good, and was of course chilly.

Food was rationed but one could manage in an extraordinary way: in the country it was easier but in London one hardly saw an egg, though one could get revolting powdered egg; half a pint of milk a day for two people was a strain, and the meat ration was laughable, but one could get sausage meat and fish; oranges and bananas one forgot about, they were for the children or the old, if they were available at all. Any little forbidden item that came one's way, or any little luxury, was a delicious treat, and any clever dodge you could learn, like marinating horsemeat and even whalemeat to make it edible, was a triumph. One saw a queue and instantly joined it, wondering what on earth one was queuing for.

★   ★   ★

Then one evening came the Blitz. The Germans struck at the City first and we could see the sky red with the reflected flames. In the morning when I cycled to work I had to make several detours as roads were roped off because of fallen buildings or buildings about to fall, or unexploded landmines. One of the girls in the office had been bombed at home; she had been in a shelter and was unharmed but her flat and all her possessions had gone; she had nothing but what she stood up in. It was my first experience of such things, and I was amazed the way she simply rejoiced to be alive, regretting nothing she had lost.

In a letter to Basil in October I wrote:

> I wonder if you can imagine what life in London is like now. It is extraordinary how soon everyone has got used to it and it all seems normal and not really frightening in retrospect. I mean at the dawn of each day you don't think 'My God, what horrors have I to suffer today?' though I must say one does suffer sheer terror during air raids at night, which thank the Lord have eased up this past week owing to bad weather.
>
> I cycle to work because it seems the only satisfactory method of transport, though after a really bad night I don't because of the glass on the roads. At night the wretched workers get desperate in their efforts to get home, fighting to get on buses, unashamedly opening car doors in traffic jams and asking for lifts, and simply surging in to the roads as a bus comes along. A lot of firms have arranged for lorries to take their staff to and from work.
>
> Conversation overheard is nearly always about war. More and more people wear tin hats. We don't take shelter when the warning goes, only when our roof spotter sights enemy aircraft coming in our direction. Bomb craters and fallen houses obstruct numerous roads and traffic diversions are one of the nuisances. Gas is cut off nearly everywhere and I don't know anyone who regularly has a bath – personally I haven't had one since Liss (some weeks before I stayed with Reggie Dukes) as we have a gas heater. Luckily our cooker is electric so we are not seriously handicapped. But when you are working you are choosy about where to have lunch, as some places boast coal ranges and can produce hot meals. Every other telephone exchange is out of order; at the office we can't use the phones at all, at home we get calls in but not out. No cuppers at tea time.
>
> Every day you wonder fearfully what well-loved building has been wrecked and you scan the roads anxiously on the way to work. Fulham is a sight to make your heart bleed. The Leicester Square Theatre and the London Pavilion are gutted. Buckingham Palace has been hit several times but you can't see much from the road. John Lewis is a terrible sight, one building completely destroyed

and fallen in, the other gutted except for the far end, where they are bravely carrying on. Bourne and Hollingsworth has a hole right through the middle where chaos reigns but all round the various brilliant departments are going on as before. The City is a nasty mess and you can get no transport further east than the Bank. The South Kensington Museum was badly burnt at one end. You can't go along Piccadilly from Sackville Street to the Circus now and Bond Street has had very bad luck. Actually everywhere has and you gasp as you go along and see chaos in every road in several places. And still the public services carry on; the buses are often quite lost as drivers don't know the districts when they get off their routes. A bomb fell at Marble Arch right through the road into the Underground.

The tubes are a pathetic sight: a large percentage of the population actually live down there. I spoke to one woman who was sitting on a rug on the platform with a little boy and a baby; she said her bigger kids, three of them, were being sent to the country the following week, but she'd got to stay with the baby as she didn't know a family to go to. Until they go the three children have to live in the tube, hardly ever going up into the open because she has to buy a ticket for them every time. We are all so dreading the outbreak of disease down there. At night when they all lie down there is only just room to walk along the edge of the platform.

One morning I arrived at work to find the building had been hit and we were told to go home. I persuaded the policeman on duty to let me in to get my knitting, which was intact in a drawer of my desk, though the typewriter on top was a mangled wreck. On my way home, I thought I would call on Nina, but as I drew near to her address there were more and more barriers and police. At last I could see down her street and No. 21 had been hit. Pleading that I had a great friend in there, I got through the barriers, and as I reached the house, which did not exist above the first floor and that was pretty damaged, a man came out on to the steps.

'Where is Miss Lynch?' I cried.

'Oh,' said he, 'she's gone to the hairdresser.' Of course.

I decided to look for another job and quickly found a most amusing one (which was 'reserved' or I would have had to join the Services and worn those stockings) with ENSA, the organisation which sent entertainments to the troops. I was secretary to the ballet mistress who called everyone, including me, 'Darling'. She asked me to make a card index of girls we saw at auditions, so that I could quickly summon up on demand three 5'6" redheads, say, or five assorted 5'8" girls who all had roughly the same measurements. One met all sorts of well-known theatre and film people, and I felt thoroughly in the mood because I had, briefly, a boyfriend in the Dutch Fleet Air Arm who used to meet me at the stage door in a red-lined cloak.

By this time I had literally got away from Brian after terrifying violence on his part, and had had to disappear. This proved surprisingly easy, considering how often one goes to London and meets somebody one knows. I gave out that I had gone home for a week, and after three days returned and packed up and moved the mile or so to Chelsea, to live with Sheila Satchwell, a friend of both Pam and Basil, whom she had met in Manchuria. She was about ten years my senior and divorced; she enjoyed mothering me and gave me a lovely feeling of safety. She was enormous fun, a rather podgy blonde with enormous blue eyes and flapping eyelashes, a mad infectious laugh and a great zest for life. She took me to her bosom as if I was an unfledged chick, and reorganised my life. From having been eking out my pay by eating a couple of penny buns and a glass of milk (twopence) for lunch, she fed me like a queen, as she was a marvellous cook.

We stole along to the mews flat at dead of night and removed all my belongings, and I sadly said goodbye to Betty and Kat. At Sheila's I had to sleep on the sofa but her wonderful cooking reconciled me to that. She had a mad cat called Poppet whose every whim had to be pandered to because he did so hate the bombing. He would terrify us sometimes in the middle of the night by suddenly zooming up the chicken wire, stretched over hardboard and fixed over the windows to prevent flying glass; the wire banged against the hardboard, back and forth, making us think something was descending on us.

Sheila had streams of glamorous people visiting her: Russian aristocrats, Polish refugees, Dutch Fleet Air Arm, Free French; also her remarkable mother and tiresome literary brother. I contributed a Hungarian sculptor at this juncture whom I had met in an air raid shelter and sat for, for a medallion – I sat for both the women, one seated and one kneeling as if for forgiveness at her feet. This was Paul Vincze who became famous; he was rather a pathetic little man, in fact, and I let him drift away.

Sheila and I were firewatchers. This entailed taking a weekly turn (often more frequently as there were very few of us, so many people having left London); we would spend the night on campbeds, dressed for action, in the basement kitchen of a large house at the end of our cul-de-sac, Woodfall Street; we covered that and Smith Street, often with only two of us and not the three needed to work a stirrup pump; one to fetch water, one to pump and one to direct the spray. One always hoped it would not happen but one night when it happened to me, I was on with Betty's half-sister who also lived in our street. It was what I had dreaded as Jena was rather grand and very county, a naval widow, willowy and fashionable, seemingly rather helpless with her long red nails and her upper-class drawl. In the event she was quite marvellous. They were dropping small fire bombs and while one was trying to put them out, oil bombs rained down and became ignited in a terrifying way. Jena and I ran out blowing our whistles hoping for help, as we knew we were not much good at hacking down front doors of unoccupied houses with the axe provided, to get at bombs on the roof, apart from only being two to the stirrup pump. Our whistles were answered by three drunken American journalists whom we soon put to work. One was very good at holding the nozzle of the stirrup pump and did not mind how near he got to the blaze – one had to take a little care of him but he was a pair of hands. I spied a fire bomb spitting away on the porch roof of our own house and was able to act as a stepladder for another journalist, rather fat, who bravely swept the bomb off with a dustbin lid, on to the ground where I could deal with it. Whenever I lost Jena, I could find her at the top of a burning building with her team. When it was all over we gathered in her little house for coffee, and I saw somebody I did not recognise for a moment; then I realised it was me in a looking-glass, wearing somebody else's Red Cross tin hat and with a completely black face.

Another night when Sheila and I had friends to dinner, I heard a noise and went outside to investigate, and there was a small bomb burning on the pavement; without calling for help (it was so small) I whammed it with a nearby sandbag as was the drill, but it was a new kind of device which exploded. Luckily I had put on my welly boots but my knees were badly burned.

When the Germans' new weapons, the V1s and V2s began, I found I was far more frightened than during the Blitz. I had thought it was all over. The first V1 I saw was when I was cleaning my teeth, and I thought it was a plane shot down; they were pilotless planes which came over in threes, crashing and blowing up like bombs, very unpleasant; if you got the line of the first two in a 'stick', you knew roughly where the third was going to land, in that line and the same distance from the second one as that had been from the first. The V2s I did not mind so much as they travelled faster than sound and you only heard them after they had arrived, so if you were underneath you had no warning; many people, however, found this hard to bear, and expected them all the time.

Life went on. I went out to dinner in a Fulham restaurant with Rex, a man I had met in the City, and afterwards, about 9 o'clock, being unable to get a taxi because the air raid warning had gone, we set off to walk back. The raid began and seemed hot in our area; they were trying to get Lot's Road Power Station on the opposite side of the Embankment, it seemed. We took cover in a nearby shelter, one of two in a wide ditch divided by a bridge serving a block of tenement flats in Beaufort Street, Chelsea. Several hours later, when we were more than sick of it, the shelter on the other side of the bridge was hit. We were shaken and covered with dust but all right. The men went out to see what they could do. After a while somebody put his head in and said:

'Could one of you ladies come and help the doctor?'

The other women were friends and relatives of those in the stricken shelter and were reluctant to face the horrors, so I went. The street was bright in a flare of gas from a holed main, and the shelter could be seen, collapsed like a pack of cards: it was difficult to believe it had looked like our own, still bravely standing in the ditch looking pretty solid. I stood looking down, and a man in the crater, ascertaining I had come to help the doctor, said:

'Jump, love, I'll catch you.'

Jump I did, but he did not catch me; we had miscalculated our comparative sizes and he was flattened. Then the doctor was not there; there was a hold-up because the heavy rescue people had not arrived so nobody could get at the people under the collapsed concrete. Ambulances stood anxiously by.

I heard a baby crying and tried to locate it. Finding the place, I called:

'Is there a baby there?'

A girl's voice replied from almost beneath my feet:

'No, the baby was the other end.'

I knew this was no longer so but having found somebody, I concentrated on her. She said she could see my feet, that she was all right but could not feel her legs. Having located her, and given a few words of comfort, I said I would get her a cup of tea, the British panacea, but I did not know you should not give liquid to somebody who might have internal injuries. Finding a way to scramble out of the pit, I crossed the road to an open front door in a small house opposite, passing as I did so an Air Raid Precautions Warden who looked absolutely ghastly. I found a wonderful old lady in the house, fully dressed in black with beads and a brooch, ready for anything. She told me the ARP man had his family in the shelter, his wife, two daughters and a grandchild. She could not produce tea as her gas was of course cut off, but she gave me brandy. I took it back to the girl who said she had discovered there was a stone pinning her under the concrete and if I could push this away she thought she could get out. The heavy rescue people were arriving but were starting at the other end of the shelter, so feeling that action was required to keep this girl's spirits up, I began to remove stones from in front of the triangular aperture through which I could now see her head. Soon I was digging like a dog, not noticing in my excitement what damage I was doing to my fingers. I came upon the body of a young boy in a green jersey, face down; upon him I had to lie in order to reach into the now enlarged hole and try to move the stone. It was not difficult and to my amazement the girl crawled out and I took her to one of the ambulances. She was fifteen and must have been the ARP warden's daughter, as I heard later that only three people survived out of over sixty, and that he had lost his family except for her. The doctor was waiting for action and when he examined this girl and found her miraculously whole, we went back to the pit where the first people had been revealed. A row of five people were sitting tidily, covered with white concrete dust, all leaning sideways from the blast, all dead. The doctor sent me away; there were plenty of people around and he was not expecting to need much help. I found Rex and we departed, the awful smell of gas and powdered concrete and death in our nostrils. It stayed with me. I thought it was in my hair, my clothes, my pillow. I washed everything furiously but still the smell remained. I went home to Irma for a week to recover and then it went away, but I wanted to get back to London. It must not be bombed while I was not there. I had become identified with London and her agony.

I rang Rex when I got back and he invited me to dine at the RAC Club in Pall Mall. I thought a drink would be better as I did not want to get caught by the air raid warning but it went even before I got there on my bicycle, nicely dressed in a Madonna-blue jacket and skirt and a white blouse. We dined early in the hope of getting it over before the raid began. We did not. We heard a bomb drop not far away, another a little nearer, and paralysed, waited for the third of the 'stick' to fall. It fell on the Carlton Club next door, with quite an effect on ours. There was a three-man band playing on a little dais in the dining room, with a glass dome above them which fell in and killed one of them. We did not know this at the time, as Rex had grabbed my hand and dragged me away from the explosion through the nearby swing doors into the kitchen. This proved to be a mistake as the chimneys belched soot and I was covered.

The initial shock over, we went to find the ladies' room for me to clean up; calm club servants told us I could not use it as the black-out curtains had come down, and would we like a drink, sir? I used the gents' lavatories while Rex stood guard outside. Then we found that the black-out was down in the only area where ladies were allowed to sit, and even in this emergency the house rules could not be bent. We were finally ushered into the basement shelter where for six hours we sat on hard wooden slats with several other men. In the corner was a partition round a bucket, which in the end I was forced to use. The others kindly whistled a noisy song but their proximity paralysed me and when they finally stopped, feeling all must now be well, I was still unrelieved. They got the message and kept up a singsong until I finally emerged, red-faced. At 3 a.m. the 'all clear' sounded and I cycled back to Chelsea. I did not see Rex again; we felt we made a bad combination and attracted bombs.

Pam was 'evacuated' to Wales, as were Cousin Nancy and her daughter Sheila, all to Borth. Pam shared a house with another girl and her twins, the same age as Richard, five, and their grandmother. One unforgettable day the boys were playing on a sand heap outside when the grandmother leaned out of a window and called them to come in and wash for lunch. Richard turned his head and said clearly:

'Shan't, you ancient bugger.'

(Such words were easily learned at the local primary school.) One can imagine the scenes which ensued, but the best bit was when Pam was putting a still tearful child to bed and he asked:

'What does ancient mean, Mummy?'

I loved going to stay with them particularly as, if I saved up my sugar ration, Pam would turn it into fudge for me.

I was not satisfied with my work for ENSA and the Tidys (still keeping their eyes on me) came to the rescue and recommended me for the job of secretary to the Dean of St Thomas's Hospital Medical School, which had just been evacuated to Godalming in Surrey. I was quite glad to go, away from the constant fear of meeting Brian, and to what promised to be a really good job. The bombing stopped as soon as I turned my back and did not resume until I returned two years later.

★   ★   ★

Professor McSwiney, my new boss, was a physiologist and his office where I worked was in the stables of the Manor House, the school's headquarters; a laboratory led out of the office, where he and a lecturer in physiology conducted experiments, mostly on rabbits, which did not please me. Downstairs were the physiology classrooms, from which soon after my arrival the students reeled in their annual exercise of swallowing stomach pumps, staggering about the garden and retching rubber tubes.

McSwiney was not an attractive character but he had a very nice wife and family; I became quite friendly with his daughter Nora. Charles Downman, the lecturer, was his blue-eyed boy, a good looking fair man, very shy and reserved, who was to become my husband. His parents, he a parson, she a passionate Channel Islands woman who had become an hysterical paralytic, had given him a strange upbringing. Charles, when his elder brother left for Australia at the age of sixteen and was never heard of again, studied behind a baize door in the vicarage, to shut out the sound of his parents' rows. He himself was a gentle, good person, utterly devoted to his research.

So began for me a period of blessed peace after the hurly-burly of that unreal London life. I was billeted on a parson's widow who had her daughter and parson son-in-law living with her. They were incredibly narrow-minded and although I liked them, I was not sorry when the daughter's baby was born and they needed my room. I moved down the hill to a baker and his wife; the wife having once been a maid to a friend of Irma's, was delighted in her old-fashioned way to give me her front bedroom and parlour, which I was terrified of soiling, and to cook for me as best she could. One of my perks was a wonderful chamber pot in my bedroom (the lavatory being outside). It had a frog in the bottom with his popping eyes staring upwards and his mouth wide open! It had been part of a collection made by Irma's friend, and she gave it to the maid as a wedding present.

I enjoyed the country walks and in winter I had Charles tobogganing in fields behind the Manor House; he had never had such fun and the staff were convulsed with mirth at old Downman becoming so human. The pathologist on the staff was a strange little man who loved to shock; one day at tea he innocently offered to show me the Anatomy Hut and I accepted. Luckily somebody warned me that even students sometimes fainted, so I was steeled to anything, determined not to please him by being shocked. He took me into this long hut lined with tables on which bluish corpses lay smelling of formaldehyde, some being dissected by fresh-faced young men. I tried to concentrate on the young men, a little hard when the professor playfully flapped a loose buttock. I hurried through and gained his office where I expressed intense interest, in my relief, in a bottled hand on his desk; instantly he whisked me back to the nearest corpse and demonstrated how the large and small tendons exposed in an arm worked the forearm and fingers. That nearly finished me but I made it and he left me alone after that.

Irma was living in the stables of an old aunt of Algy's in Herefordshire, my Great Aunt Beachie. She had become fed up with the restrictions of barbed wire at the seaside, as she once said to me on the telephone when I was living with Betty. A censor immediately chipped in and said:

'Careless talk costs lives!' and our line was cut for twenty-four hours.

We thought it was probably tapped in the first place because Betty was taking the *Daily Worker*, a Communist newspaper.

I went to stay with Irma from time to time and that was another world again. Aunt Beachie was of another age and an autocrat on her diminished estate. Visiting her one had not to wear lipstick but stockings were de rigueur; one had tea round a vast dining table completely covered by a decent white linen cloth, though there was not a great deal to eat, spread thinly on several plates from end to end. With her lived a deaf son and daughter and another daughter who was mentally retarded. With Irma, Ann and me that made quite a party. When staying there one was inevitably employed by Aunt Beachie in whatever activity was going on. I particularly remember one damson-picking season, when Aunt Beachie, in her black alpaca and an enormous picture hat, sat in the wheelbarrow sorting fruit and seeing that we were all fully employed. Even little Richard, aged two, was roped in, the lowest branches of anything being saved for him. There were frequent despairing yells as Cousin Emmie on top of a ladder, would accidentally overturn her basket of fruit on to Cousin Isabel stooping beneath, or from Cousin Joe when Pam broke down a brussels sprout plant when pursuing Richard, who had found a small axe.

Irma's life was quite difficult but she made the best of it and was always cheerful. The stairs to her mews flat were very steep and the flat tiny, with oil lamps, a coal oven and a spirit stove for heating. There was no water and every drop had to be carried up from the pump, but she managed to bath in a lovely old hip bath that Aunt Beachie had been able to provide, in front of the fire. The lavatory was at the other side of the yard and Irma (having bladder trouble) usually could not make the width of the yard in time, so kept a chamber pot in the flat; this provided the big thrill of the day when she went to empty it in full view of the house. Such a constant irritation Irma made into a joke. She had already found congenial friends around, with whom she made merry.

In due course Ann was called up, like everyone else, to do war work, and was sent to work in a munitions factory. She took it in her usual cheerful way but it was tough. She had to be on the roadside by 7 a.m. every day in all weathers to be picked up by the factory bus, and in the end this caused her to suffer pneumonia and she was very ill. When she recovered, Irma tried to get her exemption but all she achieved was permission to find more suitable war work herself. This resulted in Ann being employed in a nearby boys' school as a maid. She was ecstatic. For the rest of the war she enjoyed her independence and the knowledge that she was earning, but as soon as the war ended Irma took her away: it was not in her view 'suitable'.

Throughout this time she was a constant worry (this was mutual!). Having been left penniless and with Ann, she tackled her problems with the utmost courage and verve before she retreated to Leominster. However, there was not much for a woman of her sort to do, especially with Ann in tow, except for domestic service. With all young people called up to do work of national importance, Irma and Ann made quite a desirable team as housekeeper and maid, but Irma had not got the makings of an employee. Time and again she had to leave posts because of 'differences' with her employer. In one case Irma had taken the opportunity of her employer's absence to move all the drawing room furniture to better positions ('She had no taste at all, dear') and of course this was not in the least appreciated. Ann had to have an operation on her eye and for some reason Irma was not able to visit her so I did so. I was continually being called upon to rally round in one way or another and began to feel my mother and Ann were my responsibility rather than I my mother's. Basil was in the Army in Burma and Pam and Joe in China were a constant nagging worry.

Joe had gone back to China and was posted to Shanghai. Pam and Richard followed later, having to go via America to avoid the U-boats. In 1941 when the Japanese came, they were interned, but were better off than many, being incarcerated in an hotel rather than a camp. Food was unattractively and unsuitably cooked and the wives managed to persuade their guards to let them have the raw ingredients with which to feed the children; these were cooked on a primus stove in one of the bathrooms, in tins in a chamber pot. Pam was incredibly daring in continuing to go to her dressmaking classes not far away. She was able to go into a bar downstairs to which people from outside also had access through another door, and she would have a drink and leave through that door, walking down the street expecting a bullet between the shoulder blades. This is known as living dangerously.

A year later, they were exchanged with Japanese diplomatic prisoners of war. Joe was separated from them at Laurenço Marques, and sent straight to Urumchi in Chinese Turkestan where he languished for four years. In September 1942 somebody brought me a cutting from *The Times* which listed those on board that Japanese ship. I was so excited I could not look: and Charles did so for me and found Pam and Joe and Richard listed, whereupon to my own surprise I burst into tears of joy and relief.

Charles and I continued to go for walks together, to pick blackberries, and go further afield on our bicycles. To him this was all an eye-opener as he had lived such a deprived life. His father was the Vicar of Lambeth, a man who could deliver a really good and erudite sermon, but his private life was a travesty. His wife's illness was said by the doctors to be entirely psychological. Whatever it was, she never put a foot to the ground during the years I knew her. She had a violent temper and one had to be careful not to leave breakables near her as she tended to throw them – her moods were quite unpredictable. Charles used to go home almost every weekend to support his father and to have a horrible time.

To me Charles and the simple pleasures we shared were a blessed contrast to what really had been the horror, on the whole, of life in London, and it was not long before I persuaded myself that marriage to Charles was just what I wanted. He was a thoroughly good person, gentle, intellectual, with a quiet but keen sense of humour. He was working on shock, among other things, and invented a new apparatus for taking blood pressure around that time. He was constantly doing live experiments on rabbits which I hated, particularly as I used to feed them, but he convinced me that the animals did not suffer pain and were put down after any operation.

Charles proposed to me after a year and I accepted but was assailed by doubts thereafter. In the end we probably both had doubts but neither felt they could back out. Irma was much opposed to the marriage as she knew we were not suited, and the only thing that reconciled her a little was that Charles' mother was so opposed to it, and there was a violent clash of personalities there! We were married in the perfect little Norman church at Compton in January 1943, and Uncle Reggie gave me away. Mrs Downman was unable to be there and forbade her husband to attend. He advised Charles strongly against marriage to anyone at all.

Dr Charles Downman, my first husband.

We spent a week at an inn at Fairford, during which time Charles became ill and had to stay in bed. He never really got well though nobody could find out what was wrong; a duodenal ulcer was suspected but never found. The Dean suggested it was all due to psychological reasons connected with marriage and eventually I came to believe this to be true. He was afraid that if we had a family and I had to stop working, he could not afford to keep us, with the result that he was quite unable to make a family possible.

At first we lived in a house which was a hostel for eight of the medical students and we ran it as best we could. The boiler was a constant drag as it kept going out. The 'boys' collected road signs and filled their wardrobes with them. The bathroom was full of their drugs, some to put them to sleep, some to stimulate them for work, and so on. Charles had a skeleton in a long box under the bed, on which he had learned anatomy, and our first Christmas was spent with this skeleton being checked over beside the Christmas tree, to make sure none of the small bones were missing before it was sold for the regulation £5. The cleaning woman was constantly hysterical at finding bones amongst the biscuits in the students' rooms, as they were not as tidy as Charles. The cooking worried me a lot as I had never done much and I made some dreadful mistakes. We soon acquired a black cat called Pussyfoot.

Charles was a member of the Home Guard and had duties one or two evenings a week, and I worked two evenings at a YMCA canteen. Our walks included salvage walks, when we picked up metal and rubber thrown into hedges and gutters. An invasion test was being held in the area. I, as a firewatcher, had to go to bed dressed, in case incendiaries were dropped, and my only complaint was they did not drop any so I had nothing to do. Charterhouse boys sped round on bicycles with blackened faces, looking desperate. Charles walked round the strong-points of Godalming from 9 p.m. till 4 a.m. as they got 'bombed out', but the only time he could have given medical assistance, the enemy was between him and the casualties. I went to a lecture on fire-fighting and found that all the techniques had changed since I had done it in the Blitz. All that had been wrong! One should not hit an incendiary with sandbags or a spray, only a jet; one should not tackle it at all for seven minutes as it may explode (this leaves plenty of time for conflagration, I thought). All sorts of new bombs were described.

Charles continued to visit his parents every other weekend and at first I went with him, but his mother was so insufferably rude to me, still calling me Miss Duke, that I soon reckoned I was not obliged to go.

In March 1943 Charles was seconded to a job at the Medical Research Council in London and we had to move. The job was top secret but I put two and two together and decided it was experimenting on the effect of diving in submarines at different speeds and to different depths. I am sure he was using himself as a guinea pig as he was often peculiarly unwell, and some years later (when we were no longer together) he had a very extraordinary heart condition which kept him in hospital for six months.

We took part of a house, 80 Sydney Street, Chelsea, over an estate agency. There was a good sitting room with a balcony, and a kitchen behind it, and upstairs a bedroom and bathroom, the latter being quite a good size and it did duty, with the aid of a campbed, as a spare room. Our cat Pussyfoot came with us from Godalming and did very well.

I got a job as secretary to the Director of the Lister Institute of Preventive Medicine, just by Chelsea Bridge (now the Lister Hospital), and had also to run the large medical library. This so alarmed me that I undertook a librarian's course in the evenings; it did not help much with a medical library but gave me confidence and an associateship to the Library Association. Far from reading lots of books, as I had fondly imagined, one had to memorise the birth and death dates of every author of any significance (and they were all significant until the twentieth century), and within five years the date of all their works. Classifying and cataloguing by the Dewey Decimal System was not really up my street either. However, I was surprised and elated when I passed the examination with honours and was top in England that year. I put that down to the fact that I was a comparatively old student and took the whole thing more seriously, realising that the young ones straight from school would find the work easier.

The Lister was full of scientists working on blood problems, some of them being Jewish refugees, and I had my work cut out deciphering their handwriting in their papers full of medical terms, but I found it a satisfying and challenging job. The Director, Alan Drury, was also head of the Blood Transfusion Service, which gave another dimension to the job. I remember the uproar there was once when it was found that one hospital was using time-expired blood as compost for the tomatoes they were growing as part of the war effort; tempers ran high as opinions were divided. I was in favour of the tomatoes, even though I was by then not only a regular six-monthly blood donor, but frequently gave a few ccs for experiments, as my blood proved to be B, a rare category in England, and I was the only person in the building who could provide it.

Six years of war is a long time when one is young and it became a way of life. One sweated and rejoiced and wept over epics like Dunkirk, and guessed at what was going on between what was said in the news and rumoured by those returning from the various fronts. I never heard a whisper about Nazi concentration camps, even though I was working among Jews. Douglas Tidy was killed at Alamein and that hit me, as he had been like an older brother; it was said of him that he lay wounded in the shade of a vehicle of some kind, and when stretcher-bearers came to take him back to a hospital tent, he refused, saying that he knew he was dying and they would do better to take somebody whose life could be saved.

I was working very hard, sublimation maybe, running the house, shopping and cooking, doing my 9 a.m. to 5 p.m. job and my librarian's course. I was not only knitting for the Forces but was taking knitting orders from friends and acquaintances, and re-knitting socks and jumpers because of the shortage of wool. At weekends I did sometimes visit Charles' parents across the river at Lambeth Vicarage, wondering if Ma would be in a china-throwing mood or not.

Queuing for food often took three quarters of an hour and then one had to queue as long again for something else, such as whale meat for Pussyfoot. One was constantly on the *qui vive* for something unusual in the shops, for instance on a visit to St John's Wood once (to see Cousin Michael) I found gin, biscuits and custard powder, all things never seen in Godalming, where we were living at the time. Clothes rationing was a pain: at first 66 points for twelve months, then 60 for fourteen, and even stockings cost one point; one had ration books for meat, butter and soap and at one point they even rationed onions. One learned to be extremely frugal: I boiled up ends of soap into new cakes, even ends of lipsticks – not that they were rationed, just expensive. We made coal dust into briquettes, and rolled and compressed newspapers to augment them in the grate. Clothes were altered endlessly to give an illusion of newness; unrationed collars, new buttons and ribbons helped. Hats were unrationed but expensive; Betty's mother was a milliner and I bought my hats cheaply from her; undoubtedly my love of hats began here and she provided me with some winners.

These thrifty habits became ingrained and are one of the biggest differences now between the old and the young who have not known war; the old cannot abide waste. Heating had to be used with discretion and one year I had to bring myself to ask for it to be turned on in my office when in January we had snow and I could hardly type.

Then a great calamity overtook me which may have been due to my overwork and stress generally. I was shopping at lunch-time in Peter Jones, my bicycle parked for safety inside a side entrance, which I often did even if I was not shopping in Peter Jones itself. I was looking for envelopes to fit National Gallery postcards which I was using as Christmas cards, but as I enquired my way to the correct counter I saw some photograph frames I thought would do as presents. I took two and wandered on, absentmindedly putting them in the flat open basket on my arm in order to free my hands to look at some diaries. The envelope counter was by the front door and they had none to fit my cards, suggesting that I went across Sloane Square to W.H. Smith. Forgetting all about the frames, I went out of the front door, leaving my cycle where it was till I had finished all my chores round the square. I was arrested by a shop detective and taken upstairs while they sent for the police. I could hardly believe it, but being innocent in intention, felt it must be ironed out soon. It was not. I was cautioned, made a statement, and taken away in a Black Maria to a police station to be searched. When I remembered my cycle, they thought it was very suspicious that I had not left by the side door and picked it up.

Everyone rallied to my cries of distress when I got home, a counsel was found and in due course I appeared in court. While I was waiting among the drunks and prostitutes, I saw a very aristocratic-looking old lady in a fur coat also waiting, in the company clearly of her daughter and a fine looking Guards officer in uniform. On enquiring of the detective in charge of my case (who was being very supportive and keeping between me and the worst of the drunks), I was told the old lady was a kleptomaniac and they all knew her well! My reputation was vouched for by Dr Drury, who said I had access to his flat above the office and his wife was stone deaf so would not hear me if I had gone in, but nothing had ever been missing; by Betty in her VAD uniform which she hoped would help, though she was only part-time; by Charles looking rather bewildered. I was discharged but the judge made a statement which was reported in the evening papers that warned women shoppers to be more careful.

I worried a lot about our marriage during the three years we were together. I knew that we could not expect a family unless Charles stopped worrying about being able to support us. As it was, he paid the rent and I paid for everything else which amounted to slightly more than the rent. I made a plan that we should rent a house so that we could take one or two lodgers; thus if I had a baby I would still contribute to the budget by looking after them; perhaps this would uninhibit Charles. I found a suitable house in Notting Hill Gate and the day came when I had to sign a contract for five years. That pulled me up short. I realised that apart from babies, I could not live with this man for another five years, let alone a lifetime. I signed the contract, but having told Charles of my decision to leave him, I proposed to Irma that she come and share the house with me. She agreed with alacrity and in fact she took on the contract.

Charles was naturally rather annoyed. I did not feel it was more than this, though of course sometimes had doubts, as he was so reserved it was difficult to tell. I found him a smaller flat and moved him into it, with the cat and most of the wedding presents. I set him up with a store cupboard and taught him a bit of cooking. He refused to give evidence of adultery, which was the usual reason given for divorce, otherwise one had to desert for five years, which seemed to me a lifetime. So I decided that I would have to give evidence of adultery. Having no men friends in a position to oblige, I asked Basil, who was on leave, for his advice; he did me proud, as he produced a friend who was going through a divorce himself and had no objection to helping me get my evidence. We agreed to spend a (blameless) night in an hotel at Victoria Station which specialised in witnesses for divorce cases, we were told. It was an extremely funny experience. I wore a spectacular hat in order to be remembered and we were given a twin-bedded room with bathroom, in which we decorously undressed and dressed. We ordered early morning tea, and newspapers too, and went out for dinner. In the morning a man came with the tea and plonked it down on the nearest bedside table without putting on the light. A little boy knocked, opened the door a crack and flung in the papers. We lay there laughing helplessly. So far we had no witness. Then we thought of ringing the bell and asking the maid to draw the curtains. Although she did not appear to look at us, we felt that this preposterous request (did we not know there was a war on? hotels were short-staffed, guests had to do a minimum to help themselves) would make her remember us. I did not have to attend the hearing and it all went through without a hitch.

To add to my feelings of guilt, poor Pam was widowed, she who wanted her husband. He had been left for four years in Urumchi, in Chinese Turkestan, while his American opposite number had been changed three times. They were trying to get the old Silk Road opened because the sea route for merchandise to and from the Far East was so treacherous now with all the mines. There were Russians and Chinese and Joe spoke so many languages he could without doubt communicate with everyone, but there was nobody with whom he felt real affinity. For the last eighteen months the town had been cut off by hostile tribes and no planes could land. Finally one did land, bearing his relief, but Joe would not take off on the plane half an hour later; he quickly wrote a letter to Pam to say that they would now be able to get planes in and out and he would come on the next one, but he did not feel he could hand over a complex situation to his relief in such a short time. He said he had frostbite and waxed quite amusing about having one or two joints of toes cut off by a local medicine man, while the Mir of Hunza held his hat underneath to catch them. A few weeks later Pam received a telegram; she was bathing Richard at the time and he was standing up in the bath having his bottom washed when Joe's mother came panting up the stairs with the orange envelope in her hand:

'I expect it's from your brother, dear,' she said (Basil also was expected home), but they both thought, prayed, that it was from Joe to say that he was in England. Pam opened it and read the message out loud before realizing what it said:

'Regret to inform you of the death of your husband', etc. The quickest reaction was from the six-year-old.

'Oh, now I shall never know his face!' and a moment later with his hands clasped: 'I shall never have any brothers and sisters!' and again: 'Mummy, will you get married again?' That was a terrible time for them all.

I met Pam in London when she came up to see her solicitor, the Foreign Office, and so on. As we drove along in a taxi the tears poured down her cheeks with no grimacing, and she said:

'What can I do? I was made to cherish and be cherished.'

The Foreign Office denied her a pension because Joe had shot himself. We could not believe it and for a long time thought it must have been a political murder, but I contacted Eric Shipton, the explorer, when he was about to pass through Urumchi on an expedition, and he made enquiries and assured me it had been suicide. It was understandable: the frostbite had developed into gangrene; there was no doctor in the place; he had already lost several joints of toes when he wrote and no doubt knew that he would be losing at least a part of both legs, and that every untreated day made it more likely that he would lose his legs altogether, or even die in agony. Dear Joe, he probably took a very brave decision but how we mourned him.

After living with Irma for a year, and the war being over, I felt I had to get away: I was living her life, not my own; the house was always filled with her friends. She had been absolutely wonderful to me during that dreadful year when I wept buckets of guilt and she comforted me. I knew without asking that she would be hurt if I moved to my own accommodation in London, and that she would not understand if I tried to get a job in the provinces. A job abroad, yes, that was reasonable. I had no wish to upset her now we had at last become friends, so I applied for jobs abroad.

I had three choices in the end: a library in Washington, but I have never had any desire to live in the States; a university library in Durban which attracted me most, but the climate being good, I should only have had a month's annual leave, and no fares paid, and I felt I must keep in contact with Irma. The sea journey alone would have taken up all the month and air travel at that time was not usual. The third job therefore had it. This was to put in order in Lagos, Nigeria, a medical library which had been left to the country by an old African doctor, and to administer it thereafter; I would have two months' leave after an eighteen-month tour, fare paid.

I enrolled to learn Yoruba at the London School of Oriental Languages but did not get very far before I had to leave. It is a difficult tonal language and I always remember learning their alphabet and the African teacher telling me how to pronounce 'Gb'.

'You make your mouth as though you are going to say G – but you don't say it. Then you make your mouth as though you are going to say B – but you don't say it. You breathe in and say them both together.'

There were other combinations which worked in much the same way, and made me very glad that I hardly ever had to use the language: servants were very seldom Yorubas and I never had one, educated Yorubas spoke English.

I left England in the grip of one of the worst winters in living memory, and set off for the part of my life which I could really describe as my core, at any rate it proved to be the happiest.

CHAPTER 3

Nigeria
1947-1959

I SET OFF IN January 1947 on a banana boat for this adventure which was
utterly to change my life. There were only twelve passengers on board and
accommodation was fairly rough and ready, but I thoroughly enjoyed it all. We
called at Freetown and I was fascinated to see that even the seagulls were black
– no doubt they were young ones but I did not know that then.

Upon arrival in Lagos I was met by a fat middle-aged doctor called George
Waller, who took me under his wing. I was put into a chalet attached to the
Ikoyi Club and lived there for six weeks while waiting for a flat. During that
time I had sandfly fever which was extremely unpleasant, but I was
wonderfully cared for by my Hausa 'boy', Baku; he brought me tea and ginger
beer and aspirins and when he found I only got worse, he fetched a doctor and
I recovered.

The job proved to be fairly pointless as the medical books and journals I was
handling were out of date and nobody would want to use them. However, I
was told to put them in order because so many people, the old African doctor's
family and probably the Government too, would lose face if I did not. This
was completed in a short time, and then as there was no need for the library to
be administered as nobody was going to use it, I became secretary to the
Director of Medical Services; later I deputised for the Administrative Secretary
when he went on leave, which was the most satisfying work I had ever done,
because I had responsibility.

When I moved into a flat, I shared a cook with a girl living above, Marian,
who became a very good friend. We soon discovered that besides the cook, we
shared our goods and chattels, not just with each other, but with people whose
houseboys were friends of our cook. It was custom, and usually worked well. I
only drew the line when I found that my cut glass tumblers had gone banging
along the road in a bag hanging from bicycle handlebars. One day I found a
large dent in one of the three Georgian silver tablespoons Irma had given me
which were 'family'; Baku told me, when I questioned him, that the cook had
been breaking ice with it. I was furious; those spoons were 200 years old and
undamaged, and this silly cook had used them to break ice! Later I saw Marian,
and I had to laugh with her when she said how puzzled the cook had been at

my rage when the spoons were 200 years old anyway. I have never had the dent removed; I rather like the memory.

Soon after my arrival George took me to a Saturday lunch party. I asked him to take good care of me because I had heard of these parties that went on till tea-time before you had lunch, and I was not a practised drinker. When we got there, there was only one other girl, being held upside down at the time in rather wide shorts; I sat on a bookcase and held tight. The gin flowed and it was all great fun. George suddenly went home without telling me, driving wildly and taking with him several pedestals of geraniums adorning the drive as he swept past. People were saying how upset Joe would be and I assumed he was the gardener. After lunch we went swimming and then they began saying:

'Well, we'd better go and pick up the girls.' It was not until we got there that I realised I had been at what had been supposed to be a stag party, and all the wives, including Jo, had been sent off to the beach on their own. It took me some time to live that one down, if I ever did.

I soon met a delightful man, rotund and bespectacled, Tony Abell. I came to love him dearly but never felt I wanted to marry him. He was in my view hopelessly extravagant. He would see a case of peaches (a rare luxury) in the United Africa Company emporium, and he would not only buy it but a case of champagne to go with it. He was the greatest fun and our senses of humour clicked. He had a house on Five Cowrie Creek with a steep outside staircase down which people would toboggan on trays – usually late at night when a party had really taken hold; Tony often ended up fully clothed in the creek, one of his favourite ploys which he once did in uniform after a wedding. In the church itself he had caused the utmost mirth because as he bent down to put his helmet under the seat, the over-strained elastic which passed under his insteps and held his trousers taut, snapped on both sides with loud reports. His boys must have had quite a time with him. He told one lovely tale about Rhubarb, his Number One boy, an old-fashioned faithful. Rhubarb was sure that Tony knew everything, and when after many years his wife gave birth to yet another girl, he came to Tony and asked him how he could make sure next time to have a son. Tony, undaunted, asked Rhubarb what appeared to be relevant questions while he racked his brains for a suitable solution. Finally he hit on an idea.

'Rhubarb, do you wear your boots?'

'Mah boots, sah? No, I nebbah wear mah boots!' He went off filled with this new idea and within the year was able to report, beaming, to Tony that his wife had borne a son.

We had a hilarious time together. Tony taught me liar dice and that could occupy a group for a whole evening. I had a friend called Gwyneth Davies, he had one called John Phillips whose wife had left him and who was inclined to indulge in liquid misery by himself, so we usually made up a foursome (if not more) with those two, who eventually married. I learned to drive on Tony's car. I had had a learner driver's licence in England as Dr Drury had hoped I would drive him, but he never let me when he heard I was a learner. This licence, when presented to the Nigerian Police, resulted in their issuing me with a proper licence. I lived three miles outside Lagos, and cycled to work rather than ride in the 'mammy-wagon' provided for the secretaries, but if Tony and I were going anywhere in Lagos in the evening I would take his car home to change, and back again. If you can drive in Nigeria, you can drive anywhere; there was a great happy-go-luckiness about (in particular) African lorry drivers, who drove with their cab doors tied back all the easier to jump out in case of emergency; this they did with no concern whatsoever for the passengers packed like sardines in the back, leaving the lorry to manage on its own. They had succinct texts back and front such as 'God help me!' or even just 'Help!' I was taught to keep to the crown of the road and only to yield space when I could see the whites of the drivers' eyes, otherwise they would hog the crown of the road and never yield space. In spite of this hard training, when I took a test in England eleven years later, feeling I might have to one day when I was very old, (as in those days tests were not obligatory), I failed the first time because I had not heard of the Highway Code.

George Waller was a sailor and in the absence of his wife, who was nearly always in England with their daughter, I became his crew, so weekends were dominated by the Yacht Club races. Here I met a very attractive man called Satan Mooring, who sat on the grass by my chair one day, and I just knew at once he was the man for me. Not that I had any hope I was the girl for him. One day George made up a party to go dancing and invited Satan; he asked me to dance, discovered it was a waltz which he could not do, and backed down and did not ask me again. Little fat George danced the old-fashioned waltz magically! Then Satan invited me to a dance he and his house-mate Sam Macdonald-Smith were giving as a farewell for Satan (who was going home to have an operation on a slipped disc) and a welcome to Sam's wife, Twit; he said he would fetch me and I was in the seventh heaven. In the event dear Tony was asked to fetch me as Satan was too busy mixing drinks. I sank back into my place.

I did pluck up courage to ask him to a party I was giving; he spent the whole evening sitting next to another man's wife with whom I presumed he must be in love. Ages later he told me she took drugs, and her husband's friends took it in turns at parties to watch that she did not drink as well. Next day Satan rang to say thank you, and could I possibly come and help him buy shoes for his sister – clothes were still rationed in England. I dropped everything and went, rather surprised that he had not asked the Other Woman. We duly bought two or three pairs, and repaired to the Bristol Hotel, where we sat and told each other about ourselves.

Satan (George Rixson Mooring) was the son of the editor of the *Bedfordshire Gazette*, a farming family for generations, and Martha Rixson, daughter of a policeman, but only she was alive. He was ten years my senior. He had a brother Bill, four years younger, of whom he was very fond, and a sister Pat, who was seventeen years younger and living at home, though working. Satan had been to Bedford Modern School and then took a degree in Modern Languages at Queens' College, Cambridge, where he did a lot of rowing and actually coached. He spent a year teaching and then ten years in Northern Nigeria as a colonial administrative officer. He was a territorial in the West African Frontier Force and when the war came he went in at once. He was sent to the Arakan in Burma where he must have had a very exciting but nerve-racking time. He hardly ever spoke about it, beyond showing William, our son, how to make himself comfortable on the ground if he had to sleep on it, by digging a hole for his hip bone, and also there was a saying in the family: 'Give 'im a burst' which started there. He had been reconnoitring around the chosen campsite with a sergeant, to make sure there were no Japs in the area, when they came upon a village with a group of Japanese round a campfire in the middle. Satan, crouching in the bush, was considering what action to take when his sergeant, quivering like a dog on a lead seeing a rabbit ahead, whispered hoarsely 'Give 'em a burst, sir, give 'em a burst.' We never heard what they did do.

I later read about the exploits of his division in a book by Lucas Phillips called *Raiders of Arakan* and also John Purdy, a fellow officer, gave me the following account of the sort of bravery of which Satan was capable:

> Maungdaw, a small port on the Arakan coast, had been recaptured by the British at the end of 1943. In the first few days of 1944 'A' Squadron of the 81st West African Division Recce Regiment was dug in in Maungdaw prepared to harass the Japanese. The Recce Regiment was commanded by Col. Richard Cartwright, and 'A' Squadron was commanded by Major A.G.R. Mooring, known to all his fellow officers as 'Satan'.

> Cartwright was determined to get his troops into action against the Japanese as soon as possible. He ordered 'A' Squadron to shoot up the Japanese holding a village about 1200 yards to the east of Maungdaw. Satan told off one of his 'carrier' troops to carry out this attack, which they did. Unfortunately, unknown to us, the Japanese had an anti-tank gun in the village. When the carriers were sweeping round the village about 150 yards out, the anti-tank gun knocked out three of them in under a minute, killing the troop commander and two other ranks and wounding others.

> Satan, having watched this destruction from his advance post, took his own carrier up to each of the wrecked carriers, left the dead and extricated the

survivors. His own carrier was hit and his driver wounded, but Satan took over and brought them all back to safety. Those four men would undoubtedly have been killed if they had not been rescued immediately.

Even at the time we all thought that Satan deserved a VC but it was only our second day in battle and it was, I think, presumed that such action took place normally and was an everyday affair. If this action had taken place at a later stage of the fighting in which we took part, Satan would undoubtedly have been recommended for a high award for gallantry.

As it was, he was mentioned in despatches.

When the war was over, Satan was posted to the Secretariat in Lagos in the Establishments Department, and this is where he was when I came on the scene. When we had told each other something of our backgrounds, he asked me out to a meal on one of the three days he had before sailing but I could not. I agreed to go sailing to Tarkwa Bay with him on the Sunday, his last day, to a large picnic party. On Sunday morning I duly appeared at the Club. He was hustling rather a lot of people into a boat which had the sea to the gunwales. I said mildly couldn't we take some into our boat?

'Oh no,' said he, 'we have to wait for the Johnsons.' (That was The Other Woman.) However, when the other boat was well out to sea he decided not to wait for the Johnsons, who could, he said, hire a canoe, and we set off. What I did not know was that he had told the others we were to be left alone as he was going to propose! He gave me the helm and all the way across was thinking 'I'll do it on the next tack,' and I was thinking 'Oh dear, we don't seem to have much to talk about.' Reaching the mole round which we had to sail, he could see a little crowd of friends waiting on the shore to hear what I had said. Thus propelled, according to him, he said he was in rather a bad way about me, to which I replied 'Oh, good.' The rest happened rather quickly. It was a bit awkward with the boom slamming about, and I got a crack on the head, but we were engaged by the time we landed.

So it was, lying half in and half out of the sea most of the morning, just talking; we knew so little about each other but we were both quite sure. He did not want to hear about my marriage and divorce, he had seen the bones of it in my file! He put me firmly on a pedestal marked 'Wife' and I spent the rest of our life together trying to live up to his image of me, so it was quite a good method.

We had a reprieve as his ship was delayed for a day, so on the Monday Satan organised a most practical picnic of chocolate and cheese and grapes and champagne, and we went to the beach. I had had the dismal job of telephoning Tony to tell him the news, as I did not want him to hear it from other people. He had been away for the weekend in Ibadan and had invited me to go too, but I had not been able to get a satisfactory reply to 'Where shall I be staying?'

so did not go. It was difficult to explain to him that a long secret affair had not been building up with Satan, and that in fact the whole thing had happened that weekend. Difficult, too, to explain that one could love two people at once, and that I did not attempt: the quality of the loves was so different.

Satan went to London to have the operation on his back and we did not know when we should meet again. I had signed a contract with Government for eighteen months but under that contract was not allowed to marry, as it was considered bad for two salaries to be going into one white household. I was not prepared to break my contract and hoped I would be allowed to finish my tour even after getting married on Satan's return, but they were adamant. Satan bombarded me with telegrams and the last one which said: 'Come home and have orchids instead of cables' decided me, and I went, at my own expense.

Satan had called on Irma before his operation and they had approved of one another. She was going to a spiritualist church at that time and at their next session of trying to contact the spirit world, the medium said:

'I have a tall, thin, lame man here giving the name of George Moore – no, not Moore, Morris is it? No, Mooring, that's it.' As Satan was tall and thin and his name was George, Irma admitted she knew him and the medium said:

'You are not to worry about him, he's going to be all right.'

Irma wrote me this news and for what it was worth I wrote it to Satan in hospital. He was rather shaken as his father had been tall and thin, and lame, but at that stage neither Irma nor I knew it!

When Basil heard the news, he cabled his congratulations and added 'Presume Satari Muri is Fulani cattle owner', the telegraph office in one country or other having failed to spell Satan's name correctly.

★   ★   ★

We were duly married at Kensington High Street Registry Office in August 1947, a very small family affair, our mothers, brothers and sisters, the aunt round the corner. I was in a black dress as Satan hurried me so and I could not find anything I liked: I needed a black dress and coupons were short. With it I wore a Yoruba hat, a round pillbox in black velvet with gold embroidery which I felt was becoming, and pale yellow orchids.

To my great joy, surprise and relief, Charles Downman remarried about the same time as I did and his too was a very happy marriage to another scientist, resulting in a daughter and a son. He became Professor of Physiology at the Royal Free Hospital and died too young, at sixty-six, a universally loved man.

We went to Sweden for our honeymoon. The first night was spent in the second best hotel in Gothenburg; Satan carried me over the entrance of our bedroom, which could not have done his back any good, and I went in search of the bathroom. I could not find it on our floor or on the one below, though

Satan (alias George Mooring), my second husband.

one door said 'Badrum' (or however the Swedes spell it) but when I opened
the door it was just a black hole with the floor boards up and a few pipes lying
around. Satan did no better and when we enquired of the management they
took us to this same room and flung the door triumphantly open. It was good
value to see the surprise on the man's face. Plumbing in those days on the
continent was very uncertain and we had some wonderful experiences.

Then we went to a fishing village for swimming in the nude and lolling in
the sun, then to Stockholm to visit Anna. She had married again, a Swedish
architect called Kockum, whom we liked very much. Discovering what a keen
sailor Satan was, they pressed on us the use of their eight-metre racing yacht
for a few days' sailing in the archipelago. The season was really over, the
Swedes shut down promptly at the end of August and this was the beginning
of September, but we all reckoned (wrongly) that it would be all right, and we
accepted ecstatically. They did mention that they had not used the boat that
summer so the tackle was not in first-class order.

Off we set and the first twenty-four hours were fine except that Satan was
surprised to find that I had no idea how to work a primus stove. Also I was

extremely nervous of taking the helm which involved reading the chart at the same time as one was tacking between many islands and there were submerged rocks to beware of all the time; but I had to helm whenever we set off because I was not strong enough to pull up the extremely heavy anchor. Satan would do this and dash back to relieve me, when I would go forward and lie down on the foredeck with my feet wrapped round the mast for safety, for it was extremely windy, and stow the chain. I was a bit of a trial, as another time I hung some wet clothes on the boom to dry when we were anchored and apparently this was a perfectly dreadful thing to do. We only once saw another craft, a small motorboat with two efficient-looking uniformed men standing in it.

On the third day of appalling weather our storm jib blew away and then we went aground. Satan tied a rope to the top of the mast and rowed away like fury in the dinghy with the other end of the rope, in an attempt to tip the boat up and free the keel. Even when a boy with a motor boat came out from the shore and tried to help with that, it was no good, and we had to abandon ship. We were lucky to be near an island which was connected with the mainland by a bridge, and some very odd people, a baron and baroness, who lived there all the time, were very helpful. We had a plane to catch as we were due back in Nigeria, and after copious apologies to the Kockums and their assurances that they could cope, we left. We heard later that twenty-two yachts and two steamers had foundered in that storm!

During that first tour in Lagos we had to move house six times; Satan was the lowest form of life entitled to live in a certain standard of house, so every time a more senior person laid claim, out we had to go, whether he was in Satan's department or not. Satan's houseboy Musa, who had served as a soldier under Satan, was unfortunately not prepared to work for a missis, so he handed in his notice and the most magnificent inventory. I can see it now, with delicious items like 'Whisk glas – 9' and 'Toes plat – 2'. Baku stayed with us and we employed a cook and a small boy; Baku's beautiful wife and baby boy also lived in the compound. I was fascinated to note how she coped without nappies, particularly as she, like all Nigerian women, carried her baby on her back. A certain look would come over her face as she became aware of a familiar warm wetness, and she would go to the nearest tap, remove the baby and her cloth and rinse them both and put them back in position. In that climate, nearly always 90 degrees in heat and humidity alike, the extra damp did not worry either of them.

A couple of weeks after our return, a young couple called Nicholson lost their first baby, and the funeral of that six weeks old person was the saddest occasion I had ever attended; the tiny grave, so very deep, and the anguish of the new parents. One was made aware of the grisly history of white people in

this country, 'the white man's grave', where mortality was so high. But it was
the beginning of a new age, when medicine was available to keep many forms
of death away, and after the war children had begun to be part of everybody's
lives.

It was quite a change not having a job and of course I missed not having
my own money. I had earned £20 a month and my flat, and Satan (who
earned the princely sum of £1,230 per annum) said of course I must have my
£20 a month as before; but it was never there, so I learned to manage on the
housekeeping; it was not a thing that came between us at all. Being unable to
take a paid job I found voluntary ones quite easily. I began teaching diving to
the African girls at Queen's College which was very rewarding as they were
natural athletes. One day I had rather a shock as a girl who could not even
swim got into the queue to go off the high board. She did quite a creditable
dive, so that I did not suspect anything until one of the others dived in and
rescued her.

I was also employed for a while on going through very old files and
destroying what was no longer of use, which was considered too secret to let
Africans do. This was very interesting and one particular record I never forgot.
An Englishman asked an African in the Cameroons (German before the First
World War) which administration he preferred, German or English, being
confident of his reply. To his dismay the man replied:

'German.'

'But why?'

The answer was that if a German told an African to do something, he did it
because he knew he would be punished if he did not. If an Englishman told
him to do something and he did not want to, it was worth not doing it, as the
Englishman would try to find out why he had not done it, and in the ensuing
confusion the African might escape punishment. In short, although the
German was the harder master, the African knew where he was with him, as
he did not with the Englishman.

Satan was a polo player but did not play much in Lagos. It had been the big
sport in the North; in the southern areas there were tsetse fly, so no mares
were kept, and the quality of the stallions was not of the highest. I was able to
borrow polo ponies and go riding, which was a great joy. Even on Lagos Island
one felt one was seeing the real country and not the artificial capital, and a little
tremor of fear ran through one as one met an almost naked, surly-looking man
with a bow and arrow on a bush path. I soon learned that if one smiled and
gave a greeting, his face would be transformed into a huge grin and all feeling
of danger vanished.

Satan's sister Pat came and stayed with us for three months, but she found a
secretarial job and stayed on till the end of our tour and then moved into her

own flat. She and I got on very well, though I became a bit narked when we were introduced as Mr, Mrs and Miss Mooring and I feared people might think she was my daughter.

I was a real townee amongst people who had lived tough lives in the bush, as Satan had discovered on the honeymoon when I was unable to work a primus. Nor had I any knowledge of hurricane or Tilley lamps which we often used when electricity failed. We lived pretty civilised lives in Lagos but bush habits did arise. I remember being out to lunch one day and the ladies had retreated upstairs when suddenly there was a screech from our hostess who was looking out of the window:

'NOT on my cucumbers!'

The men were comfortably lined up doing what came naturally and what was known as 'Seeing Africa'.

Pat, too, rode, and we swam and sailed and lived a pretty social life. One party stands out in my memory, given by Phil and Brenda Rogers of the British American Tobacco Company. It was a pirate party (the name of one of the local brands of cigarettes was Pirate) and I went in Irma's lovely Spanish dress, black, with three deep flounces to the skirt and peacock's eyes on them, and a mantilla. I said I was a captive and was well paid out, as anybody not dressed as a pirate was put up for auction, manacled, on a slave platform. The prow of a huge pirate ship emerged from the bushes and one sat down on kegs. One man came striding in with a sack on his back which he dumped on the bar and out crawled his poor little wife. He was a menace as he had equipped himself with a hook – heaven knows how he managed his hand but it never showed – and when he really got going he was ripping people's shirts up the back and suchlike. In one dance I was stuck with a terrible little man, with a broken nose and an eye patch, who became rather amorous. I gestured for help from a large friend who, convulsed with laughter, came and rescued me. He then revealed that the terrible little man was in fact the wife of the Director of Education, with very good make-up indeed.

To our great joy I became pregnant and we settled down to domesticity. We continued to swim and sail, however, and one awful day I was helming the Governor's boat in a race (Satan and another officer looked after it and raced it for him) and had just gone round a buoy when a learner in the boat behind went about too soon. His boom came across and hit me in the lumbar region and then on the back of the neck and I became unconscious. I soon recovered but six weeks later our firstborn son Tom was stillborn at seven and a half months. It was a traumatic experience; the pain seemed worse in retrospect even than normal childbirth, perhaps because he was not helping and perhaps because I knew there was to be no happy ending. One nice thing happened in the Creek Hospital: a dear old black nurse was washing me and was very disapproving when she found how much whiter I was where I wore a bathing suit. She said severely:

'De good Lord He done make you white and you be very lucky woman. It no good you go lie for sun and try make you self black woman.' Wise old dear.

The doctor advised me not to try for another baby for a year but nature knew better and I was pregnant again within three months and very fit. We thought it best for me to go home to mother a bit sooner than Satan so I reluctantly set sail on an Elder Dempster ship in February 1949, seven months 'gone'. All the same I won the diving competition on board and was confident no one could tell. I booked myself into the Middlesex Hospital and when Satan returned we went to stay with his mother near Bedford until a week before the baby was due, when we were going to stay at his brother Bill's flat quite near the hospital. However, two weeks before the due date, Satan panicked, imagining the baby arriving sooner, and him having to drive me up to London in extremis, even having to deliver the baby by the roadside! The ambulance service only served the Bedford Hospital but he managed to get permission for one to go all the way to London if by gross mischance I should start more than a week early. I started that very night. He thought I must be wrong and said:

'I'll go and ask Mother!' She did not even come to check but said:

'Of course she is, go and ring for the ambulance.' The ambulance men had not yet received the order so he had to ring the Medical Officer of Health who had given the permission and the MO had to ring the ambulance men. By the time we arrived at the Middlesex at 7 a.m., Satan was in very bad shape. I was received into the system and gave birth to a perfect boy at 11 a.m. Meantime poor Satan was roaming the streets in an agony of mind. All he knew of European childbirth was the dreadful things described in novels. He reported to my ward at visiting time, 4 p.m., by which time I had lost a lot of face with the other mothers who wondered why he had not waited downstairs. He was quite expecting to be told I was still at it, thirty-six hours was the minimum he expected, so I had no trouble when I told him that although we had decided to call the baby John, it was William who had arrived – he was so relieved he would have agreed to anything. William was not a name we had considered at all, and we did not particularly like it, but this boy just *was* 'William' as soon as I set eyes on him. Luckily it pleased both sides of the family: we both had brothers with the name. The whole episode from 3 a.m. till 4 p.m. at the hospital was worse for Satan, he said, than the whole of the Burma Campaign.

It was difficult, one would have thought, to have a fun leave with a new baby, but Satan arranged for us to have a wherry on the Broads: rather a come-down after an eight-metre but at least we were waterborne. So at three weeks old William went for his first sailing holiday. We took with us two great friends, the Lawsons, he a doctor and she a nurse as it happened. They stayed with us two weeks and then we had my sister Ann and William's godfather, Oliver Hunt, a Nigerian District Officer who had become very close to Satan in Burma. Nappies were our only problem: no disposables in those days. I washed them in the river till they were all grey, but drying was difficult as Satan hated to see them flying anywhere, even on a wherry. When Billee Lawson discovered I was airing them up my jumper, a rule was made that anyone doing nothing else should sit on nappies, but I, as the nursing mother, must not put them up my jumper. Ann revealed a talent for nappy-sitting.

Ibadan

Back in Nigeria we were posted to Ibadan, the university town and capital of the Western Region, about 100 miles from Lagos. Satan was now in the Finance Department where he felt very much at home, even though he missed the bush life and the North. His sister Pat had become engaged to a policeman, Derek Fountain, and my first job was to arrange her wedding from our house. English secretaries were being snapped up by the men who had hardly seen single white women in West Africa before, and it was said that recruiting officers in London were told to recruit one for the Government (plain) and one for the boys – it did not seem to make much difference. I made Pat's wedding bouquet: it was one more facet of life one had to tackle as there were no professionals, and I became quite good at wreaths and bouquets – others became almost professional at wedding cakes.

When we had only recently arrived in Ibadan, I was sitting one morning reading, when uproar suddenly erupted in the garden and I could see men in white jackets wielding machetes and rushing wildly about. I had no idea what was happening and thought my end had probably come. In fact it turned out that they were prisoners who were cutting the grass for us, and a rat had appeared which was giving them enormous fun as they all attempted to hit it. It was the custom for prisoners to cut the grass so we did not have to have lawnmowers. Prison was not a terrible place for them; often individuals quite liked it, the food was reasonable and free, and it was all quite amusing. One man earned face when it was discovered that he used to get out at night and visit his wife, taking good care he was back for roll call in the morning.

Life was so good. I felt that at last I had found my niche in life and knew where I fitted in, which was a highly satisfactory feeling after my previous life of constant upheaval and change. We had plenty of friends, there were swimming pools and tennis courts and a golf course, there were horses to ride, above all there was my baby to delight in and bring up. I had a 'small boy' to push him out in the pram in the coolest part of the morning, otherwise I cared for him myself. It was only since the war that wives and children were out all the time and there were quite a few of us, learning how to keep our children

Us with the Premier of the Western Region of Nigeria and his wife.

healthy. In the old days malaria was the commonest form of death until the mosquito was found to be the cause. Quinine, which often made people deaf, gave way as a prophylactic to mepacrine, which made them yellow, and when I came out I was a guinea pig for paludrin. It proved excellent with no side effects and the children and I never had malaria. Water had to be boiled and filtered and a strict supervision mounted as the Africans did not see the connection between contaminated water and dysentery. Stagnant water had to be eliminated from one's environment and one of the Government rules was that no pineapples should be grown in residential areas because the leaves harboured stagnant water where mosquitoes could breed.

We had the usual number of servants: a cook, a Number One boy or butler, a Number Two boy and a gardener. Some people had three boys. The Number One boy was the boss. Our cook had two small sons called Ukuchuku and Ukuchukuman who sometimes played with our children. I was interested to find when William and Ukuchuku were two years old, that Ukuchuku had no idea how to post shapes through similarly shaped holes, and I could not decide if this was due to his never having had educational toys or to the development of his brain being slower or different. He was a good bit smaller than William, though William admittedly was a tall child.

Whilst on the subject of the cook, I must recount one or two tales about him – and me! For a children's party I asked Matthew to make marmite and honey sandwiches; careless of me, obedient of him. They were eaten up without comment until a mother asked me what this interesting taste was – it was of course marmite and honey in the same sandwich! Then came the day when I asked him to show me how he made his delicious soufflés – not only were they delicious but he could produce them perfectly if we were early, on time, or late. The only thing that went wrong in the preparation was that I found cheese bubbling away on the stove and thinking he was probably distracted by my presence, I mentioned it.

'Oh, shouldn't it be doing that?' he asked, and snatched it off the stove. The show was back on the wrong foot, I was the teacher and he the pupil. Finally when it was all ready to be cooked, I asked him what heat he would put it in at (it was simply an oven heated by wood poked in at one side).

'Well,' said he, opening the door and putting his hand inside, 'This heat.'

I tried again: 'Whereabouts in the oven do you put it?'

He came straight back at me:

'What time do you want lunch?'

I gathered that if we were going to be early he would put it at the top of the oven, if late at the bottom, if on time, in the middle. I gave up. I knew that soufflés collapsed if they weren't cooked in the middle! He continued to produce his perfect soufflés but I never had the courage to do as he did. On another occasion I had to come between him and his wife when they were having an armed row in the kitchen!

The advent of wives must have changed the lives radically of even the unmarried men, because life became more sedate. We had dances (and I was very pleased to find that Satan was a good dancer in spite of not being able to waltz, though he soon learned) and parties when we played silly games like 'Book Titles' when two teams gave each member of the opposite team in turn a book title to act, and their own team had to guess what it was. But late nights were not quite so late, and lunch-time drinking was a great mistake when you had to deal with a baby in the afternoon. We went fishing when we had a long weekend. One made one's own amusement as there was little else, and it was good. There was in fact a cinema but we very seldom went; they always seemed to be showing *King Kong* which was very popular. Once we went to see *Henry V* and were astonished at the acclaim by the mainly African audience. They could hardly have understood the Shakespearean English but they understood the story, and when Henry shouted:

'Once more into the breach…' they nearly went through the screen.

A man who was with us had to ask the operator to put up the sound as it was impossible to hear the actors.

The country around was pretty impenetrable bush. Man-made tracks had been worn over the years through trees and bushes and anything that could survive was all knitted together with lianas and creepers. The climate was humid and hot, about 90 degrees most of the time, but the humidity was 90 degrees too and one was always damp. Nobody had air-conditioning, even in the offices, and I never experienced it in my time in Nigeria. We did have electricity in Ibadan, cut as frequently at least as it is in the UK, but we were better prepared with Tilley and hurricane lamps and primus stoves.

I became involved almost at once in Red Cross work and in a fairly short time became Director of the Western Region of Nigeria. I felt that the Red Cross was needed there just as much as schools, or street clearance, or petrol pumps. One of its most important duties was teaching the women ordinary health and hygiene rules, for instance, that flies carry infection (and oh how many flies there were) so that food, dustbins and lavatories should all be covered for a start: elementary procedure at home but not abroad, where with higher temperatures it was even more important. Our main aim was to be the disaster relief organisation, but there was plenty of groundwork as well: the teaching of First Aid, mainly in schools and teaching colleges, welfare of handicapped people, in getting them artificial limbs and so on, and paying passages to the UK of people who needed urgent operations of more complicated kinds than could be carried out locally.

Most of the officers below me were African and I had some severe disagreements with them about the use of the funds we had raised for welfare. Once I discovered they had used funds to give a large cocktail party to thank people for their help, which I considered wrong – financing such a party ourselves would have been different. It being too late to correct that one, I put out a memorandum round the region, alluding to no specific occasion, but pointing out that this was not what funds were raised for; a party must be paid for by individuals giving for that purpose. A terrible scene ensued at the next committee meeting when the culprit, the Director of the Ibadan Division, accused me of slander (her husband was a judge!). In the end the chairman, a chief, suggested that all would be well if Mrs Mooring were to apologise. I then said I was sorry I had hurt Ronke's feelings but the principle stood. This sufficed and afterwards I invited her home for tea and talk. It was useless: she just could not see my point of view, though she had been educated in England and was a very nice person. She even expected me to be annoyed because her African boss had ticked her off for doing Red Cross typing in Government time on a Government typewriter! I am not at all surprised nowadays to hear of the corruption rife in Nigeria; it is basic to their lives, but I have also since become aware that money collected for welfare use must frequently be used for entertaining even in England, so I was probably just being too idealistic. Ronke and I kissed and agreed to differ.

They built a splendid headquarters very much against my advice, though there again I believe I was wrong, as it was important for the organisation to have an image. It was opened by Princess Mary, the Princess Royal, when she was visiting Nigeria in 1956. Oh, that day! We had brought in from each province a little band of schoolchildren in Red Cross uniform with banners bearing the name of their province, red on white. A programme was arranged of inspection of Red Cross units, followed by a presentation of certificates and to the Princess of a carved head of the Oba of Benin and a bouquet. Palm leaf shelters were erected for those who could not get inside.

When all was ready I dashed upstairs to change into my white uniform and gloves and, while I did so, the skies opened. Nobody moved. When I came down the palm-leaf shelters were a dripping nightmare, the children were drenched, the red on their banners had run into the white, and the whole unplanted earthen area round the building was a muddy mess. Luckily, a phone call announced that the Princess was to be a few minutes late, so we bustled the children indoors and hid their pathetic banners in the office, where there were crates of beer and orange squash and plates of cakes to entertain the provincials after the ceremony. We laid blankets on the ground for the Princess to walk over, and rearranged the inspection lines so that they were in fact rooted in the mud alongside the blankets.

When the Princess arrived, I greeted her with an umbrella which I held over her, noticing with horror that my white gloves were now filthy, and then realised I had forgotten to cancel the National Anthem, which was enthusiastically played while we stood in the rain. All went well indoors, when I had to read out a long list of difficult Yoruba names to receive awards, and then the Chief Justice's daughter presented a bouquet and my own daughter Julia (by then five years old) presented the carved head of the Oba of Benin, of which I have the only copy. After the ceremony, however, the Princess, realising we had a little time to fill, asked to see the rest of the building. The Governor's wife, Lady Rankine, who was president, and knew nothing of what had gone before, ushered her into that dreadful office full of beer and broken banners. The Princess was superb: after a catch in her breath she said:

'Ah! I see you have an In-Tray – AND an Out-Tray.' Honour satisfied, we all retreated thankfully.

Another amusing but rather horrifying event occurred, which showed us how carefully First Aid had to be taught. We had in charge of the office a well-meaning clerk called Bailus who was utterly committed to the ideals of the Red Cross. One night he was out and came across a car accident. Onlookers

Princess Mary, the Princess Royal, and me in the rain.

who were doing nothing told him a car driven by a chief known as the Carefree Prince had driven into the back of a stationary lorry. True to his race at that time, the prince had fled. Lying about the car unconscious were two Europeans, a man halfway through the windscreen and his wife (the prince's light-o'-love it transpired) on the back seat. Instantly Bailus knew his rôle and plunged to the rescue. The passenger door in the front was jammed so he dragged the man out through the windscreen! Glass was stuck into him in several places including his throat, and Bailus pulled that out. This started an artery founting in the man's neck, so unperturbed, Bailus applied a tourniquet which stopped it beautifully. He then heaved the man on his back, carried him half a mile to the hospital, and went back and fetched the woman in the same way, who only had a broken leg and concussion. Next day, Bailus presented himself before me, rather smugly, and made his report. I was appalled.

'You did WHAT, Bailus? Tell me again.' It was true. I rang the hospital and spoke to the doctor and asked how were the two Europeans.

'Well,' he said, 'the man is dead.'

'What did he die of?' I asked tremulously.

'You may well ask,' replied he, very amused in a callous medical way. 'The immediate cause of death was strangulation – but in fact he would not have survived as he had multiple internal injuries.' I turned wildly to the Red Cross Manual and found that it did in fact say tourniquets could be applied everywhere except to the neck. Poor Bailus: he had done so very well but he had forgotten that one little bit in all the mumbo-jumbo he had learned.

I sometimes accompanied a welfare officer on her town round, to gain knowledge of the people and their problems, which in spite of all the modern technology were many. For instance, one day we visited a girl who had very bad bedsores that had to be dressed by the little African nurse who came with us, crisp and neat in her pale blue and white uniform and frilly cape. The girl lived in her uncle's house and he was a witch doctor. The veranda was hung with horrid-looking dried things which one imagined to be crocodile tails, toads and even worse. The house had a mud floor and a fire burned in the middle of it, with a cauldron bubbling on it. To my horror the nurse lifted the lid and began to extract something from it. I had failed to notice, in my mesmerised entry from the veranda, that she had popped her instruments into it to sterilise. The patient's mother had been trained to have this water boiling ready for the visit. At another house we arrived just as they were patting down the earth on the threshold over Granny's grave. It had been strictly against the law for a hundred years to bury people in or around houses and when I understood what was happening I protested to the welfare officer.

'You can report it if you like,' she said, 'but I shall not.'

'Why ever not?'

'Because if I did I should never be welcomed in this area again.'

So of course I did not report it either, for I should have compromised her, and the good work she did was, I felt, worth more than the removal of one granny to the graveyard.

Another thing we applied ourselves to in Western Nigeria was disasters and we formed a Disaster Relief Committee. The chief adviser on this was a man who had worked in the West Indies and had seen what happened in hurricanes, to which we too were prone. However, before we had organised ourselves we experienced a quite different kind of disaster: we had a train accident.

It was the rainy season and a high embankment subsided, carrying the engine and three coaches over the side, one on top of the other. Satan was acting Governor at the time and was telephoned with the news at about 3 a.m. and went straight to the scene in a shuttle train. Upon his return he was able to tell me the situation and that he hoped the Red Cross could help as the local administration had just recently become Africanised and was very inexperienced. Upon his advice we decided the first thing to do was to set up a tent at the spot and to send out food and drink for the rescue workers. It was still quite early but I was surprised not to get a reply from the Red Cross office telephone. I soon discovered that the clerk Bailus had gone off to the scene of the accident in a car with the African President of the Region (the Chief Justice's wife) and the Divisional Director with whom I had had such a disagreement. This was quite useless as the road was some miles from the railway line and they were not heard of again till the next day, having been bravely hacking their way through the bush to the train.

In the meantime all sorts of needs which we could supply had manifested themselves. People were coming back from the site on shuttle trains. We had teams at the station to sort them out, sending the uninjured to a camp where we supplied blankets, food, water and sanitation. The slightly injured were taken to one hospital for treatment before being sent to the camp, the badly injured to another, and the dead to the mortuary. Here we had a stalwart team (including the Divisional Director when she had struggled home) who drew tribal markings, if any, of the dead and noted their style of dress which, if not European style, would indicate from which part of the country they originated. Very few had written identification on them, so descriptions of their appearance, colour (dark or light brown or black) and scars were very important. In the camp we had a team listing the people and their names and villages, who also discovered for them whether missing relatives were injured or dead, and where they were. A total of 200 dead was counted and many more injured.

At the end of the first day I returned to the station for one last look round and found a woman there who would not leave until her luggage was returned from the train, this in spite of the fact that she had a small boy with a badly damaged foot that needed treatment. She did not mind in the least that I should take him to the hospital and trusted utterly that I would bring him back. While I waited for him at the hospital, a nurse came and asked me to move as they were bringing a dead man out that way. I went and stood in another doorway, enjoying the slight breeze and the night sky, and was joined there by a tired young doctor. Three men came out of another doorway holding each other by the arm, went down the steps, got into a taxi and drove away. The doctor giggled.

'What's the joke?'

'Well, the one in the middle was dead.'

'What's funny about that?'

'Oh THAT'S not funny, but they've taken him away rather soon and rigor mortis will set in before they get him to their village, when they won't be able to get him out in a sitting position. Normally they have stiffened up before being removed and are taken home with their feet sticking out of the window.' This rather put me off taxis.

For two weeks after this we had a dear little boy staying with us who was about Julia's age. He knew his name which was Amadu Musa (a quarter of the male population have this name, another quarter are called Musa Amadu), and the name of his village, but we soon discovered that this too was a very popular place name. He had been travelling with his grandmother (who was killed) with whom he lived, which was the custom in many cases, to visit his parents and have his tribal marks cut into his face. The parents were unaware of the visit and, as the grandfather could not read, it was many days before he heard about the accident. It occurred to him that it could have been granny's train but the only way to find out was to travel to his son's house and see if she was there. On a Sunday afternoon when we had been visiting yet another village to see if it was Amadu's, we came home to find his extended family, about eleven of them, waiting in our drawing room, having tracked their kinsman to our house. They were all strangers to Amadu except for grandfather to whom he rushed immediately.

Not much later I was invited to a farewell coffee party by an African minister's wife and she played suitable music on her gramophone: a Beethoven sonata, *West of Zanzibar* (where we were going) and to my amazement 'The Lalupon Train Disaster', a sung description of it, which made me realise that the tradition of oral history was still in existence – when I asked if the episode of the Carefree Prince and his car accident had been vocalised she was quite grumpy:

'Of course not. He is a member of the Opposition!'

★   ★   ★

At the end of 1950 I went home, five months pregnant with my second child (again winning the diving competition on the boat!) and escorted by William, who was eighteen months old. He suffered very much on these boat trips; I used to have my breakfast with him at the children's time, but then would have to leave him in the 'nursery' while I coped with the washing and ironing in a room where I could not have had him getting in everyone's way and where it was very hot. The 'nursery' was more like a cattle pen on deck, under an overhang and with canvas sides in bad weather; most of the children settled down there after a time or two, and played with the toys provided, but he would sit huddled up hopelessly in a corner, sucking two fingers and waiting for release, if release was ever going to happen. The nannies on duty could never cope with him. He did not yell, but tears poured down his cheeks and it broke my heart to leave him. The rest of the day was all right, as I put him down for his rest in our cabin after his lunch while I had my lunch with the grown-ups, and he went to bed at six as usual before any evening activity I might wish to attend. Julia did not suffer in the same way when she had to do it, as she had William with her. Baby bottles had to be sterilised by leaving them soaking in a basin of Milton, whereas at home we boiled them. Those sea journeys were fairly trying with children as one had to keep constant vigilance for fear they might fall overboard. On one occasion when Julia was about three, I left them playing on the lower (enclosed) deck, running round the stairwell in view of the purser, while I went along the passage to our cabin to pack. After a time William came in.

'Where's Julia?'

'I don't know. A nasty lady came and shouted at us and we all ran away.'

Of course he and I went at once to find her but she seemed to be nowhere. Everyone was alerted and we searched first, second and third-class sections of the ship without success. I was frantic. I returned to our cabin in the faint hope she might be there, and a moment or two later she walked in with another mother. She had been playing with this woman's daughter, and when they were frightened they went together to her cabin, where she was feeding her baby. Not realising the situation, she kept Julia there till she had finished feeding the baby, and then brought her back. The 'frightening' woman earned my contempt at the captain's cocktail party later, when I heard her telling him about those wretched children who had disturbed her rest. I knew her for one who changed her clothes three or four times a day, never wore the same thing twice, including bathing dresses, and had nothing to do but enjoy herself. I was young, angry and exhausted!

I stayed in Notting Hill Gate with my mother and sister Ann while awaiting Julia's birth. Irma was not at all well and when I was away for a few days at Satan's mother's, she had a heart attack and was taken to hospital. I had to return with William to look after Ann and their lodger. Irma was allowed to come home before Christmas but I was tough and insisted that I could not manage if she had her usual quarters on the ground floor, as I could not keep William out of her room; much as she loved him, he was too much for her. Also the telephone was there and she had exciting calls all the time, and could call out to anybody calling at the house to come into her room. It was like Victoria Station as a rule. Reluctantly she agreed and was installed in a first floor room next to mine. In January she had another attack just after I had left her room and was stoking the boiler downstairs. Ann screamed for me and I dashed up to find Irma on the floor. I got up behind her and supported her in a sitting position but it was no good and she died in my arms. Ann was too frightened to run next door and fetch our neighbour, a great friend, but was persuaded to telephone him. He came to help but was unable to lift as he had a hernia. We had to get a policeman from the street to come to the rescue. Irma was taken away by the undertakers who turned out to be from Barkers, and spent her last few nights above ground, in their mortuary on the top floor, which I know would have amused her greatly, as she loved Barkers.

A couple of months later Julia was born, so called because I had discovered that it was Irma's third name. She was a very easy baby, unlike William. Maud Goodman, who had looked after me after my own birth, visited us and questioned me closely on the way upstairs to see the new baby, as to the exact time of her birth, and just as I was about to open the door she pronounced:

'Ah yes, the great lover.' I am not sure what system she was working on, nor what kind of love she was envisaging. Whatever the case, I was very satisfied with the daughter I had been given and have remained so.

That leave we found our dream house and were able to buy it. We were staying with the Lawsons in Devon, and were in no particular hurry, but went to see this property as part of the exercise of finding out about values. Our hearts turned over as we made the long approach. The address was Duncannon House, Stoke Gabriel, a village on the Dart, but the house was a mile outside the village, on the river. We drove along a narrow lane till we could go no further (and realised we should have to back the half-mile out again). There was a box in the hedge for milk, and a right-angled bend in the lane took us steeply down through a wood. It was June, a fine day, and through the trees we could see the river and a swan...At the bottom of the rough winding track stood three cottages, two belonging to the ferryman, and the middle one, the biggest, was the one we had come to see. An old Kenya doctor sat on a bench in the sun as he waited for us, drinking in the breathtaking view with which he was being forced to part by the illness of his wife and his increasing difficulty in getting up the hill, or of getting any domestic help who would come to such a difficult venue. We could not meet his price and were ashamed that we had wasted his time in coming at all. When we said our top price was £4,500 he accepted it at once. He wanted us to have it, we were his kind. He sold us lovely pieces of furniture for a song (a Pembroke table for £6 for instance), left the fridge, which must have been the first ever made but was still thumping away thirteen years later when we left, in the cave hollowed out of the hillside in the back of the kitchen. The garden was only about fifty yards wide at the widest point but it ran alongside the river for about 300 yards or more – a mad place to bring up children, one might say, but we had to have it, and they survived and loved it too. I feel sure it gave them a high standard of beauty and a rich start to their lives.

The house itself was early nineteenth-century, with five bedrooms and a bathroom neatly arranged round a stairwell, two living rooms and an extraordinary kitchen which, like Topsy, had just growed. It even had a ghost, though we did not discover this for some time. A tenant who was a friend of Satan's mother saw it and told her, and she tantalisingly scribbled down the side of a completed air letter:

'I must remember to tell you about the ghost at Duncannon,' but never did! On our next leave she told us it was a little woman in a blue and white striped dress and hair drawn back into a bun, twice found fussing about in the back quarters. When I knew the house better and how it had evolved, I realised she had been drawing curtains where now there was no window, and another time was found rearranging wet coats in the passage near the side door, which had been an outside area where washing would have hung. William, who of course was not told about her, probably saw her. I was tucking him up in bed one evening when he said sleepily:

'Tell Granny to come and say goodnight to me.'

'But Granny isn't staying, darling.' I replied.

'Oh no!' said he, 'Then who is it who comes to say goodnight to me every night?'

Of course while Satan was still working we could only use the house for leaves. I always spent longer in England than Satan, for the sake of the children's health. Once we survived six months apart but vowed never to do that again, so I would go home a month or so before his leave was due, and he would come for the school holidays, and I would go back a month or so after that. Incredibly difficult though it was to live there, I gave Duncannon my heart, and when we finally left it I wept and wept. The hill being so steep, cars could get down but not up again, so one turned to the river for the transport of 'loads' when coming on leave. The train took one to Kingsbridge and the ferryman, Mr Collings, would meet us there with his herring boat. We fetched coal in our own dinghy as fortunately there was a merchant who had his yard up a nearby creek. He would put sacks into the boat but poor Satan had to heave them out the other end. When we moved into the house, we did it by wheelbarrow as we did not have much furniture, but when we moved out we had to do it by barge, which took two days as the tide went down before the men loaded all our stuff on board.

The dinghy was of course essential and we used it too for picnics and to go shopping in Totnes. At first this had to be rowed, but later Satan invested in an outboard engine which made life a lot easier. When he went back to Nigeria that year I did not expect to be using it, as I am hopeless with engines, but William was soon on to me:

'Let's go for a picnic up the river.'

No amount of protests from me were any use, as we both knew that he was perfectly capable of running the engine, and even managed to start the beastly thing more easily than his father did. So in the end we did, accompanied as it happened by Jimmy Wack Wack, our greater black-backed seagull. We had inherited him with the house, though he was by no means tame. He sat on a stone post on the river wall from time to time, and we fed him, though he never agreed to be fed by hand, and the most wonderful thing was to go out and call:

'Jimmy, Jimmy, Jimmy' and have him tumbling down out of the sky to land on the post. The previous owner of Duncannon had told us they called him

Jimmy, and we added the Wack Wack because that was what he said, quietly and persistently, early in the morning when he arrived on the post until we woke up.

Then came the day when William said:

'Can Julia and I take the boat round the pool?'

This was the wide area of river in view of the house. Again in the end I agreed but made them swear to keep within sight of the house; they were after all only seven and five. A day or two later it was:

'May we take the boat down to Dartmouth?'

Of course I could not possibly agree to that, having visions of them going out to sea, but when they asked to go up to Totnes, it seemed so much safer that I let them go. They wore life jackets and were extremely competent in boats, but it was six miles and there were no inhabited houses on the banks. As soon as they had gone, their ears ringing with my injunctions, I knew I was mad, and suffered the tortures of the damned all morning. At 1 o'clock on the dot they rolled in, carrying oars and rowlocks as required, and curiously enough never again asked to take the boat out alone. When I asked how they had fared, William said:

'Well, I thought perhaps we ought to get some more petrol.'

It had not crossed my mind! Prudently he had decided to stay with the boat because there were some rough boys jeering at them (he was only seven), and had sent Julia to get the petrol from the garage. I enquired how Julia could carry a gallon of petrol, and was informed blithely that of course she didn't, the garage man had carried it for her. And how did she pay for it? He fished in his back pocket and produced the bill, signed 'Julia'.

The children never climbed on the wall; we taught them as soon as they could understand that it was too dangerous unless an adult was there. At high tide, you could drown, at low tide bash your brains out on the rocks. Otherwise it was a wonderfully free and interesting habitat. There was a cottage on either side of us, both belonging to the ferryman Mr Collings. He and his wife were good friends to us, though his daughter and grandson (four years' William's senior) were a doubtful asset. There was a little beach overlooked by the ferryman's cottage, and his old brother-in-law, who was no longer able to fish or do much except odd jobs, would usually be sitting in his oily-looking navy-blues in a shelter there, and could keep an eye on the children. He was never asked to, he was known as Grumpy Grandad, but he would have rallied I am sure in an emergency. From here the herring boats went out in the winter, and in summer they were called salmon boats. There were three or four of them, all licensed. Mr Collings owned one of them and so was entitled to half the catch; the other half was divided between the crew, so he got a share of that too. The ferry no longer brought in an income. Just occasionally hikers would want to be taken across, hailing him from the other side sometimes, coming from the nearest village of Ashe. On the hill behind there were fields and woods and just brambly jungles where high jinks went on. The only people one saw were in boats and there was a lovely old paddle steamer which plied up and down the Dart in summer. Cadets from Dartmouth Naval College sometimes became stuck on sandbanks opposite us between tides, and once or twice we had to rescue Dartington Hall students who had come to grief and had to be dried out and re-clothed. The first people to call on us came by boat. We heard the shouting:

'Is there anybody in?' but at first could not locate them as their boat was bobbing them up and down as they peered over the wall intermittently.

Rubbish was always a problem as of course the dustmen never called (though the postman did). We burnt all we could in an enclosure which had been a gun site during the war, and we feverishly made compost, but indestructibles like bottles and tins had to be broken or pierced and sunk unlawfully in a sack at dead of night in a deep place. We did not use very many tinned products and in those days many bottles were welcome back at the shop, so this exercise might only be done once in a leave.

I lost three more babies. After that first one in Lagos, Satan packed me off for a little holiday in Jos with Susan Marshall to recuperate, and this provided a lovely memory for me. While there we met a man called Hugh Mulligan (who incidentally we both thought was Satan when we first saw him, sitting down in the club dining room so we could not see that he was much shorter) who was working on sleeping sickness. He took me down to the Hidden Valley one day. This is a fantastic piece of geography, being a valley entirely enclosed by mountains. Our way down from the plateau was through some bushes to a falling stream and for a short way we walked down through it. This successfully hid the track which we eventually came out on beside the stream. It took twenty minutes to descend to a lovely cultivated country with no one to be seen at first; but soon women and children began to appear from cover, delightedly to inspect me, as hardly ever did a white woman visit them. It was a magic time until we had to make the steep ascent again.

The next baby to be lost was after Julia, in the car! I had left it too late, though I knew I was in trouble, but I would not leave until friends had come to take the children into their care. It was not safe to leave a girl child, however young, alone with Africans of either sex, as there was a belief that syphilis could be cured by contact with a virgin. Even a nanny could be bribed, so I never had one. The next miscarriage was in England, as we thought the climate might have been responsible, but life at Duncannon was too hard in the circumstances without Satan, and I had forgetfully helped to pull up a boat. That one I had to cope with on my own as the doctor did not come till the next day, and a retired midwife who did come was unable to stay because of an old lady she was looking after; she simply told me what to do. Luckily I had a German au pair girl, only seventeen, but she was able to look after the children and keep them away. The fourth lost was in Africa again and I was taking such care. I was in bed early one evening when the Governor rang up to borrow our hi-fi. It was in my bedroom and Satan fetched it. Going downstairs he slipped on the polished wood; he saved the hi-fi but winded himself on the banisters and was making the most appalling groans. I forgot my need to take care and dashed to the rescue, and that was that. We decided that, as I was then nearly forty, we should just give thanks for our pigeon pair, born near in age and perfect.

Until they were eight the children were a pretty full-time job for me. To keep them fit in that humid heat, I took them to private swimming pools nearly every day and, in one garden we had, Satan and the gardener hacked out a small pool of our own; we were immediately moved to another house! There was a lovely pool in the bush we occasionally visited with other families. William was swimming well and diving before he was five. Julia might have done the same as up to the age of seven months she was like a little frog in the water as I held her, but William caught ringworm from wearing the driver's hat and we were unable to go swimming for several months, by which time she was old enough to be afraid. However, she was very competent by the time she was six and in her teens was captain of swimming at the Godolphin School. They learned to ride tricycles (William at fifteen months to the frustration of the mother of the little girl whose tricycle he was borrowing, she being three and quite unable to ride it), then bicycles, and I taught them to ride – stallions were all we could get as it was tsetse fly country; it was quite a game teaching a small child on even a pretty quiet one, as one's own was trying to bite the other one all the time. Whatever William learned to do, and he was a natural athlete, he insisted Julia should learn too, and she, who knew fear as he never did, was incredibly brave in her determination to master whatever he decreed, for she loved him very much. We collected butterflies together, we learned the alphabet and numbers.

Then at four and a half William went to the University Staff School, rather to Julia's dismay. At six and a half I found he no longer knew his alphabet and still could not read or write. I knew why; he was always dreaming of some physical exploit he was going to try when he was free of this tiresome classroom and I could not blame the teachers. But I had to face the fact that in two years' time he was booked in to a preparatory school for which he had to be able to read, write, do elementary arithmetic and French! So I wrote home and joined the Parents' National Educational Union.

In the meantime one day William came home from school in tears because he had been knocked about by an African boy, Wilfred Enahoro, the son of a Minister. Satan comforted him:

'I must teach you to box, my boy.' Early next morning an urgent little figure appeared the other side of our mosquito net:

'Daddy, you said you'd teach me to box.'

There and then, standing between his father's knees, he had to have a lesson. He came back from school that day covered in blood but radiant.

'It's all right, Mummy, it's not my blood, it's Wilfred's.'

Teaching them was a highlight in my life, it was so rewarding. The courses were very well organised and if one did one's homework one kept one jump ahead. The main thing was that one felt one knew the children so much better than before, how each brain worked and how to get the best results. I was not supposed to teach Julia before she was five but it was not possible to stop her learning. There was William fretting to get up the nearest tree, and Julia busy absorbing over his shoulder what he was supposed to be learning. Before he went to boarding school I decided I must tell him the Facts of Life, and bought a booklet from a magazine called *The Family Doctor* which told one how to go about it. It began with the story of banana flies, carried on with the life of chickens, and by the time one got to human beings it was fairly obvious what happened, only of course William had not been paying attention.

'Do you mean so-and-so, Mummy?' asked Julia, using her own words to make the matter quite clear.

'That's right,' said I, a bit red in the face.

William came to. 'Mummy,' he said in appalled accents, 'that's NOT what happens, is it?'

'Well, of course it is,' I said tartly, embarrassed, 'and if you had been paying attention you would have understood.'

This he ignored in the grand manner. 'Well,' he said finally '*I* shan't be getting married!' I felt I had done him everlasting damage but he married at twenty-two and seemed to live happily ever after.

He was a wonderfully co-ordinated youngster, and very determined when he decided to conquer some skill. However, although Julia endeavoured to do all he wanted her to do, she did not damage herself like he did. He broke his arm falling off a sofa, was knocked unconscious by a car in England, running out from behind a bus, was cut and badly bruised by pulling everything down on top of himself when scaling the trunks piled up in the garage. Once he came in screaming from playing on the sand heap under a tree in Nigeria, and screamed for two hours, so that I could not discover what had happened. It transpired in the end that stinging caterpillars had fallen off the tree on to him, and a week or two later it happened to Julia in another garden, with the same results. One was always on the lookout for snakes and scorpions and deadly bacteria; they must never take their shoes off for fear of catching burrowing worms called jiggers, often caught in a house from the servants' feet. But on the whole it was a good life.

Julia was a joy to teach, she understood so quickly. Maths came easily to her. On one occasion I bought a book on 'Space' as I felt we must keep upsides with technology! It was all news to me and the first time we went through this book with large pictures on every page, I was amazed and bemused. The next time I brought it out there were cries of:

'Oh, we've done that!'

'Well, we have been through it, but we don't know it,' I replied. I opened the book at random, pointed to a picture and demanded to know what it illustrated. In her own words, but very clearly, Julia explained the pull of gravity. They both loved books and would lie quietly during our afternoon rests, or if they woke early in the morning, looking at pictures or, when they could read, reading avidly. I always read to them from the beginning and never had to choose more babyish books for Julia's benefit.

We began to travel by air and this soon became compulsory. That held other difficulties than those experienced at sea. I shall never forget having a small child wanting to perform the daily evacuation at take-off time when everyone was strapped in. I had a potty with me and was forced to allow its use on my lap, but the stewardess was adamant we could not leave our seats for any reason. I had my revenge by handing her the pot, decently shrouded, for disposal later, when the child was asleep on my lap. Another time at Paddington Station I had to produce this object when we were waiting for our porter to bring us a taxi. There was a drain nearby, down which I expected to empty it, but the little darling produced a major contribution and I could not. I popped the pot into the bag just as the taxi came with the porter hanging on outside, and thought I should be able to empty it at King's Cross Station. Unhappily we had hardly any time to catch our train, so I promised myself I could do it on the train. The train was very full and kind people, seeing this poor young mother with two small children and a great deal of luggage, ushered me to the window seats of one of those carriages with four or five seats a-side and a long corridor outside. I put the dreadful bag under my seat (next to the heater) while I settled the children and the luggage, and then just did not have the nerve to get up and carry the thing to the lavatory. Finally I arrived at Granny's house carrying it before me.

Then came the years when the children themselves had to go off to school by air, first of all William alone. It was the most awful torture and one could not at first comfort oneself with the later knowledge, imparted by one of the co-travellers, that as soon as the children boarded, a new world swallowed them up; they drank the plane dry of forbidden Coca-Cola in no time, and had a very enjoyable trip. Julia used to see my distress as soon as William had gone and, unknown to me, determined never to cry at parting, so I never knew she minded until she told me when she was grown-up. They both hated boarding school; eight years old is too young to go away from home, but there was nothing else we could do except for Satan and me to live apart, an idea we did not entertain. All we could do was vow that at least I should be with them every holidays and this we stuck to. I had hoped that Julia's intelligence and ability would make it all easier for her than for William, whose interests lay outdoors, like the majority of boys. The difference only meant that she had to make no effort and that he worked very hard for his good results.

Leaving William at his prep school in Weston-super-Mare for the first time was bad. The moment of realisation came when he saw his bear on the bed that was to be his, and I was hustled away. A friend, John Morris, who with his family was overlapping with me at Duncannon, which they were having for their leave, was accompanying me on this trip, his wife Nan looking after Julia and her own children. He, a doughty colonel, had been impatient with Nan when she had begun to lament about leaving their own son the following term, and had said:

'Oh pull yourself together, woman, be like Patricia, she wouldn't cry.' Little did he know. I emerged from the school in floods. He gritted his teeth and said:

'We'll go and get a drink in a pub.' Alas the pubs were not open for another half-hour and he was obliged to drive all that time without fortification for either of us. When we had downed a stiff whisky, he said:

'Tell me when that begins to wear off and we'll stop again.'

On one occasion the horrors of the separation were particularly underlined. William had been given a letter by his headmaster's wife at the beginning of the long holidays, with instructions to give it to us. In the letter she was informing us that William was booked to have an operation on an eye muscle to correct a squint, two days after the following term began; and she was asking if she could have our official permission. William forgot about the letter, I did not search his Macintosh pockets, and the Macintosh was not seen again till he was returning to school. Holding it on the airstrip, I realised there was a lump in one pocket, reckoned it was probably sweets, by now in a horrible state, about which I could do nothing, and I let him go with it. A cable brought me the horrid news and we could only cable our permission and not be with him. I sent an SOS to all sorts of people about visiting him and having him for convalescence, and things worked out in the end without him being unduly disturbed, but it was the kind of nightmare one had to expect in this life of separation.

★   ★   ★

Satan had been quietly moving up the Western Region hierarchy and was now No. 3 as Minister of Finance, so I had to combine a good deal of social life with my nursery life. I never left the children alone, none of us did. If we were in we had other people's children to stay the night, if we were out they had ours, and it worked well. Interesting people visited the country, tiresome Members of Parliament came, and new cadets had to be asked to a meal or for the night on their way up-country.

One hardly ever met an African at a meal, but at cocktail parties, though even there the blacks tended to group together and the women separated out from the men, just as the whites did. The Nigerian wives often had no English at all, and with what little they had I found the conversation very restricted: babies, food, operations and clothes. I did discover that a Yoruba man's robe, called a *riga,* took ten yards to make, and that the Premier for one had eighty or so *rigas* in his cupboards; some were in broderie anglaise and we were able to discuss the cost of that, and where to buy it.

We were working towards integration, but it was slow work. The uproar when it was decreed that the English Club should be open to all was a pointer, but in the end it was. Nothing much happened; most Africans did not even want to join. A few well-educated and evolved ones, mostly judges, did join, were very welcome, and were the first to blackball an unsuitable member of their own race trying to join. One Minister's wife, a very elegant addition, who wore stunning slacks and skin-tight tops in brilliant colours, learned to play golf at Simpson's in Piccadilly, and thoroughly distracted the chaps from their game whenever she played. Even she was heavy-going when one tried to fraternise and one found oneself discussing what was available in the local shops. She told me an interesting fact about her hair, which was straight and drawn back into a bun on top of her head; she had it straightened and every three months she would comb it out and wash it, then pomade it and smooth it, with an artificial bun on top. It was very effective and the pomade kept her insect-free.

When both children were at school I did what work I was allowed to do. I taught shorthand to a girls' school and to male clerks, though the latter frightened me so much that I took a shorthand teacher's course by correspondence, and that encouraged me to do a journalism course, as a result of which I had two articles printed in *The Times* when we were in Zanzibar 'by our special correspondent'. One was about a slave I met and one about a trip to Uganda. For part of the summer holidays, which were extra long in Nigeria, I ran a little school in our garage. Several mothers were teachers and it kept the little ones interested and busy. I made my own clothes and Julia's (occasionally William's) and did embroidery, and a lot of gardening, and collected stamps and butterflies with the children in the holidays. We always had cats and I also kept chickens. I bred Rhode Island Reds with local hens because the Rhode Island hens were hopeless mothers in the tropics; they had no idea about snakes and birds of prey. But I had one awful tragedy with them: I shut them up at night in a wire run, and one morning came to release them and found just a collection of skeletons, the mother with her wings over most of her chicks, but two stuck to the side of the cage, all eaten clean by driver ants. These were a horrid hazard, and we kept our bed legs in large tins of kerosene – if too small the ants would make a bridge of their own bodies, dying in the act, over which their brothers could swarm. On one hilarious occasion when we had a dinner party, the first two guests arrived at the double, tearing off their clothes as they came and shrieking:

'Ants! Which way is the bedroom?' The other four guests performed an exact replica of this performance, as there was a line of driver ants across our drive, and they all arrived before we had time to investigate and warn. It certainly broke any ice there might have been.

Our cats were Siamese and we liked to have a pair, but it was hard to keep them going. One dear one was a great hunter, and came home with a very bad leg wound. We reckoned he had been in a trap. Another time he went missing for several days and we feared the worst, but he turned up in very bad shape, trailing a trap. His leg had been well nigh severed. We drove him the 100 miles to the Lagos vet, who amputated the leg, a front one. He did very well for some time on only three, sitting like a tripod, but then his hunting instinct overcame him and he disappeared, that time for ever. We had difficulty in breeding Siamese because it seemed that the female always preferred an ordinary moggie. Perhaps it was not the race but the individual. Who knows? We did achieve one spectacular litter, when we had shut her up with a Siamese and were confident this would be a pure bred litter. She produced two Siamese, one grey Persian, one ginger and one tabby.

When Tony Abell went on leave one year, we looked after his parrot. All went well until a day or two before his return when, to my consternation, I could not find the parrot. The boys and I looked high and low, but he was not to be found. When Satan returned from the office I ran out to break the awful news to him and, lo and behold, the parrot stepped down off the back axle and walked into the house. He must have ridden to the office there, and stayed there all day till he got home again.

We never owned a rock hyrax but we knew one quite well. He was about the size of a large moggie, with very short legs so rather heavier. He had thick dark hair and hooves like an elephant of whom he was a relation. He simply loved to eat roses which was a trial but his owners loved him so much they grew roses for him. He was very friendly and would make himself comfortable on your shoulders. He was not on the list of pets who had to be in quarantine if they came to England, presumably because they were not expected to come. So he came on leave with his owners and lived happily in a London flat with them. In the wild his kind would always relieve nature in the same communal place, so this chap naturally learned to use the lavatory. This was ideal in the flat and I was delighted to be invited to witness this habit. He was asleep on top of a cupboard when I arrived but descended at his usual time, walking down the side of the wardrobe on his suckered hooves. Making sure the coast was clear (we were hiding), he then belted down the corridor, ricocheting from wall to wall on all four feet till he reached the loo. This he used efficiently except he did not use paper. Tiny deer were sometimes kept as pets. One we met was devoted to Smarties.

One of the nicest things to happen was that somebody left his squirrel with us when he retired. He was called Lumpers (the nickname given to the lump sum compensation being offered to people required to leave because of Africanisation of the service). We put his 'nest', a cardboard box, on top of the wardrobe in our room. One day I was annoyed to see him running along the landing, trailing one of my stockings which he took up to his nest. When I investigated I found, among other remnants, a Union Jack, still recognisable as such but shredded! Later we had another squirrel called Littley, brought in by the gardener when I was in bed following a miscarriage. This one was a baby and I brought him up in a bag pinned to my dresses, and fed him at first with a dropper, and he was a truly delightful, if destructive, pet. I took him with me when I visited a blind school outside the town. He chose that day to leave me for the first time. Previously he had come out of his bag and run around my person, but never left me. That day he caused pandemonium because he leapt on to a blind man, who had no idea what it was and slapped at him. Littley got away on to another shoulder, and so on until I could get him back to me, where he was rather thankful to be by then. When it was explained to the blind men, they enjoyed the joke very much, and it probably gave them something to talk about for some time.

In the mornings Littley would come down from his box and have a lump of sugar when we had our early morning tea. Then he would sit on the end of our bed having a wash and brush-up, particularly his beautiful bushy tail. After that he would go out of the window and eat coralita seeds or whatever was on offer, until breakfast time, when he would appear in the dining room. He liked to sit on Satan's shoulder and be given titbits, and on days when we had prunes, he would have a stone to open up. He would discard the bits and eat the kernel, and Satan would have to go and change his shirt before going to the office. He would be at the front door mat to greet Satan at lunch-time and would run up his trouser leg into his pocket, turn round and peep out. When I went out in the car I would ask the driver to drop me at the end of the drive on

Me and my second squirrel, Littley.

the way back, so that I could walk up, calling Littley out of the bushes, and it was lovely to have him emerge from some leafy hiding place and land on my shoulder. He was very partial to ice cream and I was angry one day with Julia, when I left her in the car with an ice cream and Littley while I shopped, and I returned to find him gibbering with frustration because she would not share.

There came a very difficult time for Satan. Everything was being directed towards independence for Nigeria and gradually all the ministries were given to Africans. The last to go was the Ministry of Finance, but go it had to, and there was no comparable posting to which to move Satan. He was asked if he would take demotion to permanent secretary to the Ministry of Finance, and train the new minister, who was an elementary school headmaster with very little experience of government. Satan agreed and began a difficult task, although luckily the minister was a nice man. We had heard a horrid tale from Ghana which made everyone nervous. A great friend of Satan's was Chief Commissioner of the North there, and was summoned to a minister's office and treated with short shrift, particularly noticeable when Africans are normally very courteous. He was not offered a chair so, it being very hot and exhausting, he perched on the edge of the very large desk. Not for long. The minister said:

'Please stand in my presence.'

When it was time to prepare the Budget, Satan coached his minister in procedure and left him to work it out. He eventually came, beaming, to Satan and presented his plan, costing £13 million. Satan made a show of reading it but had to point out that the Region was working on a £3.25 million budget.

'I know,' said the minister 'but I can't do everything I want for that amount. I came to power promising free education and a free health service for all my people, and this I must give.'

Patiently Satan maintained that they only had £3.25 million to work with and that the minister must have another try. Away he went rather grumpily and made his alterations. Returning, he flung down his budget on the desk and said defiantly:

'£9 million. Last price.'

No arguments Satan could bring forth bore any weight.

'But where are you going to get the money, then?' asked Satan wearily.

'Where DO you get money from?' countered the Minister, and to his surprise, Satan found he had to explain about taxation: rates, indirect taxation, poll tax – poll tax? What was that? When the Minister understood that every adult in the country paid sixpence a year, he was overjoyed.

'Aha!' said he. 'We will raise the poll tax to ten shillings and sixpence!' (That was a mere two thousand per cent plus mark-up). Appalled as Satan was, and as much as he warned that there would be riots (What are the Police for?) the minister went ahead and levied a new poll tax of ten shillings and sixpence. He got it, in spite of casualties in the police and among the people during the inevitable riots. The sad bit was that, although he built his hospitals and schools in remote parts of the bush as promised, there were not enough trained doctors, nurses and teachers to staff them, and gradually they fell into ruins. But that lay some time ahead.

Not long after this Tom Shankland, the Deputy Governor, was sent home with Ménière's Disease, and Satan was moved to that post. The post of Governor itself was vacant for three months between the departure of one governor and the arrival of another, so all of a sudden there he was acting Governor, and we moved into Government House. It was a huge house on top of a hill, with a feeling of space and light, though those views were of solid, impenetrable, dark green bush. We did not enjoy living there, particularly as the servants were adept at turning a dishonest penny at our expense. For instance, when visitors stayed, drinks were served in their rooms, and, however abstemious they might really be, they appeared to get through large quantities of alcohol and soft drinks in their rooms and there was little we could do about it. Except that the next time Satan had to act, we did not move into Government House. The children, however, enjoyed the house very much, with its vast number of rooms, and were soon enlivening the place with games of hide-and-seek with their friends.

One had an entertainment allowance but it certainly did not cover what one was expected to do. We were annoyed by the way droves of MPs came, expecting to be fêted, and when Adlai Stevenson, whom we rather liked, came from the States with an entourage of eleven, one felt things had gone too far. One of his entourage was the woman editor of the *Chicago Herald Tribune*, rabidly anti-British and permanently sloshed. Others were not only Mr and Mrs Ronald Tree but her daughter from a previous marriage with her newly-wed husband, presumably on their honeymoon.

Ernest Marples, then Minister of Transport in the United Kingdom, was one guest we did not care for. We had heard he was a keen tennis player, so we laid on three of the best players we had to give him a game, and they were no mean performers. However, when I put this plan to him tentatively, he scotched it brusquely, saying:

'Oh no! I'm rather good. I should prefer the court to myself with a couple of ball boys to field my serves.'

He elected to play at 3 p.m. which was some revenge to me, as I heard him pounding around at a time which was almost the hottest of the day, when everyone rested. Office hours were from 8 a.m. to 2 p.m. officially, then people lay down for an hour after lunch. After tea, if they did not have to return to the office for meetings or extra work, they played games or swam, as it was important to keep fit in such a climate.

At our first meal with Marples he brought up the subject of the notorious Geoffrey Bing, my first cousin, who was at that time adviser to Nkrumah, the President of Ghana. Marples had just been there and had met Geoffrey. Usually I managed to fend off derogatory discussions of Geoffrey by early announcement that I was related to him, but this time I missed it and Marples told us that the reason Bing was such an awkward, if clever, fellow was that his grandmother was Chinese. This was news to me, but it was a nice moment when I left the room with the ladies, to whisper to Satan as I passed, projecting a glance at a picture of a Chinese girl which happened to hang behind him:

'Granny!'

Not long after this I had the chance of going to Ghana with the Bromages in their car, so I was able to check the truth of Marples' statement. Geoffrey's mother, Irene, who was my father's sister, was visiting him and I thought she might be having a horrid time, as most Europeans shunned Geoffrey because he had begun his adult life by being a Communist. Now he was being chummy with the President who was not popular with most of the Europeans, who felt that Geoffrey must be responsible for or at least compliant with many of Nkrumah's controversial actions. I had Army friends with whom I could stay and was rather excited by the jaunt. The Bromage limousine was tied together with string, but the company of these two tiny people, he a district officer, she a doctor, made up for anything. They bubbled with mirth. We were impressed by the quality of the French road through Dahomey, far better than the English ones in Nigeria or Ghana, but gathered that the excellent quality finished on that one road, as the others were far worse than those in Nigeria. None of their interior roads were tarmacked and most were full of potholes.

My aunt seemed perfectly happy and did not require to be rescued. Soon after I arrived, she excused herself, saying how sorry she was but she was due at a Christian tea party in Geoffrey's place. I could not imagine him ever going to one, let alone bothering to find a deputy. He took me on a sight-seeing drive which was very interesting and he was good company, but I was rather disconcerted at the way Europeans cut him. I asked him about the Chinese ancestor; he said it was true, on his father's side, as his forbears had lived in Dutch Java, the name Bing being Dutch, and that it was his great-grandmother. He was a very interesting man and it was sad that the family had drawn away from him because he was as a young man a member of the Communist Party; he had been an MP, had fought very bravely in the Spanish Civil War, had been parachuted into France during the war, and altogether seemed to have had a lot going for him. When Ghana blew up, he fielded a spear in his back and was invalided out.

It did one good to get away from the big town and the one environment, if one could. I only once went on tour, which Satan had been doing most of the time in the North before the war. We did a tour of the Western Region when William was seven months old, leaving him with the Lawsons (the doctor and nurse who had been with us on the Broads). He did not know me when we got back after three weeks. We stayed in rest houses or with friends, looked at new projects, like bridges being built or a new crop tried, visited schools and courts; to me all quite new, to Satan nostalgically familiar. He once told me how he had got a road built in Northern Nigeria before the First World War. There was no money in the vote for this project which was much desired by the two villages it would unite. So Satan bought three cows (which the vote could afford) and tied them on long tethers at the halfway point. He told the people that the cows would be given to the village which first reached them on a road that they had built. This appealed to the people and they set about building a road from each end. When the first village reached the cows they rejoiced exceedingly, and after killing the cows, invited the other village, which arrived within a day later, to feast with them. The tour we made of the West was never again possible and we contented ourselves with a long weekend at Olokomeji, a pool fed by a river, in dense bush, where fishing could be had; or an expedition with guests to Ife to see the famous mysterious bronze heads, when the Oni, the chief, would treat us to warm champagne. Once when we had him to dinner in Ibadan, I offered coffee to this charming old man, saying:

'Black or white?'

'Well,' he said with a twinkle in his eye, 'seeing that I am black, I think I'll have white, thank you very much.'

If we had some local leave, we all went to Lighthouse Bay beyond Lagos, where we borrowed a hut and stayed in delicious isolation, running over the blazing sands to the sea many times a day and getting brown as berries all over. Before I was married I had been there when a dreadful tragedy took place on Lighthouse Beach. My party had found the waves too weak for surfing and were sitting on the beach when we became aware of a woman calling out for help, standing in water up to her knees but quite unable to move because of the undertow. We formed a chain and got her out, also another woman, and then noticed several surfboards being washed about unattended. In the end it transpired that what probably happened was that the colonel of the regiment's small son had got into difficulties, his mother went to his rescue, the colonel to hers, and a subaltern to his – they all drowned. So I knew the dangers of that coast and stood careful guard. We would take a boat to Tarkwa Bay and then hike across it and overland to Lighthouse Bay. Our servants would have gone ahead with our belongings and food, and a caretaker saw to lamps and water. To have a shower, he would put water in a container above and by pulling a string we could tip the bucket up; our sandy bathing suits would be rinsed in the water that was caught below.

Once I was lucky enough to be invited by Susan Marshall, the wife of the Chief Secretary in Lagos, both of whom were good friends of ours, to accompany them as Susan's interpreter when they went on an official visit to French Dahomey. We visited the Alake of Abeokuta before crossing the border. His people and the Dahomians had been traditional enemies for centuries, and he sent a message by us to the King of Dahomey:

'Tell him that I will be very happy to let him have a copy of the ceremonial umbrella captured by us from him in the last wars.'

This message was not delivered as it was clearly meant as a serious insult.

Our first job on arriving was to visit a factory of some kind, an exhausting procedure, and we were all parched with thirst upon emerging; we were offered drinks which looked like squash, and downed them with gusto, only to discover that they were at least half gin. It was like that most of the way: the French colonialists seemed to drink alcohol all the time, though they soon learned that we were odd enough to like tea or even just water sometimes. We saw a model village which was wonderful, but were informed on the side that there were not any being lived in or even built. We asked the French District Officers if they had the same difficulty our chaps had, that when a weighty decision had to be made, permission had to be sought from the mother country first, which took a long time.

'Oh no,' they replied, 'that would never do here; you would get a decision and then poof! The government, it would fall, and you would have to start again!'

The same old France. One good thing, I thought, was the way the French took local wives. They seemed to have no colour bar and any black man, if he had the qualifications required, could apply for any job in Dahomey or even back in France. These black wives were apparently just as well educated as their French counterparts would have been. They entertained us royally, including a magnificent ball held at an outdoor dance floor.

We had a very bad experience in Ibadan with a temporary white mission dentist, who without anaesthetic began to tear flesh from William's jaw which was growing up between tooth and gum and giving pain. I stayed in the waiting room with Julia, believing that children behaved better without their mothers, but when I heard his yells I left Julia with somebody else and dashed in. The dentist had all but finished, he said, so I simply held William's hands and made comforting noises. Then the man said he just wanted to take an X-ray so I went out again to comfort Julia, but fainted dead away in the waiting room. To my rage the dentist had another little go, when I did not dare return for fear of fainting and making things worse. William suddenly flung open the door, scarlet in the face and unable to speak, gestured furiously to us to follow and we went down to the car. Luckily it was a gubernatorial one at that time, and very large, as William was quite unable to sit down, he was rigid, and had a very high temperature. After this I used to drive the hundred miles to Lagos to take the children to an African dentist. The African dentist in Lagos was a darling and gave them a shilling every time. I always found that Africans were better at things like injections too, and would prefer to be given one by an African nurse than by a European nurse or doctor. They have great manual dexterity and gentleness.

Once, returning from putting the children on a plane in Lagos, the driver Sam and I came upon an accident and could not get by, though we had been warned not to stop for accidents even if one was involved, but to report it to the nearest police station; they were lynching people who may not even have been drivers, black and white alike. On this occasion a car had tried to pass a lorry which did not wish to be passed and swerved out at the critical moment; the car was badly damaged on the passenger side and a well-dressed black man was slumped there unconscious; both drivers had vanished. A great many people stood around, some off the lorry and others who had appeared miraculously from the bush, as always happened when an accident occurred. Nobody was doing anything, so I got two men to help Sam put the injured man across our back seat, we turned round and drove back to the orthopaedic hospital just outside Lagos. It was Sunday and nobody was about but I managed to flush out a couple of orderlies to take the patient on a stretcher, then I went to the swimming pool where they said the duty doctor would be, and alerted him. Returning to the ward, I found they had stripped the victim and had him under scratchy red blankets with his poor head jammed up between the bars of the bed, while they were busy going through the contents of his pockets. He was a dental student, and I fear was probably lost to his country by the way things were going, but there was no more I could do.

Sam was a great character and very good with the children. One day, driving to Lagos, Sam suddenly stopped the car.

'Why have you stopped, Sam?' I asked anxiously.

'I go shit, madam,' he replied politely, and did just that.

Ju-ju played quite a large part in the people's lives and sometimes encroached on ours. I know that Satan was careful to comb any hairs from his brush and to collect the parings when he cut his nails, and put them down the lavatory, and he admitted he did this to prevent any servant from thinking he could use them for ju-ju purposes.

We had a servant (known as a small-boy) who became convinced that the Number One boy, John, was putting a ju-ju on him. John was an unusual character and it was quite likely that he was! He was light-skinned – his mother was a Jekri from an area where European seamen provided many of the local ladies not only with a living but with children; he was very intelligent and an excellent servant; we liked him but felt there were hidden depths. We found we were unable to talk the small-boy out of his belief, and even when I prepared food from out of our fridge in front of him, he would not eat because he was convinced any food would poison him.

One evening when we were expecting the Governor and his wife, among others, to dinner, we emerged from our room all dressed up to find the small-boy lying on the dining room floor. He refused to go to his quarter so we had to ask John and a man we had hired for the evening in the small-boy's place, to carry him there. They had difficulty as he put his hands round the door jamb so that they could not shut him in, but eventually they tied his feet together so that while he was untying them they could lock him in. The guests duly arrived and we regaled them with this story; John kept up the interest by periodically coming to whisper developments in Satan's ear: the boy had set fire to his bedding: he had stuck a knife in his belly, etc. At last the police arrived and took him away and next day we took him to the asylum sixty miles away for treatment, but they were unable to persuade him to eat even so far away from John. Finally we sent for his brothers in the country, and they took him home and we heard no more till years later, when we were the other side of Africa, we had a letter addressing us as 'My father and my mother', thanking us for having saved his life. We never made up our minds whether John had put a ju-ju on him, but all that was needed was that the boy should believe that he had.

One day when John was serving supper to the children and I was sitting nearby, I heard the following sinister exchange:

William, excitedly: 'John, today at school we learned about people who used to eat people in the old days.'

John, calmly, passing the pudding: 'Yes, Master William, they still do.'

One gradually grew to understand the people a little more but often it was the hard way. The wife of one of our servants came to me one day to see if I could stop her three-months-old baby crying. I asked her all the pertinent questions I could think of, and coming to no conclusion, decided to take them to hospital. On the way I discovered that she had fed it the contents of a whole tin of Heinz spinach for babies, bought from an itinerant seller who came to the house with such delights in a basket on her head. Knowing that I had bought some for Julia (who was a couple of months older and only had two teaspoons of it a day) she also bought some, but being unable to read, administered the whole tin at one go. The hospital issued us with a beer bottle three quarters full of some calming mixture, but warned me to administer it myself, or the woman would be likely to give large quantities at one time, thinking the more the better.

It worked both ways. I had several enchanting little camellia bushes lining the drive, and planned places to plant a few seedlings I found under one of them. When I came to move them, they were gone; the gardener had thrown them away. I was cross, but he said he could bring me some more from the bush. I did not believe him, but he brought me several roots next day of a variety I had never seen, a creeper, with huge flowers but authentic shapes and leaves. He was amazed that I so valued a mere bush plant.

★   ★   ★

Sir John Rankine was the new Governor who arrived in due course, and Satan sank thankfully back into the job of Deputy Governor. Sir John was a dour man, who found it difficult to make friends, earning himself the nickname of 'Jolly Jack'. When he first came out, it was Christmas time and his really jolly wife had stayed at home to be with their daughter. We therefore invited him (reluctantly) to have Christmas dinner with us, and we did our best to be friendly. Satan had to show him the ropes, because although he had been British Resident in Zanzibar, he had never served in Nigeria. We had heard that when he was appointed to Zanzibar, the old Sultan had groaned and said:

'I have suffered the father, must I also suffer the son?'

John's father had also been British Resident some years before. Anyway,

John was certainly very grateful to Satan for the support and friendliness, and many years later, when he was a widower and we met at reunions, he was almost pathetic in the way he clung to me. He liked children, though again he found it difficult to show it. At one cocktail party in the Government House garden, when we arrived in the line to shake hands with the Rankines, we were horrified to see William, standing beside the Governor for all to see, filthy dirty with red laterite, as he had been making a run for his cars on a heap of the stuff at our gate; he must have run up through a bush path between our houses.

'What are you doing here?' I hissed.

'I want to catch Mrs Rosser,' he replied, 'to return this car which belongs to Lindsay.' Sir John actually had a twinkle in his eye.

Not long after we had all retired, I reminded him of this occasion and he said:

'Yes, I knew William quite well. He and Julia used to push their bikes up to our front door and whizz down the hill to yours, and I used to watch them from my office.'

It is amusing to think that the ceremonial guard at the gates had allowed them to come and go, but of course they and the children had got used to each other when we had lived in the house.

In 1956 the Queen visited Nigeria. The excitement leading up to it knew no bounds. The Governor's wife decreed that the main spare quarters in Government House must be done up and refurnished, but when it was finished she realised it still was not as good as the Governor's quarters and that those would have to be given up to the Queen. So these had to be done up, and as she had rather taken to the furniture she had bought, she wrote to somebody on leave asking her to buy more. One thing was a kidney-shaped dressing table with a glass top which inevitably arrived broken; the Public Works Department, however, could cut glass and cut a new top which was dropped on the stairs. A third was made and placed in position with sighs of relief, but on the very day of the royal arrival it was found, mysteriously, to be cracked, and that was the way the Queen had to use it. The electricians put in extra points, the rooms were decorated, the parquet floors were polished. The floor polishers broke several of the electric points, these were mended and the decorators had to return, they dripped paint on the floor and the polishers were sent for... Holes were dug for bunting poles and they frequently fractured water pipes and telephone cables, then it rained and again the exposed and damaged cables were affected and communications became desperate. There were several nervous breakdowns.

When the Queen and the Duke of Edinburgh arrived, the first event was an investiture at the House of Assembly, organised by the Premier, Obafemi

Awolowo. The Queen and the Governor and their spouses were on the stage in full and very splendid rig, with the Premier. The Deputy Governor, Tom Shankland, who had returned (and Satan was Permanent Secretary to the Minister of Finance again) sat in the front row with his wife and the rest of the hall was filled with Africans, some with servants fanning them. Satan and I were squashed into a box with the wives of people being invested, one of them breast-feeding a baby. We were lucky: all the other Europeans were outside on wooden stands. I was disappointed as both the Queen and Duke looked grumpy people, and the Premier was a bore showing us all the gifts the country was showering on the Queen, before presenting them to her, almost saying:

'Look at this lovely fly whisk, isn't she a lucky queen?'

As they left the building the Duke was heard by Tom Shankland, walking behind, to say to the Premier:

'Why are all those white people sitting outside in the sun?'

Tom nearly fainted as we spent our lives not discriminating against the Africans, to such an extent that we were really discriminating against ourselves in these days leading to independence. The Premier too was taken aback.

'Well, your Highness,' said he, 'we couldn't all get into the hall.'

'I can see that,' replied Prince Philip with asperity, 'but the Civil Servants should have been in the front rows.'

How refreshing to us all: no discrimination at all, but he knew the senior people were nearly all white, therefore it happened to be white people who should have had precedence. We later heard he had cramp up on the stage which helped to account for his grumpy appearance.

The next time we saw them was at a garden party at which neither of us was to be presented, so I was just having a lovely time staring when all of a sudden Lady Rankine, who was escorting the Prince, introduced me. She knew her next stop was a Red Cross person (it was Bailus) but she could not see him, so thought wildly:

'Patricia will have to do, she's Red Cross.'

The Prince knew his programme well and could not place me, so asked:

'And what do YOU do?'

What did I DO? I never stopped. My mind whirled and all I could think of was those buff forms one has sometimes to fill in. Occupation: housewife.

'Housewife!' I exclaimed in triumph, and he had a good laugh.

In the evening of the second day we were immensely fortunate and John Rankine, so grateful to Satan in his funny way, invited us to dinner. He asked nobody more senior than Satan, still doing the Permanent Secretary job, so we sat on the right of the Queen and the Prince at the narrow part of the table so that we were nearly opposite one or the other. I knew so many little details of

Julia (being useful) and the Premier of the W. Region of Nigeria.

the preparations: that the Queen must have no arms to her chair or her skirt got crushed, that she did not use fish knives and forks or even large knives and forks, and so on. I was amused when she was handed a large dish of fish completely masked in a thick sauce, and when she helped herself an enormous amount of fish came up out of it. She giggled and said:

'Whoopsey!' But one had to be very careful; she was surrounded by a very regal aura which was maintained too by her staff, and however informal she sounded, one never forgot who she was.

The Duke was very naughty at dinner: on his other side he had a Mrs Ojo, wife of a leading African who was next to the Queen. Mrs Ojo had little English and in fact only said 'Yes please' in answer to all the Duke's attempts at conversation. He soon realised this and modelled his questions accordingly. I got nervous as Mr Ojo was listening and his English was very good, so I diverted the Duke by asking if he had eaten palm oil chop, the national dish of southern Nigeria. He had not, but upon hearing that the first person to help himself to *foufou*, the farinaceous substance served with it, was expected to hurl a spoonful at the ceiling where, with luck, it would remain at least until the meal was over, he was determined he must eat palm oil chop. The Queen was not keen and pointed out that next day they were lunching at Ijebu Ode (with John and Gwyneth Phillips) and dining at Government House, Lagos, so there was scarcely time to order a change, and the following morning they were leaving. But he insisted, and I heard later that the Government House cook had to lay it on for him the next evening. That would indeed have caused uproar as one NEVER had it except at lunch-time and the 'bangers' of palm oil nuts would have been picked off the tree at dawn. Whether or not he was able to get any *foufou* stuck on the very high ceiling I was never able to find out. It would have left a nasty grey stain.

We had some good holidays when we went on leave. So often it was in the winter so we took a few weeks somewhere in the sun on the way. The first holiday abroad was to Portugal. We were about to be caught for British income tax because we would have spent one year in four in the United Kingdom, so I said:

'Why not spend that money on a flip abroad instead of on tax?'

Satan said if I could arrange a holiday that did not cost more, he was agreeable. We left the children with his mother and an au pair girl at Duncannon, and we went second class by Blue Line ship destined for South America. Satan was not amused but it was in fact hilarious. We were met by a steward who dropped our bags as soon as he heard we were second class, and we had to find another man to show us to our cabin in the bowels of the ship. The passage to it was too narrow to stand in squarely, you had to sidle, and the cabin had no porthole. There was a large hot pipe going from floor to ceiling in the middle and the bunks were under the bulkhead from, as it were, the waist down. We felt claustrophobic and, with ten shillings, Satan was able to encourage the steward to let us have his own cabin, which had two portholes and a basin, but was not very clean. Meals were in shifts and the first shift, we discovered too late, rushed out and bagged all the armchairs. We also inherited their table cloth. Breakfast tended to be curry and rice, the evening meal at five o'clock was hotpot and buns. We sat at a table with a Lascar seaman with lovely and unexpected blue eyes, two waiters who had been working in Jersey all summer and who thought Satan was lovely and kept taking his photograph with one of them in it, and a woman with dyed hair whom we called my friend; she was, too, as she had us to stay for a night when our money ran out on the way home.

We stayed at Albufeira on the recommendation of a Portuguese surgeon who was a friend of Tom Lawson's. Now it is the 'in' place to go, but in 1952 it was not a resort at all. There was one 'pensione' with two rooms to let, of which we had one, and a shared bathroom which had no plug in the bath. There was a plug in the basin but the water did not drain away; Satan bent down to see if he could unscrew the joint underneath, only to find the pipe was twisted round and not connected at all. A box by the lavatory for used paper (newspaper) was on the understanding that plumbing was not made for paper. The bed appeared to bear a lovely fluffy duvet and I bounced delightedly on it and nearly broke my back as it was filled with dried leaves which crackled dreadfully and let me straight down on to the hard wooden slats. But it was a good holiday, swimming in the rather cold November sea, eating the good lady's picnics of an omelette in a crusty roll, with wine, and exploring this very poor area. Every inch of ground was cultivated, even where it had fallen into a hole from erosion. The local children wore no shoes and even in this cold weather, often no trousers.

Several times we went to Malta because my aged godmother Wilhelmina Hayles, my mother's cousin, lived there with her retired naval husband, and they missed seeing the family. We could stop off there on our flights without having to pay extra fares. It was a strange three-way set up. Aunt Willie had very mixed blood like my mother but her father was English and she never admitted to having anything so appalling as Maltese relations (which she had). So visiting her was one thing, with no allusion allowed to the Maltese relations; visiting them was secret and separate. The third connection was Satan's with government officials. A national lottery had been organised in Nigeria with the help of a Maltese called Mifsud, to whom Satan had been kind. His kindness was repaid twice over when it leaked that we were coming to the island. To our surprise we were given the red-carpet treatment at the airport and one was bemused by officials and my cousins, all with huge flashing eyes and outstretched hands, greeting us on all sides. The principal cousins were a very British, very big and handsome major, Freddie, and his extremely foreign, small, dapper and I'm sure corseted father, Captain Armando Stagno Navarra. We were worried like bones, and our time divided up, Satan going off to several official occasions, I being trotted round Valletta with Armando, and later we all went to a meal at Freddie's house, which was built into the walls of the ancient city of Mdina. Anxious that my children, who were whisked off to nursery quarters to have tea, might be facing eating peculiar food, I made a sortie and found them sitting up to table with Freddie's seven sons, consuming Kellogg's Cornflakes and Heinz Baked Beans. (Freddie later had another son and then at last a daughter.)

Aunt Willie and Uncle Trevor lived in a large apartment almost entirely obscured by photographs in silver frames, mostly of their one child Trevor, who at the age of sixteen was tragically drowned at the Battle of Jutland. Uncle Trevor was nearly ninety but insisted on taking me sight-seeing, he carrying William half the way on his back and I struggling behind with the baby. He was a good guide, throwing in colourful remarks like:

'I can see your Aunt Willie now, coming down those steps in a beautiful ball gown, white with gold embroidery.' And his old blue eyes would be faraway and full of memories. Subsequent visits were paid to them in the hospital where they were given rooms for the rest of their lives and where people called formally on them, even each new Governor coming to pay his respects to the oldest British residents.

Once when I visited them, Trevor greeted me and then went into Willie's room ahead of me to proclaim my arrival. She was blind and very deaf, so he went right up to her and before mentioning me, bawled:

'Have you had your pudding, dear?' She misheard him and clutched anxiously at him.

'Haven't you had your pudding, dear?' and they went on like that for several minutes before they were satisfied that all was as it should be. She looked terrible and it was an effort to kiss her, but as soon as my cheek was against hers she became familiar, for her skin had the same unusually satin quality as my mother's. That time I had an appointment to speak at a Women's Institute meeting (I was staying with a judge and his wife who had been in Nigeria) and when I gave this as my reason for going, Willie instantly said:

'Ah, please give the women of Malta a message from me.' And gave me some stirring thoughts to pass on. She had been quite a power in the land for years and I was aware of the veneration in which she was still held when I passed on her words.

The last time I went, I only had Julia with me, aged about seven. Trevor met us in the hall in his dressing gown, a little agitated. He wanted me to look at Willie's jewellery, spread over his bed, and choose items for him to leave to the matron and one or two others, then to take the rest with me. I protested; it seemed to me a horrid thing to do, though now that I am old myself I can see his point of view: they had no further use for these things and they wanted to make sure they went to the family and not to strangers. He had made his will and written a memorandum in triplicate for the hospital authorities about improvements that should be made, his affairs were now in order and he could set about dying peacefully. He seemed to have decided that the time had come and it was no use waiting any longer for Willie to go first. I was in tears when I left, I always was; they were so old I was sure each time I should never see them again, and I forgot the jewellery. Reaching the taxi I turned to see that Julia was still with me, and there she was, tears streaming down her cheeks too, and clutched to her chest was an airbag.

'I've got the jewellery, Mummy.'

That was indeed the last time and they died within a few weeks of one another a little later.

The judge I had been staying with had an artificial leg with which he coped wonderfully so that one might never suspect unless one had seen him swimming. When his first child was born, his wife enquired anxiously of the nurse at her bedside:

'Is it all right?'

'Oh it's fine,' rejoined the nurse, 'except it has a wooden leg.' The nurse was very much confused when she understood that in that case it was taking after its father!

One holiday was to Majorca and we developed whooping cough amongst us on the way. We saw something of Rome, though Julia got rather fed up with the armoury at the Castile Sant Angelo (which William adored), so we took her to throw pennies in the Fountain of Trevi, a custom supposed to ensure one's return. But:

'I don't want to come back to this beastly place!' she declared and refused to throw pennies.

William began to cough. We reached Nice and found that the Lagos clerk had made a mistake and there was no booking on to Majorca for us till the following week. We took a large room with four beds and a wash place in Juan les Pins (much cheaper than Nice). Julia was coughing by then but neither child was really ill, and spent a lot of time riding hired velocipedes on the promenade. Then Satan caught it. The landlady was suspicious and kept asking me if they had whooping cough, but I stalled, pretending I did not know the French word – well I did not, but I knew what she meant. We knew we should not be allowed to fly if we were known to have whooping cough. The doctor had told us this but he, anxious to be rid of our infection from the neighbourhood, did not betray us and said the flight would do us good. Julia was caught at the airport by William, explaining to some official that we had whooping cough but luckily he did not understand her. After a talking-to about not coughing, she nearly blew up at the gangway when we were held up for a few moments, and was puce in the face as we entered the aircraft.

That was a lovely holiday: a month in a villa at Puerto de Pollensa, again a place which is now where everyone goes, but in 1956 very remote. £15 a month we paid for the villa on the waterside, £5 for a maid of all work literally. She did the shopping, washing, cooking and cleaning; and £5 for a boat. The bay was only three feet deep for a long way out and the children messed about in the boat nearly all day, with some American children who had also had whooping cough. Julia fell in once, in her winter coat, and afterwards said to me in wonder:

'I lay on the bottom and looked up through the water and I could see all the others looking at me over the edge of the boat!'

I learned enough Spanish to be able to cope with the maid, though I was rather thrown when she replied at length to my carefully composed and rehearsed speeches, and the children learned enough to ask her for more bread, please, at meals:

'Mas pan, por favor.'

William was one day sitting on the wall on the road side of the villa when some boys came along who threw stones and yelled at him; he, after a few attempts at conciliation, was suddenly inspired and in his most terrifying voice shouted:

'Mas pan, por favor!' Naturally they thought he was mad and ran away.

We sampled octopus one day. The woman was much against our doing so, but Satan had said we must not be insular, so I ordered it for lunch. Unfortunately for me, I saw the horrid thing sitting on the kitchen table and knew I should not be able to eat it. Cooked, it smelt dreadful. I helped Satan first, and as his plate was passed down the table, both children remarked:

'Pooh!' I fear Satan was the only one who braved it, and he had to, but it was very rubbery, very strong, not how I later encountered 'calamares'.

In the last few years of our time in Nigeria two very disturbing things were happening. One was the so-called Leopard Murders, when people were killed on bush paths with leopard claw marks on the back of their necks. Our brother-in-law Derek Fountain, who was Commissioner of Police in the Western Region, was convinced that the murderers were men and not leopards; the Resident in the area involved believed they were leopards. After a lengthy enquiry, a hundred men were convicted and hanged.

The other disturbing item was the steady disappearance of little boys in the Abeokuta District. Most of them were orphans but, even so, it was disturbing. Eventually it was discovered that they were going into a local chief's house and never reappearing and the police were able to clear the matter up to everyone's satisfaction. The reason for the killings was to extract the pituitary glands from the skulls, to be used to induce fertility in childless couples. Two years later I read in the *British Medical Journal* an article about just such a discovery recently made!

In all these years of marriage I had found that my intuition about Satan had been absolutely right; it was as if we had been made for each other (as they so aptly say) and I often gave thanks that we had met. He was a very strong character and I was happy for him to be master, so was quite surprised later on to find he thought he had to fight to keep on top! He was known by the Africans of the North as 'The Iron Man' and I can imagine they found him strong but fair, and I never found him inflexible. To me he was gentle. He stuck to his guns if he considered something right, but then I seldom disagreed with him. Over decisions about the children we agreed that he should have the last word about William and I about Julia, and we only once disagreed. William had failed his Common Entrance exam for Wellington and Satan decreed that he must stay at home for the summer holidays and go to a crammer. I could imagine William's horror and disbelief and my heart bled for him; I was convinced it would make no difference and it did not, he failed again, and I had to control myself and not say 'I told you so.' I loved everything about

Satan, including his looks which were by no means classic. He was six foot three inches, and lean; even when we met he had very little hair but he still had left the curly tufts which may have given him his name. His face was long and lean and pointed, dominated by large tilted blue eyes which could freeze a man in disapproval, I was told, though was not favoured with such a look myself. Perhaps I was wrong to say his face was dominated by his eyes, as his nose was large and hawkish. As soon as we became engaged it occurred to me to hope any daughter we might have would escape that nose, though when I met his sister I was reassured: her profile was exactly his and it was all right. But so far I have not encountered that nose in any of the descendants, though I am always hopeful.

He was being honoured. In 1955 he was awarded the CMG. In 1958 he was knighted. This was a knight bachelorhood and in fact meant more to us than anything, as it was given specifically for his work in those difficult years before Nigerian independence. Of course I was pleased but in a curious way, although not expecting honours, I was not surprised and delighted like his mother was. This was the man I had always thought was wonderful so subconsciously I was not surprised that others thought he was quite good too. If it had been my son, I now realise I should have been amazed that my own flesh and blood should have achieved it. I never looked ahead nor expected honours or advancement, nor increases in salary. Money never meant a lot to me. When I married I did not enquire or even think about Satan's income. If I had, I should have done better to have married Tony who had private means. Money was the commodity that in my life had always been there but was in short supply, and it was quite fun seeing what could be achieved with what was available. We went to the Palace on both occasions for Satan to be invested, and took his proud mama. The photographs show the pale gauntlet gloves she chose to wear, which he said made her look like the chap who took 'the good news from Ghent to Aix'. He felt pretty awful himself, in a Moss Bros hired morning suit.*

At 51 he decided to retire and receive £8,000 'Lumpers', or lump sum compensation for loss of career, because independence was coming the following year, 1960, and there would be no further employment for him. Years later Simeon Adebo, who was Minister of Finance when we left (the only African to have come right up through the Service like a European), wrote a book called *Our Unforgettable Years*, and in it made two references to Satan which are worth quoting:

---

*When he went to Zanzibar as British Resident he was made a KCMG (Knight Commander of St Michael and St George), which honour Kenneth Maddocks also had, plus the KCVO (Knight Commander of the Victorian Order) given by the Queen when she stayed with him in Fiji.

1955. On 1 July, the effective date of my transfer (Lagos to Ibadan), I reported at the Ministry of Finance and was taken to see Mr A.G.R. Mooring, the substantive Permanent Secretary, who was then acting as Deputy Governor. Mr Mooring was not a stranger to me, for I had already met him several times at inter-governmental conferences in Lagos and I had always liked him. His first reception of me made me like him even more. He spoke to me kindly, said that he and his colleagues were happy to accept me into their fold and he wished me every luck. I replied that I was equally happy to be with them and would do my best to prove worthy of their association...

1959. The Premier (Chief Awolowo) was kind enough to refer, in his farewell statement, to members of the European staff who had left after giving valuable service to the Region. One who left in the latter part of this year was Sir George Mooring. He and his wife were about the most popular expatriate couple in the Region. His relations with Ministers were, so far as I could judge, impeccable, and they left him in no doubt of their appreciation of his generous understanding. Two days before he and his wife were due to leave our wives, that is to say, the wives of senior officials, went to the Moorings' house and, on behalf of the Administrative Class of the Region made a special presentation to Lady Mooring. On the actual day of their departure – 19 October – we gave them the most spectacular send-off of my time in Ibadan. We lined out, black and white alike, along their entire route through the Secretariat, cheering them as they went.

It was for us a most unexpected and moving demonstration. We had sold our car and asked the Governor if we might borrow one of his, and we were lent the shopping car, a Ford Estate. As we drove out of our drive, we were rather horrified to be joined by a posse of motor cycle outriders before and behind, who escorted us down the hill to the Secretariat, a stop we had not envisaged. The whole human content of the building was in the compound, and Simeon made a farewell speech which nearly reduced us to tears. We were saved by his humour, one bit of which I remember: he had studied the way such speeches were made, and had looked Satan up in *Who's Who*, and at one point said:

'He married Patricia Downman, and they had (as usual) one s. and one d.'

This brought the house down as it was clearly an African joke that European families normally consisted of one son and one daughter, and of course the Europeans all enjoyed this gentle humour at their expense. We were driven on, and I did have a little weep; luckily I did not let go completely, for we were again stopped unexpectedly, this time at Police Headquarters, where our brother-in-law Derek Fountain was the Commissioner, and there the police officers and their wives were all lined up to say goodbye. The farewells in Lagos have not imprinted themselves on my memory, but as we steamed out of the harbour on board the SS *Apapa*, the military band on the Yacht Club lawn where we had first met played 'The Hausa Farewell', and that was hard to bear.

Satan was keen to spend his £8,000 (when he got it, which he never did) on buying a farm. I was very apprehensive about this; he had farming in his blood but no experience. But then the Colonial Office offered him the post of British Resident, Zanzibar. He asked me what I thought, but I felt I was too biased to say, and contented myself with saying I had always wanted to go to a place beginning with Z, but that it must be his decision. He was torn. We were dining during that time with an ex-governor of Eastern Nigeria, Clem Pleass, across the river from Duncannon, and Satan felt it was permissible to tell him in confidence and ask his advice. Clem said:

'Let me think about it. I will tell you after dinner.'

As we pushed our chairs back at the end of the meal, he said:

'How silly of me, Satan. Of course you must go. The Queen has asked you.' And that was the end of that.

CHAPTER 4

Zanzibar
1960-1964

THEN BEGAN perhaps the most interesting four years of my life. It was as though in Nigeria I was being prepared. I had become aware of how a country was run. In England everything was so complex it had been difficult to understand and I just accepted what came my way, but in Nigeria one knew the man who was the head of, say, the Agriculture Department, one knew the men working under him in the various offices of that department, and one met the agricultural officers doing their bit in the bush. Similarly one could so easily see the structure of the other departments: Education, Public Works, Police, etc. and the way they worked together. In Zanzibar it was even easier to see as it was all so small. As the wife of the British Resident too, for the first time I had a rôle to play; one was expected to do more than be a hostess and to take as much interest as one wished in all the voluntary organisations (more, I swear, than in any other country, great or small). There was so much of interest to learn about, to see, to help with, and everyone was keen to show me and to include me because my position alone could be of help, and anything else I could contribute was a bonus.

Satan had had to have a medical before going to Zanzibar and they discovered to our surprise that he had filaria, bilharzia, and gardia lambia cysts; the treatment left him a shadow of his former pretty hearty self, and we decided he must travel by sea in an attempt to build himself up. I could not go with him because it was still the school holidays and I had to take Julia to a new school. Apart from the emotional side of the exercise, William and I had a terrible time getting back from Exeter to Duncannon. Snow had fallen, unseen by us, while we were having tea with Pam Davidson, a good friend who was to be extremely kind to Julia while she was in that area. It continued to fall heavily while we parked poor Julia, which took a bit of time, and our progress towards home was very slow and skiddy. William was wearing his school suit of grey flannel shorts and jacket which was most unsuitable for the stalwart rôle he had to play, continually having to get out and push the car out of difficult places. He was only eleven so I could not let him drive while I pushed. Finally we became very stuck on Telegraph Hill, where a garage man helped William to turn the car around and he advised us to go round by the longer sea road, where icy conditions would not be so bad. We had to battle on

The Zanzibar Residency.

because the next day I had to drive William to Weston-super-Mare to his own school, and myself carry on to London and get my plane to Mombasa.

Here I joined Satan, who had a heavy cold, and together we boarded the Sultan's yacht to sail over to Zanzibar. Instantly we sensed the difference between West and East Africa, and between being a governor amongst old friends and one in an unknown territory. Two ADCs greeted us on board, one Arab, one English, both very respectful. We invited both to have a drink with us at sundown before sailing. In the event the Arab did not come, but sent an excuse about a grandmother. We later realised that he had never sat in the presence of his seniors, Arab or English, and that he was probably nervous of having to say he could not drink alcohol. From the beginning we felt the shadow of the Raj was upon Zanzibar and things were far more ceremonious and grand than in rugged West Africa.

Our arrival was ruined by torrential rain and I huddled ashore under somebody else's mackintosh which was too small to put on properly. The reception arrangements on the quay were cancelled but the inhabitants of the town still lined the streets, white-clad men on one side, black-clad women the other, bearing banners reading 'Uhuru April 19th.' (Uhuru meant freedom). As this was already 23 January it was rather a daunting reception, and the unsmiling faces of the people also disappointed us. Not even rain or disagreement with one's rulers would have stopped the laughter and goings-on of a Nigerian crowd. We felt at once we were in foreign territory, though at

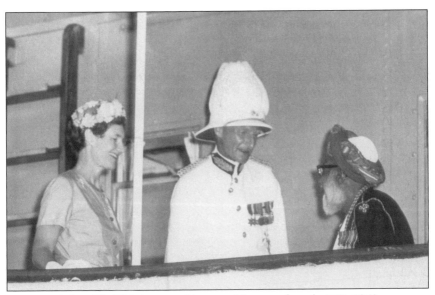

Sultan Khalifa being greeted by us on his return from the UK, 1960.

least for Satan the Muslim North of Nigeria had prepared him for dealing with the 80 per cent Muslim population of Zanzibar.

We soon found that protocol was strong. To start with, our car was driven at never more than fifteen mph in order to give people in the streets time to stop, even to get off their bicycles, and bow, and as it would have been unthinkable for any other vehicle to overtake us, our progress soon became a procession. Our drivers were extremely loath to change this system but when they found the Resident leaning out of the window to signal cars to pass, they decided to increase their speed to twenty-five mph in order at least to keep the procession! The Sultan was never in such unseemly haste and wherever he went in one of his numerous scarlet cars, ceremony was observed and traffic congested.

As Zanzibar was a Protectorate, the Sultan was nominally the ruler and on Mondays Satan used to have an audience at the Palace to 'advise' the Sultan, who in fact did no governing at all, but knew his people better than any European could. I would accompany Satan on these occasions in order to advise the Sultana of all the doings in Zanzibar about which she did NOT know. In fact she was better informed by far of the two of us, and intensely interested in politics. However, she was also very interested in fashion and other feminine topics so that it was possible to avoid any sensitive subject. We would arrive promptly at 11.30 a.m. (me in stockings and a hat), and the guard would turn out and blow bugles and Satan would take a salute. The heir to the

L to R: Satan, Commissioner of Police, Sultan Khalifa,
Seyyida Nunu, Prince Abdullah (the next Sultan).

throne would be waiting for us at the top of the steps, we would go up in a lift
and as we stepped out the Sultan would be there to greet us ceremonially. The
Sultana should have been there too, but was usually late and servants would
have to bring her barbaric jewellery for her to put on when we were sitting
down. Sultan Khalifa was the most charming little old man of eighty,
courtliness incarnate, always calling me 'lady' in a loving voice as if I was a tiny
piece of delicate porcelain. He had a diamond on one finger as big as the
proverbial pigeon's egg. He was much loved and revered by his people and
respected by the British. The Sultana and I would peel off to another room
and have a good half-hour on our own, and then join the men for coffee or
sherbet (both tepid) and sticky cakes.

The Sultana, Seyyida Nunu, (known irreverently by the British as Floozie),
was the Sultan's second wife and was not the mother of his son. She was large
and flashy and wore very modern but rather unsuitable dresses under a
carelessly worn purdah garment, or *buibui*. She was a highly intelligent woman.
We would have brisk exchanges of news while her jewels were being arranged.
She would have far more to impart than I was able to, and I had very
interesting little interviews, discovering much about the customs and

the culture of her people, about slavery, about her view of history, about individuals.

When Sultan Khalifa died about a year after we arrived, his funeral was an amazing demonstration of love and despair. I was at a window in the Palace with the women. Satan, in uniform, followed the coffin. He found it very difficult to keep his feet, let alone his position. The crowds of men swarmed and wailed and waved their arms, all intent on even momentarily helping to carry the coffin, which soared waveringly over their heads. When the second Sultan, Abdullah, died, Satan had a police escort and I could see the ring of red berets around his white-feathered helmet, going fairly steadily towards the mosque, which Satan did not enter.

After Sultan Khalifa's death, Seyyida Nunu was plunged into forty days of mourning, when she was not supposed to have any visitors or to go out. I was therefore intrigued when I received a message from her demanding my presence at the Palace. Satan quite rightly guessed that she was anxious to know about her pension, so duly primed me. For the first time I was taken to the private quarters, padding shoeless along a wide corridor lined with keening women sitting on the floor and throwing their arms about. I was interested to see that one of them was white, perhaps Circassian. In the royal bedroom my breath was taken away by the most magnificent silver four-poster double bed. Instead of curtains it had mosquito nets, and instead of a roof it had diagonal silver shafts supporting in the centre a huge silver crown. On this wonderful bed lay the Sultana, dressed in white, the colour of mourning, wailing intolerably. I sat down beside her and waited to be noticed. After ten minutes with no abating of the terrible cries and the casting of the substantial body about the bed, I decided to leave, but I had barely made the first movement, when she stopped wailing and plied me with financial questions. I was able to tell her what she wanted to know, and knew she was satisfied and I dismissed, when the keening began again. She later retreated to Oman from where most Zanzibar Arabs originated.

The man who succeeded to the throne was Khalifa's one son, Abdullah, and I had less fun with his wife. She was much older than he and was the daughter of a previous Sultan. She was extremely old-fashioned and had no English. Her youngest son Harub, a very beautiful mystic, would interpret for us and she would fire questions at me. The very first one set the standard:

'Do you believe in life after death?'

She was interested to know what went on in the world outside purdah, but clearly had had little opportunity to find out, as her ignorance was abysmal and her questions extraordinary. She was so orthodox a Muslim that she never read anything but the Koran, which would be lying on the coffee table between us. Seyyida Nunu had not bothered with books at all but displayed lavish ornaments such as an exquisite dhow crafted in gold, and an immense ivory crab with ruby eyes.

The third Sultana I had dealings with was the wife of Jamshid, Abdullah's eldest son, and she was a very different proposition. She was a beautiful girl always dressed in the height of fashion, by which I mean she really did wear the sort of thing one sees in *Vogue* but would never dream of wearing oneself. On the first occasion it was white satin with a red rose at the hip to match her nail varnish. She would have a copy of the latest novel on her coffee table and would want to discuss it. She had been educated at the German convent and had gone to England to do a social welfare course. I had great hopes that she might start her countrywomen on the way to rejecting purdah, but she was not prepared to do so. She always wore the black *buibui* when she went out, would not come to our house, would not take her place at the head of any of the women's organisations –

'My husband would not like it,' she would say. Life must have been particularly hard for her.

When the old Sultan Khalifa died in 1961, the feeling of solidarity which he had engendered in his people disappeared for ever. Abdullah, his heir, was a solemn character who was not at all charismatic. On the day of the swearing in of the new Court at the Palace, he sent his son Jamshid to take his place. Satan, so fed up with him forever making excuses for not doing what he should, on this occasion took it upon himself to go into the royal bedroom. It was not long before he realised that there was an emergency on his hands. Abdullah was a diabetic and had concealed from the doctors the fact that he had developed gangrene in both feet. Some weeks later he succumbed to his gangrene, following the amputation of both legs by a surgeon flown out from England, which he bore with the utmost fortitude. Jamshid, his heir, was something of a playboy; women, pigsticking and fast cars were his interests, not necessarily in that order, and he dabbled in politics. Again, he showed bravery when he was faced with revolution.

I had known so little about Zanzibar before we knew we were going there that I even had to look it up on a map. It turned out to be just as I always imagined a tropical island to be: surrounded by sandy beaches and low coral cliffs full of exciting caves; covered with coconut palms and in this case clove trees; a clear blue sea and sky and brilliant sunshine reigned most of the time. For about five months of the year, from May to September, the climate is delightful, and not too hot, but the other seven months are hotter than is comfortable, temperatures being about 92 degrees with the highest possible humidity. However, we were used to this in Nigeria and here we had sea breezes to cool one a little bit. Air conditioners were an innovation at that time and were presenting a problem: the moisture which is extracted from a room is supposed to be thrown on to the outer air and absorbed, but as the outer air was saturated and could absorb no more, water just poured continually out of the air conditioners. We had never had one before, but here we had just one installed at our own expense, in our bedroom, shared by the children in the tower room adjoining, thus ensuring us all a good night's rest.

The territory was composed of two main islands, Zanzibar and Pemba, and many small ones, some uninhabited. The capital was known as Stone Town, a collection of very tall stone buildings huddled together along tiny lanes too narrow for cars on the whole. One of these lanes, which did admit cars to get through the town, was called Suicide Alley and had unbelievably, two-way traffic. The houses were embellished in many cases by great black doors with huge metal studs for repelling elephants: rather unnecessary on Zanzibar as elephants were not part of the scene. A hippo and, on another occasion, a crocodile were washed up on Zanzibar when Tanganyikan rivers were in flood. Otherwise larger wild animals were confined to pig, tiny deer, and leopards not much bigger than cats, one of whom took a puppy from our dachshund's litter. Outside the town, where most of the rich lived, sprawled Ngambo, the African quarter with its mud huts and teaming life, and beyond that again was the harbour with its dhows and fishing boats. The Catholic Church and the Anglican Cathedral thrust their towers skywards to give a diverse outline to the town, though they were obediently less high than the Sultan's Palace.

There were a great many communities: Arabs and Africans, Indians of various kinds such as Goans, Parsees, Ishmaelis, Hindus, Muslims, Christians, Singalese Buddhists, and a few Chinese. Even these groups were subdivided: there were the Arabs whose Omani forebears had conquered the islands and who were permanently settled there; the Manga Arabs who came in their dhows on the north-east monsoon each year, and traded in the rural areas until the winds changed and they could return with agricultural produce and timber; and those who visited from the Hadramaut for longer periods and engaged in town trades and running shops and eating-houses. Africans too were in three groups: those who were believed to have been the earliest inhabitants and who were mostly living outside the plantation belts, the Watumbatu, Wahadimu, and Wapemba ('Wa' meaning people and the rest of each word being the place where they lived) – these people were pretty mixed, being descended from the Bantus of East Africa, the Shirazis from the Persian Gulf (a name given there to anyone who was not Arab so that in itself allows for variation), and Arabs; the second group of Africans was just as mixed, being descendants of liberated slaves from all over East Africa, being found in towns and plantation belts; and thirdly the rather temporary Africans who came over from various mainland areas to help with the clove harvests, some of whom remained, and from whom most of the Police Force, it was realised after the

Issa Nasser, the Arab ADC, and me on tour at Kojani.

revolution, were drawn. The Europeans were mostly British, mostly government servants, missionaries and traders, and there were a few interestingly
different people: German nuns in the convent school, a Swiss trader and his
wife, one or two South Africans, a Polish doctor and his wife, one or two
Americans setting up a space tracking station. It was difficult for us to make
close friends of any but a very few of the Europeans; the local people expected
us to remain on our pedestal, which was trying.

With all these different nationalities, a walk through the town was an
exciting and colourful occasion. A fierce dhow captain from Oman or Muscat
might be swaggering down the street as if he owned it, with sandalled feet,
belted nightshirt with lovely curved silver dagger stuck in his belt, an orange
Kashmir turban and a beard, and the expression of a hawk; he would have a
group of followers clustering round, never deviating from their positions
beside or behind him all through the narrow streets of the town, never mind
the crowds. Pairs of Indian ladies in the most beautiful saris would be seen, a
coffee seller with his brass pot and clutter of little cups, a few rickshaws, a
sturdy African pushing a 'homali' (man) cart or pulling a rickshaw, which was
all the transport some of the streets could accommodate; Goans often in
European dress; Muslim women in their black *buibuis* and the men in their
white gowns and little caps; old men with beards sitting on the stone benches

outside the houses – altogether it was a fascinating display. The whole scene was pervaded by the smell of cloves which were the basis of the territory's economy.

There were other islands in the Protectorate to be visited, notably Pemba, said to be the home of the University of Witchcraft, though when I laughingly taxed the Prime Minister (a Pemba man) with this, saying I had never seen it, he replied:

'Ah! But it is invisible.'

When the children came with us on tour, it made the visit easier; we were seen to be human, and as far as I was concerned I had to try and make engagements that they could enjoy or make other arrangements for them. We travelled and lived entirely on the Sultan's yacht; the officers were quite happy occasionally to take them underwater swimming, and one day an agricultural officer took William somewhere so that he could fell two trees with his scout axe: bliss!

There would be *barazas* (meetings with speeches and coffee), tea parties, receptions on board for a hundred people at a time, during which people were brought up to us at the rate of two in four minutes, which was trying conversationally; inspections of waterworks, of projects of various kinds, of plantations of clove trees and of cloves themselves in different stages laid out on cloths on the ground to dry, pink when they were fresh, darkening to nearly black when dried; visits by me to schools, though if my children were there it was holiday time and the schools were closed; to hospitals, waterworks, bridges, jetties, the new airstrip, the electricity station. At one reception I thawed a lot of giggling shy women by getting them to guess the children's ages and then Julia departed saying:

'Now guess Mummy's', which was immediately translated and laughed about, but they DID, and then began questions such as:

'Is this your first husband?'

We stopped short of showing each other our operations, but that party was a distinct success.

Less successful was taking Julia to an Arab child's birthday party – the Sultan's great-grandchild. We just sat in rows and never spoke to our hostess; they had a puppet show in a passage so about twenty children out of eighty could see; even I could not as I stood back behind all the children and it was too far away. Endless group photographs were taken; finally cakes were passed round but nothing to drink, and many little tots were begging for water as it was so hot. Another time an Indian lady doctor gave a very successful party for me in Pemba when she handed round photographs of a baby ossified in the womb and extracted after eighteen months.

Wherever we went I would make sure that the people knew in advance that

I should want to see any old buildings, mostly mosques, in the vicinity. In this way, the bush around them would be cut back and possibly they would be preserved a little longer for a posterity which might appreciate them. Some were as early as the eleventh century. Satan was usually too busy to accompany me on these expeditions, as he was having to meet with the local government people and elders to discuss their problems.

On one occasion we went to an island where it seemed no white woman had been before and there was great excitement amongst the female population. None of them wore purdah garments. I was borne off in triumph for a private *baraza* of my own. A card table with a cloth on it was set up quite near the beach, the cloth being held down against the wind by the most lovely conch shell, and they set about having their demands translated by the schoolmaster. Their main worry was that they had no water at all on the island, and had to fetch every drop by boat from the mainland. I knew in fact that one of the things Satan was going to discuss with the men was the building of a concrete catchment area for rain, so I was able to give the ladies a little bit of hope. It was expected that the islanders would be able to pay for the concrete itself, from the sale of a special kind of seaweed that grew there, which could be turned into nylon elsewhere, and of course they would provide the bulk of the work force. When I left, the ladies presented me with the conch shell which I had admired, and which became the first shell in my collection.

★   ★   ★

The Residency itself was a delight and had the reputation of being the most attractive of all gubernatorial houses. Built in 1903 on the site of a Cormorian settlement, the householders were given new houses elsewhere and five hundred rupees as compensation. But one old lady refused to go; she had lived there all her life. As she was forcibly removed she cursed the house and all who were to live in it, and certainly illness and death dogged the first few Residents until the place was exorcised; then it was said the old lady's ghost haunted a gravestone which stood in the lane between the Residency and the Chief Secretary's house.

The house was situated on the waterside with a lawn running down to the beach and our own jetty from which we swam. We became familiar with a number of underwater markers and could find our way unerringly to the habitats of interesting fishes such as a fire fish and one that looked like a crocodile but was completely flat and lay on the bottom. The garden had been stocked by a previous Resident's wife with bougainvilleas of thirteen different kinds and colours, and my predecessor, Lady Potter, had collected samples of many epiphytic orchids of East Africa and planted them in various trees. There were old guns on the front lawn, one mounted on a replica of the earliest known type of carriage used at the siege of Boulogne in 1547, and two mortars on the front steps were from a British ship of 1850. The house was a miniature castle with a tower and crenulations; the ground floor had a black-and-white tiled entrance hall with much brass and copper about, and potted plants; it was traditionally all servants' quarters downstairs, kitchens, store rooms and minor offices. A gracious stone staircase twisted up to a veranda between a huge semicircular terrace (where receptions were held and where we sat every evening after dinner under the stars with the sea gently lapping), and the ballroom, a beautiful room with three huge Austrian chandeliers – surplus from a gift of eight to the Sultan – many lovely Persian rugs, and English and French antique sofas, tables and chairs. In spite of the apparent size of the house we only had five bedrooms, but space had to be given to a private sitting room, an office for Satan and one for me, two dining rooms, one large and one very large, and a flat for the housekeeper. There were two rooms unused in the tower but they were rather damp. Everything was on a large scale. I had no wish to change anything in the house, and it was well appointed. Before we left I collated all the facts about the history of the house that I could find, and wrote a leaflet with the idea of leaving it for future occupants but it was probably not wanted.

We had a housekeeper, rather laughably called Mrs Cope (like Happy Families), whom I would interview each morning and be told what we were having to eat. My first interview with her rather unnerved me as she produced a list of linen she said we needed to order, amounting to £150. As this was the annual sum we had for all household replacements, and as it appeared to me we had a good supply of linen, I cut this by half and was not very popular from the beginning. In fact when we left four years later there were still unopened packets of sheets in the cupboard, so I finally felt justified.

Also working on the ground floor of the building were the ADCs (Aides-de-Camp), one Arab called Issa, and one Englishman who was changed several times; also the Private Secretary, Joyce Leverett, who was my mainstay as she knew it all, and we communed together daily. During our tour there, she and Bill Dickson, one of the ADCs, were married, a very happy event.

The staff of about six housemen, three gardeners, three drivers and three guards was all paid by Government but we were for some reason expected to employ a bedroom boy whom we paid personally; the one we were presented with was a mean-looking individual and we became almost sure he was a spy. They were all Africans who did not speak English – in fact it was preferred that they should not do so, on the understanding that they could not report conversations overheard – and were of very different tribes. Mohamed, the head man, had been in the Residency for years and was a great support. He was tall, thin and aristocratic-looking, impassive, though we felt he grew fond of us and he clearly enjoyed the children; he was dignified, quiet and weary-looking, and was never observed actually to be working, but was always at hand and in charge. When we left, the domestic staff approached the Private Secretary and asked her to buy us a present for them; they had collected a rather odd amount of money. She felt that they should choose something themselves and we should appreciate it more. She was quite right: the small silver ashtray inscribed 'From Staff 1963 Residency' touched us to the heart and we felt they were our friends.

The first day after our arrival we retired to our room for a post-prandial nap from which in Nigeria we were accustomed to being roused with a cup of tea. Nothing happened, so we rang and asked the room boy to bring it. He came staggering in with a vast silver tray laden with silver, china, cakes etc. We gathered it was not the custom to have tea in the bedroom, so next day went down to the library, where we usually sat, and called for it. The same thing happened and there was no obvious place to put the tray. The third day we tried the ballroom and were rewarded by seeing the tray carried in from the shady veranda over the porch, where daily it was laid on a suitable cloth-covered table, and a cool breeze swept through. Much later the Sultan lent me a book of old photographs and I was amused to see a picture of this veranda clearly labelled 'The Tea Veranda' in 1903 when it was built; in such ways were successive Residents and their wives taught how to behave.

On the whole we ate English-style meals but took full advantage of the tropical things available: kingfish, for instance, avocados, mangos, coconuts, and we often ate curries which the cook made particularly well and variously, no doubt having learnt from local Indians. We (and he) made one bad mistake when we had Mrs Indira Gandhi to lunch and gave her an extra hot curry, presumably because she was extra important, but unfortunately she did not eat hot curries! On one occasion we were able to get some palm oil nuts from the Agricultural Experimental Station (they were not generally grown in Zanzibar) and I showed him how to make a palm oil stew, of which we had been very fond in West Africa, where we had it once a week as it is particularly rich in vitamins. It looks terrible, orange and oily, but tastes delicious and is surprisingly light, and helped to offset the effects of any gin one might have imbibed. We did eat very well at the Residency, and it was a treat after the hit and miss methods of the Nigerian cooks, many carrying on a tradition of cooking originally imported, we always thought, by early missionaries. The children, I was told when they were grown up, stoked up in the streets of Zanzibar town from barrow vendors on roasted cassava, sugar cane and Turkish delight, water ices and other more dubious delights. It was one of the joys of the place that they were perfectly safe in the town and were able to make their own way to the Sailing Club where the young used to gather. I too used to wander the narrow streets of Stone Town, sometimes with the dog, in search of a piece of jewellery or to visit somebody I wanted to paint. The horrors of the revolution were to make a dreadful contrast to the peace and trust when the British were there.

I collected pearls from a fisherman who used to come along the beach and I would meet him when walking our dog. I wanted a ring with one large pearl in the centre and smaller different coloured ones round it. When I had made my collection I took them to my tame jeweller, and he escorted me into a back room of his shop. Here, in his workroom, he placed a tin tray on a table and fetched a large Heinz Tomato Ketchup bottle full to the brim with pearls of every hue, which he emptied on the tray. He was not satisfied with my matching of sizes and picked out better ones in this extraordinary setting.

Social life could not be as free as we should have liked, but it was very enjoyable and brisk. It was not possible to have any local people to a meal because if one invited one person of a certain standing, say the head of the Parsee community, it would have been necessary to have the heads of all the communities to the same party so that nobody lost face. We therefore had parties called 'receptions', really drinks parties, but they could not be called that because the majority of the guests were Muslim and not supposed to drink alcohol. Previous Residents, we were given to understand, gave and went to enormous tea parties, but after going to one Satan decreed that it should be the last, and I was in complete agreement: they were at a hot time of day when one did not want to dress up, they were in gardens in the sun, the flies would swarm on the sticky cakes and the tea was a curious beverage that just might have been coffee. The only locals who ever dined with us were the Sultan and his sons, but not their wives, and an Indian millionaire who could not be fitted into any category, not being a true local, so nobody could take offence.

At first only heads of departments invited us anywhere, but when people realised we would accept invitations elsewhere, a few exceptions also invited us. Life was never dull, in fact we had to ask the Private Secretary, a very nice woman, not to continue to have lunch with us as she had with our predecessors, because we never saw each other to talk to till we went to bed, probably too tired to talk.

I was invited to an Arab wedding on one occasion, which was of great interest, and another time we both went to the Palace for the engagement party of the Sultana's adopted daughter: it was too late when we discovered it was for ladies only, but Satan was not the only European man who made the mistake and they soon made themselves scarce. There were many such ceremonial events to which we went, but they were often far too long.

Our day started with the raising of the Union Jack on top of the tower, and the bugler sounding 'The Reveille', and at sundown the flag was lowered and

'The Last Post' sounded. I always found this moving, but particularly the last time it was played and I insisted we kept the last flag to be lowered which I sometimes fly from a bedroom window in Aldeburgh on suitable occasions.

The Chief Secretary's wife, Penny Robertson, was extremely helpful in introducing me to people and explaining the intricacies of what was virtually my work there, if I was prepared to do it. My day, having breakfasted, walked the dog along the beach and seen Mrs Cope, began usually at 9 o'clock in my office, where I had an extraordinary amount to do. Some of the work of course was connected with the children, arranging their travel, their half-term and exeats and so on. The Private Secretary would come to see me about entertaining: people who should be invited to meet certain visitors, people who were simply due to be invited, and to co-ordinate diaries – above all, about the all-important seating plans which could cause terrible high feeling, I discovered. I once protested at having one particularly boring man next to me whenever he frequently had to come to dinner, and was anxiously told that once when he was not given his proper place he had actually written a letter of protest the next day! So I relied very much on the Private Secretary and did what I was told. Other work concerned the many organisations with which I had to involve myself in the island.

Later in the morning, there would be visits to schools (there were about 560 of them and I managed to visit most of them), the leper colony, the TB home, the Old People's Home for those with no relatives, the various women's associations, welfare organisations (which proliferated), the hospital, the Girl Guides, and the St John Ambulance Brigade. Sometimes I would have to speak, which meant more homework. Having a garden and lots of flowers, I did the cathedral flowers every Saturday as well as those in the house. There was a great deal of entertaining as nobody officially visiting East Africa wanted to miss a visit to lovely little Zanzibar, so that I am sure, even if there was no need to come, some of them manufactured a need. There were commissions and Members of Parliament, the GOC from time to time, members of the Fleet and the Air Force, the Governor of Northern Ireland and party, the Archbishops of Canterbury and York, Lord Mountbatten, Herr Willy Brandt, Mrs Gandhi, education experts, ambassadors and consuls and commissioners, Father Trevor Huddleston, African Presidents, and Americans setting up Project Mercury, the satellite plotting station. Many of these people stayed in the house, others just came for a meeting and a meal and a whizz round the town, others were staying elsewhere.

Lord Mountbatten came to stay for a few days with his daughter Patricia about two years after his wife died. He had had one journey overseas since her death and found it difficult on his own. They were charming guests and I liked him particularly very much. Curiously, Satan did not! Later when we met the Duke of Edinburgh, Satan got on with him very well but I found him awkward.

One particularly enjoyable visit was by a Russian scientist called Professor Bogorov, who arrived on a ship which requested permission to survey the reef, explore the island and various other things which Satan was obliged to refuse. He arranged for guided tours for the crew, and at my insistence we invited the professor and the captain to lunch. I so much wanted to hear the ADC introduce the professor, whose name was pronounced 'bugger off'. The ADC utterly funked it. As we were having a drink before lunch, standing about in the ballroom, a bird nesting in the chandelier above the professor laid an egg which landed at his feet; these little birds were manikin finches which were persecuted by the crows that had been imported by the Parsees to deal with their dead exposed on Towers of Silence, and the finches were in the habit of trying to build nests in our chandeliers. We were fairly new at this stage and nobody had told us of this but the Public Works Department had ceased the custom of cleaning out the chandeliers from time to time, waiting to see if we would give the order. I picked up the egg and held it out to the professor, explaining how it came to be there and he behaved in a delightful absent-minded professorial manner by putting it in his pocket. But later he proved himself to be very much on the ball. At lunch, thwarted of hearing his name, I said to the captain:

'What difficult names you Russians have! Do tell me how to pronounce yours!' (which had no vowels to mention), and when he obliged I said:

'And the Professor's?' whereupon the professor, from the other end of the table, exclaimed:

'You want to know how I say my name? It is Bugger Off.'

When I thanked him, he added:

'And you want to know what it means? It means Son of Bugger.'

I deserved it.

After tea we usually took time off for exercise unless it was quite impossible: swimming, tennis (we had our own court), golf, and at first I was able to get some riding on one of the only two horses on the island, both superb Arab stallions belonging to the old Sultan who felt a man was not a man if he did not own a horse. At the weekend we sailed and picnicked and went skin-diving. This was sometimes at Prison Island which one could book for a day or a weekend. It was built as a prison but never used as such, possibly because they discovered too late that it had no water. It was a superb holiday venue with a rest house, and an avenue of trees almost the length of the tiny island, perhaps half a mile. Rocks all round made an interesting coast line, and kapok trees dropped their scarlet seeds around. A large number of giant tortoises lived there, each with his number painted on his shell – 'races' were run sitting on their oblivious backs. It was fascinating to see them very slowly trying to get a large seed into their mouths, infinite time and patience being required.

Julia and I became keen shell collectors and I built up an almost complete collection of the shells of Zanzibar, all found by us and never bought. That was unthinkable according to the Conchology Society which we had to join. Shelling introduced me to yet another world within the world of Zanzibar. At least once a week a party of us would make a shelling expedition by boat – one fitted on one's mask and flippers, slid into the water, and left behind one's ordinary life on land. One did not swim strongly, just gently moved the flippers. The hands were covered with gloves, to protect them from coral scratches or stings, and one hand held a short pole with a hook on the end with which to turn things over if necessary. A bag tied round the waist was ready to receive those shells one wanted to keep. A shirt kept one's shoulders from burning and one rather stout party wore an apron back to front to keep another part of her anatomy away from the sun. Below lay a dream world of infinite complexity; clumps of coral of different gorgeous colours and shapes; cliffs, ravines and plains of coral and weed; and fish of such diversity that one saw something new every time. Their colours and shapes were almost outrageous. God must have had such fun thinking them up: stripes and spots and stars and patterns, elegance and downright ugliness, menace and beauty, all were there. We would be so entranced by these gentle journeys that we only brought them to an end when we became so cold (in these balmy tropical waters) that we clambered with difficulty into the boat, blue and shaking, very ready for a hot drink and a big towel and to exchange news with each other.

On one occasion very early in our tour we took our launch at a weekend, a fellow officer of Satan's, who knew the ropes, being in charge of the party. I was a little alarmed that we went beyond the reef, where one could expect to find sharks but Satan said:

'Don't interfere; Henry is in charge and he knows the ropes.'

Two visitors were with us who had no gear with them so Julia and I lent them our masks and flippers, and by the time they had finished with them everyone else was back on the launch. I had forgotten my fear as nobody had seen anything alarming. Julia (aged nine) and I set off to put a distance between us and the boat and were idling happily along when suddenly an enormous shark (bigger and bigger in my imagination) crossed our bows about twenty-five yards ahead. I turned to look at Julia; she was looking at me and inside her mask was mouthing:

'SHARK!'

I mouthed 'SWIM!' back at her and with her hand on my shoulder we set off pretty briskly, forgetting that making splashes might indicate a creature in distress and therefore easy prey. One of the very worst moments in my life was stuffing Julia, flippers and all, up the rope ladder and expecting at any second to be munched in half myself.

Shells, we learned, favoured different habitats. A little golden cowrie for instance lived in golden coral. Other cowries, called hump-backs, lived on the underside of bushlike coral and one could only find them at particularly low tide when one lay on one's back on the sand and wriggled in under the coral, hoping to be lucky. Some shells favoured very deep water and so were precious rarities. In the end I gathered almost a complete collection of the shells of Zanzibar, which I housed in a cabinet of drawers made from a beam of teak taken from the Sultan's Palace because it had dry rot at each end. Shells have to be kept in the dark to retain their colours, and here again the variety of shapes and patterns seems unending.

I joined a painting class in an attempt to meet people on an equal footing, but I became so interested in the painting that I did not have much time to make friends. The teacher was an Irishman who came to Zanzibar to paint murals in the Catholic Church, but, when he became a Muslim in order to marry a Muslim girl, the Catholics felt it was unsuitable for him to carry on with their murals. So he fell back on teaching and I believe he was a better teacher than an artist: he was able to draw out from each pupil what talent they had, though I thought little of his own. We worked on top of an Arab house, low walls around and a roof above. The hours flew by! I found I had a flair for portraits and would pay a beggar, or a fisherman or an orange seller a shilling to sit for me; there was only one thing they liked better than doing nothing and that was being paid for it. I did a few 'commissions' for local people but when I came to England I had to give it up because the sitters were so interested in the painting and wanted it to be flattering, and I became inhibited! I also joined in a rifle shooting class and shot in an East African competition for the Zanzibar team.

I am particularly fond of animals and, as well as a Siamese cat called Napoleon whom we inherited, we took on another one we called Wow; they did not care for each other. Then we became stuck with a dachshund puppy somebody asked us to bring over from Pemba as a present to a couple who had just lost theirs, but as they were just going on leave they did not want it; Honeybun became a part of our lives for the next fourteen years. She was a great character and eventually returned to England with us. She had a difficult life as we were often on tour or on the mainland and had one leave from Zanzibar. Returning from one tour, we arrived when she was out walking with a friend; we were having tea when we heard the sad slow clicking of her claws on the ballroom floor as she plodded in, despondent and alone. We spoke to each other loudly and after a moment of silence suddenly she erupted through the door, all smiles and paws. When we were away for any length of time we left her with a friend who had Honeybun's sister, and when the friend was away we had the sister.

I had always longed to have a bush-baby and we had two at different times. When very young they were no trouble and would sleep at night under my chin, holding on to my ear. When he reckoned it was time to wake up, one of them had the tiresome habit of prising one's eyes open with his busy little fingers, to make sure one was there. Also if he suspected you to be eating something he would like to share, he pushed his fingers into your mouth in the hope of hooking out a tasty morsel. But they are nocturnal animals and as they grew they became more and more active at night. One early morning we were woken by distressed cries and found that Fundi (Swahili for workman) was being mobbed by crows in the gutter above the ballroom, and Satan went inching his way along to the rescue, wearing, to my apprehension, only his sarong which he slept in. I was also mightily afraid the gutter would give way, but all went well and Fundi was delighted, making the return journey even more dangerous by running up and down Satan's arms, and round his head and neck.

On the very day we were having the Archbishop of York (Dr Ramsey) to lunch, a hunter brought me a very young bush-baby, which took up its position on the back of my neck with its hands and face buried in my hair. What with the cats, united for once, circling round and the staff not yet being trained in the ways of bush-babies in Residencies, I was forced to 'wear' him for lunch, for he had never let go even when I was changing. At lunch he took fright, however, and struggled up through my hair to a position of vantage on top of my head, where he sat rolling his eyes and twitching his ears at the assembled company. Nobody said a word. The Archbishop did not even notice until his chaplain drew attention to it, when he seemed to register that there were two of God's creatures sitting on one chair, and got on with his lunch. I have never known a joke fall so flat.

This brings me to hairdressing. I would always try to make an appointment on board a liner calling at the islands, and to get a good haircut when visiting Nairobi or Dar es Salaam, but there was a little hairdresser with whom I made do whenever I was desperate, as I have always been bad at doing it myself. I was rather disconcerted on my last visit; I asked if I could use her lavatory but she said she had not got one. Not believing her, I asked how she and her assistants managed.

'Oh,' replied she, 'we use the basins in the lunch hour.'

We were very lucky to have an excellent and painstaking Government dentist; this was a help after the bad experience the children had had in Nigeria. Luckily none of us had any serious medical problems, so never had occasion to test the facilities but I know we had some very good people indeed.

★   ★   ★

On our first Sunday in Zanzibar, when the doctor had confined Satan to bed with his very bad cold, I went to church with the Private Secretary, Joyce Leverett. I did not realise that even there protocol was observed, and being shown into the front pew I knelt at the first (very splendid) kneeler; upon rising I noticed that Joyce had pointedly left a space between us which I realised was mine, and that I was in Satan's. After the service she shooed me out before everyone and I had to march out alone and meet the clergy at the door. It seemed odd to be doing these things, but I hoped nobody guessed that inside the British Resident's wife there was only me. It was always rather daunting the way the National Anthem was played when we appeared at official functions and I never got used to it.

The Cathedral Church of Christ is a memorial to the official end of the slave trade in East Africa, having been built by Bishop Steere on the site of the slave market, the altar having been placed where the whipping post had been. The Bishop's only qualification as a builder was that he had an architect friend in England. Plans, advice and materials took long weary months to come by sea around 1875. A new medium was used: Portland cement and crushed coral, which gave a pinkish glow to the walls. The building, simple, tall and narrow, with just one nave, held six hundred people. The rounded chancel was lined, Eastern fashion, with the Bishop's throne and thirteen canons' stalls locally carved in dark wood and backed with tall copper panels representing Old Testament characters. In the centre of the chancel and approached by a long flight of steps, stood the altar, faced with gold mosaics and bearing six gold candlesticks and a crucifix.

One day when I was arranging flowers at the foot of the altar steps for a service to be taken by the Archbishop of York, a rehearsal of the procession took place. It flowed up the steps and came to a halt, and the last person was a bored little man who stopped level with me. After a moment or two he said to me gloomily:

'Hope it goes better than it did in Dar.'

'What happened there?' I asked.

'Well,' replied he, 'he lost his place – didn't know where he'd got to at all – in a dream he was.'

'Go on,' I urged. 'What happened then?'

'Oh, he turns to me and says "Where am I?" Well, I didn't know where he was either, did I? But I has to think quick, so I says "The Lord be with you."'

'And was that right?'

'Oh that's always safe,' he answered, picking his teeth, 'But it WAS a bit tiresome as we was on the air.'

A gallery at the back was intended for purdah ladies who, despite conversion, would certainly cling to their customs. During the building years the Bishop used to stand on the rising walls and preach to the populace on Fridays, the Muslim holy day. The tower had a fine clock presented by the Muslim Sultan of that time, on condition that the tower should not be higher than that of the Palace.

One stained glass window is in memory of British sailors who died in Zanzibar in suppressing the slave trade; another is in memory of Livingstone, who equipped his expeditions from Zanzibar. There is also a crucifix made from the tree in Northern Rhodesia beneath which his heart is buried.

Black and white marble tiles and black marble pillars were imported from Italy. When the Bishop was away for a few days, the workmen put in twelve of these pillars upside down, and so they have remained, an interesting curiosity. When work reached the roof, the Bishop was uncertain how to proceed, so whilst advice was awaited from England, worship continued in the roofless church for two years. The final result is slightly crooked, a vaulted roof sixty feet high and twenty-eight and a half feet wide, which experts say is only held aloft by miraculous powers. Some years after our return to England I was sent a photograph of the Cathedral with, to my horror, the recognisable figures of Julia and her friend Helen Horsfall on the roof; I had never known that while I was arranging flowers one day, they had amused themselves by climbing the tower stairs and letting themselves out.

Bishop Steere was, among other things, responsible for the only Swahili textbook in existence for very many years, and from which I was instructed by one of the Anglican nuns attached to the Cathedral. It was a joy because one came across unexpected sentences like 'The angry European killed the wicked cook.' I did not progress very well with the language but the old nun and I very much enjoyed one another's company and she was intensely interested in the town doings I could report to her.

I was privileged to meet the last known slave on Zanzibar. Persis was a delightful woman, certainly over ninety, with a wicked chuckle and a keen mind in spite of the physical frailty of age and the fading of her eye. Through an interpreter (our 'tame' bishop, Frank Thorne, long retired, who still flitted about the precincts in his pink robe, with bare feet), she was very ready to talk of those far-off days, which were quite clear in her mind. It was in 1879, when she was certainly as much as eight years old, that she was captured in her village near Likoma in Nyasaland. The fear of slave traders was always with her people and Bona, as her name was then, knew that if they came she should never betray which was her mother or they would certainly be separated.

When a neighbouring tribe, the Wangone, swooped on the village, Bona had her baby brother on her hip. He was not wanted as he needed too much care, so he was dashed to the ground and left. Some of the men who resisted were killed, the rest, men, women and children able to walk strongly, were herded together, the village was burnt, and they all returned to the village of the captors. There were quite a number of captives from other villages marshalled there, and after a few days Bona was one of those bought by another tribe, the Wayeo, and began the long march to the coast. Surprisingly, Bona does not seem to have suffered on this march. The children were left free to run around, the traders treated them kindly and fed them from their own bowls. The adults fared worse: they all wore wooden yokes round their necks, which were chained to the slaves in front and behind. Fifteen of them shared one bowl of rice. But adults and children alike must have suffered from being torn from their homes and families; for instance, Bona's family was not bought at the same time as she was, so that she never again saw any of them except one of her brothers.

So she could not remember how long it took to get to the coast, but 'Safari, sleep, safari, sleep' repeated until we stopped her, gave the impression of a good long walk. Bagamoyo was their destination and here she was sold again to a small stall-holder. Her description of this part of her life was graphic:

'Bona, do this, do that, fetch this, take that, go there, come here.'

One day when she was at the well, she was overjoyed to meet one of her four younger brothers. She told him where she was working and whenever he was sent to buy coconuts he used to buy them from her, as she was trusted to sell these. The cackle with which she told us that she always gave him his money back brought to us over the years the child's sense of secret triumph over her hard master.

After some months at Bagamoyo she was sold yet again to an Arab and shipped on a dhow to be taken to Zanzibar, about 200 miles north. She lost contact with her brother for ever. This time children and adults alike were just tipped into the hold and there was not room even to sit. The ship sailed after dark, but she had been under observation by a ship of the British Navy which was lying in wait. About 1 o'clock in the morning the Naval ship crept up on the slaver and arrested her with grappling irons. Three Britons boarded her and were received by the Arabs, sitting on mats over the hatch. They gave horrified denials to the suggestion that they might be carrying slaves, but a woman down below cried out:

'We are down here!'

The British went into action and Bona could hear the clash of swords. The Arabs were disarmed, the children were taken on board the naval vessel and the dhow was towed to Zanzibar. A sackful of peanuts was given to the slaves left on the dhow, but the children were given hard-boiled eggs and ship's biscuits. Bona had been in captivity for probably a little more than a year.

Archdeacon Hudson of the Universities Mission to Central Africa in Zanzibar, chose fourteen of the children, including Bona, to go to the mission school at Mbweni, but the records do not make it clear whether he had to buy them. The Sultan had already signed a treaty with the British not to allow slaves to be shipped from Zanzibar, but the trade was still legal within the island. Persis (as Bona was renamed) in fact said that some of the adults of her party were sent to Mombasa and that Sultan Barghash bought the rest; but she added that Queen Victoria very soon wanted to see him about this and then all were set free.

In 1881 Persis was baptized with her new name and in 1885 was confirmed by Bishop Steere. She gave us these dates herself and they were later verified in the mission diary. She remembered Miss Caroline Thackeray, sister of the author William Thackeray, with affection and admiration. Miss Thackeray was a missionary in charge of a school for girls and among Persis' reminiscences we came upon an amusing contrast to the walk from Nyasaland to Kilwa: the daily constitutional taken by the girls of the mission, two by two, with Miss Thackeray in front and Miss Mills behind.

When Persis grew up, she taught at the school for fourteen years, during which time she married Isaac Chimwai, a mission servant. She had five sons and a daughter but surprisingly only two grandchildren, as she said all the others died. She was living in a clean little house with her daughter to care for her, and her day was made by a gift of tea, as she told me when I gave her a bag of coffee. She died a few months later.

★   ★   ★

When I first arrived, I was horrified to find that the Red Cross was only a committee, which never met. Fresh from the train disaster in Nigeria, I felt that Zanzibar should have a working Red Cross in case of a disaster, but I was begged not to get it started as they had so many organisations already which had to be financed; furthermore they had the St John Ambulance Brigade for First Aid, and an excellent Welfare Department. I saw their point, but we compromised: we would have a working Red Cross committee, concentrating on disaster relief, and would do anything except raise money. It was surprising how much we were able to achieve without doing so.

Almost at once a hurricane hit Mauritius and the Indians of Zanzibar were so eager to send help that before I had collected my wits, the Mayor had appealed on the radio and the Scouts and Guides were making a house-to-house collection of second-hand clothing. Keen for the Red Cross to make its mark, I said we would get free shipping for the collection and would sort the things at the Residency. You live and learn. It was quite funny. On Sunday when we returned from the beach we found an enormous heap of clothing dumped in the very large dining room, reaching from wall to wall and quite high in the middle. Teams of ten women, Indians, Europeans and Girl Guides, worked on it for a week and packed sixty-one sacks of men's, women's and children's clothing. When we found some dead bedbugs we started filling other sacks with insanitary or very worn clothing, but we could not destroy them for fear that word would get out. Nineteen sacks were labelled in code for the Red Cross Field Officer in Mauritius, to be destroyed, but it was humbling to be told later that nothing was destroyed, they had needed it all. Money collected was also sent through the Red Cross. Later we sent help to Kenya and Tanganyika when they had floods or famines, and the British, Indian and East African Red Cross Societies sent help through us when Zanzibar had floods.

Then one day a fierce little person fighting her corner came to see me. Plain, aggressive Doris Jones was completely lined with gold. She was a sort of district nurse who toured the island checking on ex-patients, and she made it her business to list all the handicapped people she came across. Now she came to me to demand that somehow the Red Cross should provide a centre where such people could come for assessment, minor treatment, and assistance to get more major attention that might be available. Doris, about to retire, offered to run it as a volunteer.

Having pledged that I would not raise money for the Red Cross, Doris' demand was quite a poser. But word got around, no doubt mainly by Doris, and a football manager donated twenty-five pounds to the project from a game without being asked. Then an Indian millionaire donated one thousand pounds which was about twice as much as we had been envisaging, so we were in business. After much futility we did eventually find harbour in a disused building in the hospital grounds, which we put in order, equipped as a day centre, and opened. Doris ran it until the revolution. I hope and pray it still exists.

I sometimes went round a district with an Arab Welfare Officer on her visits. One day I said to her how wonderfully honest the people of Zanzibar seemed to be.

'Oh,' she replied, 'they are not nearly so honest as they used to be. When I was a child' (she was about 35) 'it was the custom when the Africans had parties for weddings or anything else, for us to lend them jewellery and other valuables for the occasion. Nowadays we have so many people from the mainland that we can only do this for people we know by sight.'

Apart from amazement at such a standard, I was struck by the resemblance to the custom in ancient Egypt, when the Egyptians also followed this custom with the Israelites, but the Israelites made their exodus complete with Egyptian spoils. This tale illustrates how benevolent slavery could be. The slaves often suffered terribly immediately after capture (probably by their fellow countrymen) and during transport, but more often than not afterwards they were kindly treated and those born in captivity did not appreciate the meaning of freedom. Certainly when they were freed, many of them stayed on with their employers. Slavery still existed unofficially in Zanzibar when we were there, the only difference being that if they wanted to leave their masters they had the law on their side. Parents would take children to rich Arabs and ask them to rear and educate them in return for their services, and when the girls grew up their masters would provide dowries for their marriages, and take them in again if they became divorced; they were in effect members of the family.

Purdah was one of my problems, trying to help the women in the next generation to live in the modern world. The system was good while it worked in their kind of world but now the menfolk wanted their country to keep up with global developments. They did not seem to understand that you could not educate girls, even to university standard in some cases, and hope to keep them in purdah afterwards. As soon as such girls returned from overseas they had to put on the long black silk *buibui*, a garment which also covers the head, sometimes face and all, and observe the strict rules of behaviour laid down; no man might see her face except her immediate family, she might not go out alone, and she could not join in any communal activity, play games, or even read books except the Koran. Very few families in Zanzibar were quite so strict, but many still forbade the showing of the face and they nearly all wore the *buibui*, though sometimes with the face piece thrown back. A few girls were so bold as to play netball but always in the confines of the Portuguese Fort, which had been re-designated 'The Ladies' Club' and where the Girl Guides met.

★   ★   ★

The annual Queen's Birthday Parade and garden party, when one shook 450 or so hands and kept trying to freshen up the smile on one's face, recognise people, and remember something relevant to say to some of the visitors, was one of the more trying social events. Others (for me) were football and hockey matches to be attended, though I often had some other engagement and Satan coped alone; Remembrance Sunday ceremonies and wreath-laying; investitures which took place in the ballroom; occasionally an endless religious ceremony on the playing fields, us sitting as still as possible for hours under a 'shamiana' or open marquee, with the Sultan. Events put on by different ethnic groups had to be honoured; once I even had to help judge a sari fashion show and learned a great deal about what was and what was not considered correct.

There were St John Ambulance Brigade events, and I even attended a course to encourage the others. This was extremely funny because the ladies (men were taught separately, of course) were so modest about being bandaged that it was almost impossible to teach them a number of the more tricky ones. There were Girl Guides and Brownies to be visited, too – Satan saw to the Scouts and Cubs.

The Hindu community would annually use their meeting hall for the treatment of patients needing eye operations. A Hindu surgeon would come over from Dar es Salaam and perform the operations and a week later return to remove the bandages; the patients meanwhile were tended by the community on grass mats on the floor. One such return trip I was privileged to go round with this good surgeon and I shall not forget the old bearded man who, on having his bandages removed, saw me and cried:

'Is it an angel?' He had had cataracts for years and also had probably never seen a white woman before. Indeed a treasured memory!

In all of these activities I was of course supported and encouraged by other wives who did most of the donkey-work, and in my turn I gave them support and encouragement. One usually found there were the enthusiastic few who could be relied on wholeheartedly, others had to be coerced a little. Still others were not interested, and in fact hated being on the island altogether, though they were the ones who did not even take advantage of the more distant beaches or nearby islands. So it was doubtless just a feeling. But the ones who did help made up for all the others; they were tireless and resourceful.

I organised a show of national dances which was a great success and fun to do. We had Scots reels by the Gordon Highlanders who were stationed with us after election riots; various gently sinuous Indian dances; thigh slapping German dances, which the German nuns taught to Goan children, though I fear they did not show nearly enough vigour; some Swiss and some English folk-dancing, and an Irish jig. I was delighted to get the African umbrella dance performed, the first time ever on stage, and they insisted on borrowing Europeans' umbrellas – that was a very colourful number. The real triumph, though, was getting an Arab sword dance. At first they were very boring, just standing twiddling their long curved swords in the air, their drummer with his back to the audience; but after a talk from the Chief Secretary, who spoke Swahili very well, and a suggestion that they might pretend to chop each other's heads off, they compromised and produced a lively dance pretending to try and cut each other's feet off! The Scots, I discovered at the second rehearsal (having myself been on tour when the first took place) were all wearing different coloured underpants; when I complained, I was told more or less to pipe down as at the first rehearsal they had not worn underpants at all, and on a stage it mattered! I think everyone found the whole show a diversion from

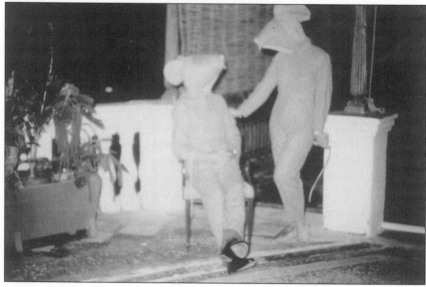

Rats.

the excellent plays put on by the Amateur Dramatic Society, and also it involved so many different groups in something which was purely for entertainment.

All the time Satan was having to work towards independence, although he did not feel the country was ready for it. At the first elections there were dreadful riots and more than seventy people were killed and many injured. It was after that we had British troops on the island; before, the Police Force was the only armed body of men, and when the British finally left, the Army was withdrawn, although the Sultan begged for them to remain. When the Coldstream Guards replaced the Gordon Highlanders, one of the officers took me up in a helicopter from our own lawn to take photographs. I was hardly able to operate my camera, as the kind man had had the doors removed to make my views unrestricted; however, I did get several good ones, including a gem of the Residency. Another kind officer, who was having lunch with us, asked if he could take Julia over to the mainland for a few days; he had been teaching her to waterski and had become fond of her. I felt it would be too awful for William not to be included, as Prince William of Gloucester was in the party and it was all rather exciting, so I said no. But he said to Julia:

'Well, pack your bag, you are coming back to Kenya with us.'

She was so thrilled I had to agree and she went off squeezed between the prince and the colonel's wife. When she returned some days later, her first remark was:

'What can I have to eat? I didn't have any breakfast.' But her second was:

'Oh Mummy, I'm in love.' To my surprise it was not with the prince but with a youth called Nicholas Tollemache, who had been of the party. The colonel and his wife were staying in an hotel and Julia slept on their balcony. The boys had a tent in the grounds and Julia was included in their mess arrangements, laid on by a sergeant-major.

To some extent Satan discussed his problems with me, but I never felt I was anything like an *'eminence grise'*! I know my opinion about people influenced him very much and I had to be careful in making a decision about a person because, if I later changed my mind, he might not change his. But of course it was a relief to him to have somebody he could say anything to, and know it would go no further. This was one of the reasons I hated having to leave him in order to go to England and spend time with the children in the good climate. We arranged matters as a rule so that we were not separated for more than three months, though one awful time it had had to be six in Nigeria.

Although my life was on the surface happy and carefree, I was, maybe subconsciously most of the time, aware of danger below. I remember one night when sleep was difficult to achieve, I lay there planning where I could hide the children if I heard 'them' swarming up the tower stairs. Julia would fit nicely into the 'well' on top of the wardrobe but I never could think of anywhere for William.

One day an ominous little display was made on the Post Office steps. Twelve dead rats and a mouse were laid out there, each with a label round its neck giving the name of some eminent person on the island, for instance 'H.E.' for Satan, and to our amusement the mouse was labelled 'The Minister of Health' who was an unusually small Arab. It was very near New Year's Eve, when the Europeans always had a fancy dress party at the English Club, and because of the narrow streets precluding traffic, they had to walk to the party. The locals knew this and enjoyed the fun. That year I made up a party of thirteen of us and had a little tailor make us all grey boiler suits with pink satin tails. Satan of course could not go into the town for a fitting so the tailor came to the house, and it was very funny when he held the fat pink tail against Satan's behind, asking me:

'Here? Or here?'

I made a prototype head out of radio gauze, boiler suit cotton, wire for whiskers, buttons for eyes, and everyone made their own. We each wore a label round our necks to match those on the rats at the Post Office. One very small woman had the label 'Minister of Health'. It was a particularly successful fancy dress and the crowds loved it. We felt it had taken the sting out of the demonstration because we had laughed.

A great deal of my time, inevitably, was spent on the children: arranging

William (with the cook) and the fish he gave to the Sultan.

amusements for them, planning their journeys and seeing that people met them at various stops and upon arrival, arranging extra tuition for them in maths, Latin, riding, dancing, guitar. We gave William a Dabchick in which to learn sailing the best way, and we had a share in a sailing dinghy. William went deep-sea fishing with an Arab and another English boy in a small outboard motorboat, and the first time, when he himself caught seventeen huge kingfish, he took the best one, which was as long as he was, to give to the Sultan who had been a keen fisherman. William commandeered the second best car (he would have taken the best but the drivers just would not agree, and wanted him to take the shopping car), had the fish inside on the fur rug instead of in the boot, and sallied forth to the Palace, quite unknown to us. At the Palace, in spite of the car, he was denied entrance and had to send his fish in with a message. The Sultan responded with a photograph of himself and the Sultana.

The day the Dabchick arrived, both Satan and I were caught up in meetings, but William saw no reason to wait for us. He rallied two friends and they set off to sea in this minute boat, intended for learning to sail single-handed. They were all about eleven. A fourth boy, aged ten, simply could not squeeze on board and watched enviously from the shore. All went well until a squall overturned the boat. With its solid hull it could not sink and they soon righted it, but as soon as the third boy tried to get on board again it would turn over. They soon became exhausted. Their friend on shore set off in his father's dinghy, rowing furiously. Other people had noticed them, and three policemen came dashing to the rescue, tearing their clothes off on the beach and throwing themselves fearlessly into the sea. As only one could swim, just a little, they did not get very far. The Port launch was sent out and reached them after they had already been taken in tow most efficiently by their little friend, and all the boys were indignant that the Port officials took over and made the rescue theirs.

The contrast between being the governor's lady, being treated with deference and red carpets, and being a housewife in England was pretty sharp; I usually had an au pair girl in England as we lived in such a remote place where we could not get domestic help. If I wanted to nip to the shops it was a help to be able to leave short fat little legs behind in the care of somebody else, because getting up the hill to the car was a slow business. I was often to be found painting walls, digging in the garden, battling with cooking, cleaning and washing. One did feel that this was what life was all about, and it was difficult to take the pomp of Zanzibar seriously, though it made a lovely change.

★   ★   ★

We no longer took the opportunity of stopping off on our way home as we had from Nigeria, in warm climates such as Malta, Majorca and Portugal, because now we were able to choose the time of our leave, and we chose summer. We rather missed the early sea journeys we used to make to and from Nigeria, when one met and made friends with people from other territories or from different regions of Nigeria, but with little children both sea and air travel were very wearing and I was usually alone. When Satan became more senior, we travelled first class and that certainly was a great improvement, using VIP lounges at airports and having more room on the planes. One scene stays in my memory at Entebbe airport in the VIP lounge, when William slammed down his airbag which had a bottle of whisky in it, which of course broke. Whisky flooded the bag and the floor, and the one with resourcefulness was Julia, who came flying from the lavatory trailing clouds of paper to mop up the mess. We were forced to dry William's thick underwear which he was due to change into quite shortly, in the first-class cabin, resulting in a heady atmosphere of whisky fumes. Twice, we travelled from Zanzibar by Lloyd Triestino ship, once for Satan's only leave from there, on our own, and once, the last time, with the children, and that was blissful: excellent food and accommodation and a gentle transition from one world to another.

When on tour in Zanzibar inter-island, we used the Sultan's yacht which was very pleasant, sleeping and entertaining on board, but it had to be carefully planned because it was normally used as a passenger ship to the mainland. On one occasion we were told it was the custom for the Resident to go and plant a Union Jack annually on Latham Island, to maintain British rights to it; Satan fell for this and it was duly organised, two nights away on the yacht with a few friends. It turned out to be a guano mound, quite unoccupied, in very rough waters, and there was no question of Satan being able to land, let alone in full uniform as he had been informed he would be expected to do! It had been a good way to spend a weekend which he refused ever to do again.

We were extremely lucky to be within such easy reach of the East African game parks, and into the bargain I had Basil serving in Uganda and my cousin Val and her husband Mervyn Cowie, the Director of the East African Game Parks, in Kenya. We took every opportunity of visiting the parks; the Uganda ones when we went in 1960 to their Independence Ceremony, the Kenya ones whenever Satan had to go over for a conference, and the Tanganyika ones I visited on my own, and we all went on our last journey home.

On one trip we were given a lift by Sir Richard Turnbull (the Governor of Tanganyika) and his wife in their plane, to a conference in Nairobi Government House for the governors of all the East African territories. The plane was un-pressurised and we flew too high for my stoppings, which throbbed mercilessly. Beatrice Turnbull was most concerned and kept wailing that all the aspirin was in the boot. Upon arrival at Government House I lay on my bed and was restored with brandy. We were a little late in joining everyone before dinner. Walking the length of the ballroom to reach the small area beyond the last pillars which was used as a sitting room, we saw Julius Nyerere (who happened to be staying but not for the conference) standing on a plinth trying to squeeze himself between the pillars and not succeeding. (Primed by brandy I forced myself through and made quite an entry.) Throughout the evening I was impressed by Nyerere's ability to join in with the fairly undignified proceedings when we were all able to let our hair down: it was Satan's birthday and we sang 'Happy Birthday' for instance, and after dinner the men played 'hockey' on the billiard table. For a Catholic mission-trained African amongst public school educated men who had reached the tops of their particular trees, it was a remarkable performance and I recognised his greatness.

My impression of Uganda was of a rich agricultural country of great beauty, peopled by happy people, mostly with large behinds, wearing bright colours with great panache. Nowhere else in East Africa did I find the people so

Four governors: L to R: Patrick Renison (Kenya), Frederick Crawford (Uganda), Richard Turnbull (Tanganyika) and George Mooring (Zanzibar) with a Colonial Office Official.

relaxed and smiling, like they were in Nigeria, so I felt at home instantly. Of course they had a lot to smile about, they thought, at that time, because it was at the time of the Independence Ceremony. We were put up by kind people to whom we had been allotted, and entertained at other houses too. We were lent a car with a driver who had a different silly hat for every occasion, and became more and more drunk until, for the Ceremony itself, our host had to drive us himself. The Duke of Kent performed the ceremony, and the Duchess enhanced the occasion with her beauty and her lovely dresses and her charm. The actual lowering of the Union Jack for the last time and the raising of the Ugandan flag was a very moving moment.

On one occasion I was sitting with a number of other women on a wooden bench in the House of Assembly gallery. We had little cards with our names on them on the bench-back in front of us, but whoever assessed the size of the ladies had got it very wrong. I was next to Mrs Obote (her card said) and she was determined to sit bang in front of it; every time we sat down I had to be very quick or I would have been sitting on her lap. I later found that she was in fact Mrs Obote's 'sister' (whatever that might have meant). Mrs Obote herself had in some way displeased her husband and he had forbidden her to attend, sending this other woman in her place.

When all the official business was at an end, an expedition had been
organised for a few of us to the Murchison Falls and to the Queen Elizabeth
Game Park, all of which was magic. Sir Andrew and Lady Cohen were of the
party but I found no sympathy between us. At the game park we were allotted
the chalet which the Queen Mother had slept in and we had a lovely adventure
there. In the middle of the night I was woken by Satan's hand over my mouth.
I got the message and kept quiet while he tiptoed across to peer out of the
window. I joined him and saw a vast hippo quietly cropping the grass under
the window and moving steadily to the corner of the building, round which he
disappeared. Satan nipped across the room to the front door which was in a
convex recess. His plan was to be at the corner of the recess when the hippo
turned the next corner of the house, and thus to get a very good view of his
face. To his utter consternation he came face to face with *another* hippo which
was as surprised as he! Seeing them thus grazing reminded me of Laurens Van
der Post's tale from the bushmen of South Africa about the hippo:

> The First Spirit made the hippo to live and feed on the land but the hippo so
> loved the water that he begged the First Spirit to reconsider and allow him to live
> and feed in the water.
>
> 'No,' said the First Spirit 'I can't do that, because you have such a big mouth
> you would eat far too many fish.' The hippo was very sad and went away. But
> then he had a brilliant idea and came back to the First Spirit:
>
> 'Sir, might I live in the water if I promise not to eat fish, but to come out on to
> the land at night and eat grass?'
>
> The First Spirit considered this proposition and allowed it, on condition that
> the promise was rigidly kept. That is why the hippo spreads his dung by swishing
> it around with his tail, to show everyone that there are no fishbones in it.

Basil had been transferred from the Sudan after sixteen happy years and was
now in Uganda. He had become as a father to his people. Eccentric that he
was, he had directed them in the building of a Greek theatre complete with
plinths bearing busts of local people, sculpted by a local man whose talent Basil
had discovered and fostered. Here they learned a few Greek plays before the
whole project took off and they composed and acted their own plays. When
the Sudan became independent, he was sent to a station over the border in
Uganda, only about 100 miles distant, where the language was much the same.
Not long afterwards a stream of distressed refugees began to pour in from his
old station. The Northern Sudanese, much hated by the Southerners, had
taken over the jobs vacated by the British, and atrocities occurred; this
included the massacre of the Police Force in Basil's district of Madi, when they
had obediently collected up all the arms they could find in the area and piled
them up on the barracks yard for inspection. They were gunned down. Finally
the Southerners erupted, the Northerners sent more troops and chaos ensued.

Basil applied to the Governor of the Sudan for permission to go across and help to calm the proceedings, but was told quite rightly that the British could not interfere in the domestic affairs of an independent country. So he just went. He knew so many of those refugees. His presence certainly helped. To start with he was a white man, which they knew meant law and order; look closer and it was Mr Duke. Confidence began to return that all would be well. Basil's successor, a Northerner, was holed up in a store room in the District Officer's house, with a spear in his back. Basil rescued him and the Northerners realised that he was acting impartially, so he was able to liaise between them and the locals. But there was quite a row about it in England. The Sudanese Government accused Britain of placing spies along the border but of course they were only there because of their knowledge of the language and customs. After much publicity and hard speaking, Basil's action was recognised as brave, sympathetic, but unwise politically.

When I visited Basil in Moyo, Uganda, I was amazed to find that hardly anyone lived in towns; they lived in homesteads scattered over the district and used their town as a centre; here would be the shops, the district office, post office, hospital, rest house, a mission and so on. At Moyo too there was a football stadium which Basil had had built and which brought the people together for pleasure as well as business. We used to go and sit on it in the evenings to watch the sun go down over the distant mountains. The main crop was cotton, sent off by Nile steamer to various destinations, and some cassava too. It is unfortunate that cassava, the staple diet of so many African peoples, is a root with practically no food value at all.

Besides Basil's wife and baby son, there were no other Europeans except the Italian missionaries. Theirs was the only Christian church, Catholic, built by themselves, tall and graceful and most beautifully decorated. Compared with the square white architecture of most of the other buildings in the town, and the round thatched huts of the people, this was a great marvel. The Italians ran a boarding school.

Visitors made for interest, whether welcome or not. Once Basil told his staff that the Governor was coming for a meal when on tour, and he begged the No. 1 boy to use the hatch, instead of plodding down the verandas and letting the food get cold. In the event, the first course went smoothly, and then to Basil's horror a long black leg came through the hatch followed by the rest of the No. 1 boy and then a dish of roast meat. Naturally.

The Nile ran strongly not many miles away. The ferry was a perfect Heath Robinson device and I was not surprised when we failed to make our target and were swept downstream, leaving two of the crew stranded on the shore where they had leapt. Back we chugged to the other side where the current was weaker, and again crept upstream to a suitable point from which to bear down on the opposite landing place. This time we were successful and the patient machine went up in my estimation. In the meantime we had had plenty of time to watch the coloured and the black and white kingfishers which dived and swooped around us.

Every man we met carried a spear. Even men on bicycles had spears strapped to their crossbars: they never knew when they might get the chance of 'beef'. Nearby was a pocket of white rhino, so misnamed by the mispronunciation of the German word for wide, because these rhino are distinct from 'black' rhino mainly by their wide mouths, used for cropping grass only. The 'black' rhino, which are more dangerous, have pointed mouths and can raise their heads higher to get at bushes, as well as grass. The local African knew that if he could kill a rhino he could sell the horn quite profitably as an aphrodisiac. White men interested in the preservation of the species had been attempting to foil them by removing the rhino to game reserves where they would be safe. One day Basil took me to see a half-grown rhino being caught for this purpose, lassoed from a lurching lorry and secured by ropes round the legs. These were very difficult to apply and many men were needed; a big hole was then dug into which the lorry could be backed on runners and the rhino dragged to the lorry. He was similarly unloaded at the camp and imprisoned temporarily in a log cage until he could be transported to a game park. This one's mother had been captured the day before, and their joy when they were reunited was lovely to see. Rhino kept for a few days in captivity become very tame; indeed one which was released because it fought with another one, stayed near the camp for several days and clocked in for his regular meals, but at the end of that time he was found, speared and hornless, on the road outside the camp.

Not far away was a lonely earthwork on the bank of the Nile, with faint traces of brick buildings within. With a stone memorial at the edge of the river, this was all that was left of one of Emin Pasha's line of forts on the Nile. Indeed later, when I wanted to discover exactly who Emin Pasha had been, I found it quite difficult to find that detail in any East African library. It was hard, in the quiet vastness there, to imagine the busy station life built up by this German Muslim who was Governor of Equitoria, appointed by Gordon on behalf of the Khedive. Something of the streets which cut the six-acre fort into four could be seen, and the corners where guns were mounted, but the jetties had been swept away and the thatched huts of the Egyptian soldiers and their families had disappeared completely; no gardens and crops surrounded the ditch and the noisy market which sprang up outside had melted away. The men who brought order to this province found themselves at one time an isolated pocket of peace while all around them the Mahdi's rebellion brought death and devastation. Finally they too were forced to leave.

This part of Africa probably still manages to remain remarkably unchanged, in spite of the activities of western newcomers. The cleft stick* would still be extremely useful if one's transport broke down.

Staying with the Cowie cousins in Nairobi was always a great pleasure. Their house was well outside the town in what might be called a suburb, though very unlike our ideas of such. The bush came right up to their garden boundaries, and often wild animals could be seen on the lawn – even giraffe and warthog. Val had been hit by polio when she was fourteen but, wearing callipers and using two sticks, she had not let it stop her. In spite of loving parental protestations, she found a tutor to get her through the school examinations she had not been able to take, then went to London to train as an occupational therapist, and worked in a military hospital. Later she had gone to stay with Basil in the Sudan, and even later with people she had met who worked at a Tanganyikan game reserve. From there she went to Nairobi where in due course she met and married Mervyn Cowie. When she had children she gradually began to use a wheelchair more, because it freed her hands from sticks, to attend to the children. We had some wonderful safaris in the Nairobi Game Park with them, once with David Attenborough who was also staying with them, and who I saw swoop on a snake in the garage, grab it behind the head and pop it into a nearby urn which it could not get out of. On one of my visits there was a woman staying who was studying lions for a thesis. She maintained that one could recognise individual lions by their whisker spots, and in the end she was able to prove it. Three cubs were sent off to two zoos and a couple of years later she went to see the two who were together. She instantly saw that one was not the one registered as being there, and her subsequent enquiries established that there had been a mix up at the airport, which of course nobody noticed or thought important. I went lion-watching with her at dawn a couple of times, and learned a great deal.

On one safari in Kenya we were so lucky as to be present at the birth of an elephant. A party of elephants grouped themselves round the mother, facing outwards, while two 'aunties' helped her by leaning against her sides. After about half an hour the baby tottered out of the circle, heavily escorted and lifted up by loving trunks when it fell down, and slowly they drifted away, weather eyes being kept on our silent watch. We went to a reception at Government House that evening and I was so excited by our adventure that I was telling a high-powered group the story. The wife of the GOC East Africa, known as Little Audrey, could hardly bear not being the centre of attention but soon reversed her position by exclaiming:

'But Patricia, didn't you know that elephants have a party after a birth and toss the foreskin from trunk to trunk!'

---

*In former days a message would be sent by a runner carrying it in a cleft stick.

There was a moment's awful silence, then a General said:

'I don't think you mean the *foreskin*, Audrey; it would be the after-birth.'

The Tanganyikan safaris included visits to the Leakeys, archaeologists working in the Olduvai Gorge. Here we learned about geological levels, and saw the remains of giant animals, even a goat, which existed in one era, though so far no giant man has been unearthed. Mary Leakey had just discovered Zinjanthropus man which was very exciting. But even more exciting was the young wildebeest which they had adopted. Oliver had been found beside his mother on a lonely track; she had been killed and partially eaten. The Leakeys were in their Land-Rover and the little calf followed them back to the camp, so in a way he adopted them. He transferred his love for his mother to vehicles, which was a bit awkward, and whenever anyone left camp in a car, Oliver had to be distracted with a bottle of milk; to drink this, he would kneel down on his front legs as he would to his mother and you had to lower the bottle for him. He was very undisciplined and would snatch bananas off the lunch table if he felt so inclined. A little monkey, who often sat on Oliver's head, actually stole food off my plate when Oliver pushed in between me and the next guest at the table. On my second visit, I was ushered into Mary's tent to wash at a small iron tripod in the corner; unknown to me, another tent led out of this one, where Oliver and the dogs slept at night to keep them safe from predators, and while I was washing Oliver came out, saw me and gave me an almighty biff in the backside with his now quite powerful horns. I was quite frightened, which amused him mightily, and the rest of that visit was enlivened by Oliver endeavouring to catch me unawares. He became quite a problem and eventually was used as a stud so that wildebeest could be studied at close quarters as never before.

The Ngorongoro Crater was one of the best parks and we had a wonderful visit there. Our Land-Rover broke down, however, and we had a tiresome walk of several miles back to camp at dusk which was a little hair-raising. In the Serengeti we once spent five hours looking for cheetah, and eventually found two lying in a tree. There also we saw hyena cubs frolicking in the open near their den and wondered how such little charmers could become such depressing-looking creatures as their parents. We drove behind a jackal for miles because he would not get off the path which ran through miles of flat open grassland, but just ran on ahead. And in all these parks we saw lion and elephant in large numbers and Satan took myriads of photographs of them; our albums are full of photos of distant herds and of equally distant marching soldiers which he could never resist taking. One day we met a Masai man who wanted to be driven in our Land-Rover. He sat at the back with the children, doing his best to find out if Julia was a girl or a boy. He took us to his people's settlement and I went into one of their 'houses'. It was like something built by another kind of creature – a long worm-like structure with a bend near the entrance which was a defensive measure, the whole made of mud and dung and patted smooth. Inside it was difficult to see, as the only light came through windows made by pushing a finger through the wall. They seemed to be friendly but Satan, who knew so much more than I about tribal groups, was very wary.

Once, at Amboseli, we were chased in our car by a rhino we had not noticed, but as we had to zigzag to avoid the branches pulled down by elephant, and the rhino charged in a direct and very fast line, we were able to escape. Here, too, we met three ostriches whose eggs had been found abandoned and the birds hatched and brought up at the camp; they were so thoroughly convinced that they were not ostriches but people that they would never dream of stepping over the line of stones round the camp which marked the boundaries beyond which we were not allowed to go; they would wait patiently at one of the gates in the fences between chalets, for somebody to let them through, when all they needed to do was to walk to the end of the fence and go round it.

★   ★   ★

A memorable journey I made was with Peggy Hawker, the wife of the Financial Secretary in Zanzibar, when we travelled by dhow, bus, canoe and Greek caique with a cargo of salt to the island of Kilwa, the first settlement on the coast by Omani Arabs. An archaeological dig was being conducted there by Neville Chittick, then the Director of the British Institute of Archaeology in Dar es Salaam. The most notable detail in our adventures was the variety of lavatories: there was one on the dhow which hung over the side; luckily, as we only spent a night on board, sleeping in the captain's cabin, I did not have to use it, but Peggy was made differently and had to make frequent visits accompanied by me to help her over the side and give her moral support. (This reminded me of how I had told the children never to sail close to a dhow when the wind was in the wrong direction or they ran a certain risk from these 'long drops'.) On the bus trip we had occasional stops of three minutes flat in which to find cover in the most unlikely places. At the Kilwa camp there was a house in which we stayed, sporting a room called the lavatory: very large, with a long slit in the concrete floor, and a piece of wood, fixed between two poles, was supposed to support you if you could balance on it; if you preferred there was a movable seat you could balance over the wood, but it was often missing as people came to borrow it to sit on while sorting pottery nearby. The worst lavatory of all was on the Greek caique: it was a doorless sentry box forrard, facing not only the bridge but another sentry box used as a cookhouse; there was in fact a door leaning up against the side which you could hold on if you

insisted on privacy but one had other priorities. This was a day trip and we
lasted as long as we could; finally Peggy broke and said brightly to the captain
that the time had come to use the loo; very shyly this Seychelles-born Swiss,
who had served in the Tanganyikan Navy in the war, asked if she would not
rather have a potty in his cabin, and produced a rusty enamel model which
looked like heaven to us, our only worry then being which way the wind was
blowing.

The bus drive was enlivened by the fact that the brakes did not work and a
man was ready on hills to jump out with a couple of big rocks to put behind
the wheels. At one place a magnificent eland broke cover on the left and leapt
over us and off into the bush the other side. At the Rufiji Ferry the landing
place had broken down during storms and was being built up by just one man.
We settled down with positively African fatalism to wait, and after an hour
heard that the man had gone across to mend the other side now. A van full of
cigarettes sported a gramophone but only one record which was an
advertisement 'Shillingi moja tu' (only one shilling) and one did get a little tired
of it. Peggy had her hair done in tiny plaits by a fellow woman passenger, amid
screams of mirth from all the others, which helped later on to keep her cool.
After another hour we went across the ferry, everyone quite calm and
philosophical about the delay, which made it restful.

We were met by a canoe, which took us over to Kilwa where we beached in
the shadow of the beautiful Arab fort built on Portuguese foundations. There
was a party of three archaeologists and the wife of the leader Neville Chittick.
Living was pretty primitive – the meat I brought with me was welcome and
eaten with yams and seaweed, boiled three times to get rid of the salt. Ants
abounded and covered one's sandshoes but once sprayed with 'Off' they died
there.

There were five archaeological sites on the island. The largest, which was
the earliest excavated site on the Tanganyikan coast, was built some time after
the twelfth century, because it resembled Arab places of that date in Arabia, and
it had probably been built by Shirazi invaders. It was thought to have been a
rich trader's establishment. There was a hexagonal bath with stone seats all
round it, well-preserved latrines (of far better design than those we had been
sampling recently), bidets and places for putting water jars and a huge
courtyard with about seventy holes for coconut oil lamps (which leave no
black trace) in two of the walls. Every room had central draining holes with
little covers, for sluicing water over the floors, several inscriptions and, above
all, a lovely intact blue Yuan vase thought to be early thirteenth century.

There was a Stone-Age site where all sorts of artefacts had been left and
were now to be found on pinnacles of sand, due to erosion. The Great
Mosque, partly thirteenth-century, partly fifteenth-century, was in a wonderful

state of preservation, with seven domes still intact and many Persian porcelain inserts in the walls. There were two washing departments with stone foot rubbers* and loos, but here were found human and animal bones in some numbers, probably bearing gloomy witness to the invasion of the cannibal Wazimba in 1600 when the place became deserted. There was evidence of three earlier floors underneath. Behind the mosque was a complex of houses across a narrow street, covering about three quarters of an acre and with at least seven occupational levels underneath. This was where I was put to use, working out what the foundations meant, what a house consisted of, and so on. At other times I worked on piecing pottery together, which was not nearly such fun.

There was another smaller domed mosque on which Neville was doing a great deal of repair work. He had an ingenious way of raising some of the money: goats being a great nuisance on the sites, leaping from high places over his wire fences and causing a lot of damage, he would have them captured and locked in his bathroom, and when the owner came he had to pay a shilling to reclaim each one – one hoped before bath time. As the people still use this mosque and it would by now have fallen down without Neville's attentions, it was really quite fair. Another bonus he brought to the people was a number of extra wells; they only had two in use but he found a goodly number more, and cleared them of debris. He would tear about the island along its sandy paths on his bicycle, from site to site, supervising.

A Portuguese fort and the remains of an eighteenth-century walled town with a lot of interesting features, some of earlier date, were two more sites. And there were two other islands we visited, one of which, Songo Songo, had not been visited by Europeans since a German archaeologist sixty years before. We were to pick up a boat at Kivinje on the mainland, and while we waited we went shopping: one man tried to buy a hat but there were only plastic trilbies. I bought some gripewater for Neville's baby, and another man bought cement and lime for use at the digs. When the boat came we had to wade out through deep mud, the men rescuing things from their shorts pockets, the African foreman carrying a picnic basket on his head. When it was lunch time I opened a tin of corned beef, the boat lurched and the beef slipped out as the flap door I was working on fell open and the beef slipped down towards the engine; I managed to knock the flap shut with my knee and neatly caught the beef in the opening – as one chap said:

'Is this what they call pressed beef?'

Neville got a bowl to catch it and although we had to scoop one bit off the filthy floor we ate it all, as there was nothing else. Food was always the

---

*Corrugated places to rub your feet and clean them.

problem and everyone was sick of the tough little chickens which provided the only fresh meat. Songo Songo was the perfect desert island to look at, with yellow sands and palm trees and coral cliffs, everything sparkling and clean. The local chief welcomed us to his house, to which we were taken by fishermen, and offered Neville a chair which Neville quickly offered to me – a dirty trick as I have never seen a more dangerous object, possibly a nineteenth century German deck chair, with a head and foot rest, one arm rest and a sliding seat; it was very uncomfortable and I was sure that at any minute it was going to shut up, with me inside.

We were taken to see the water supply which was not a well but a great chasm in the coral floor; we went down cemented steps, terribly steep and high, about thirty feet, and there were a lot of women down there, and a small puddle of clear water. Then we heard voices right in the rock and Neville dived into a dark crack armed with a box of matches, followed by the rest of us. The matches were not much help and after a while we came to a crossroads and in various crouching positions we shouted and waited for light. A little tin lamp appeared on a ledge ahead of us and on we went until Neville found a dipper, a coconut on a stick, and feeling about he found water, tasted it and declared it delicious and icy cold. I held the lamp down and to our horror we found ourselves to be standing on a three inch ledge over the water which was down a man-sized slit which would have been tricky to get out of. Going on we found another way out and realised that the journey was obviously one-way.

Crossing the island was wicked as it was coral rag, jagged, sharp and irregular. The foreman had no shoes and had a very bad time. We came out on to a small plain where we found the remains of a house and a mosque but no cut stone except gravestones. We were set to look for 'pot' and before long were finding early celadon and weald ware, and a gravestone with an inscription, early Persian ware, Islamic monochrome and an ancient piece of gilded glass. I also found a wound glass bead of an unusual colour and finally, triumph, a coin of the earliest Sultan of Kilwa, dated 957; only two others had been found anywhere and none in this area, so it was a great find. Celebrating on the roof of the launch with a bottle of wine on our way back, I mentioned that we had not seen the solitary palm tree which seemed to be growing out of the sea which we had noticed on the way out. It was discovered that the crew had never before been out of sight of land and had no idea of navigation. We had to do the best we could by the stars, and eventually got back safely, very late at night.

The caique which took us back to Zanzibar was fifty-seven feet overall, loaded with brown sugar, elephant tusks and Indian cloth piled some way above the rail, and we got quite good at skipping about on top. A dicey-looking dinghy perched nonchalantly over all. Dolphins played round the bows and we were only a few feet above them as they rolled, sometimes in glorious unison as if they had learned every movement for a chorus.

Uhuru

At the end of the summer holidays in 1963, Satan travelled to England with Julia, taking her back to school and himself attending a conference in London to determine the date of independence for Zanzibar. To his dismay it was fixed for 10 December, giving everyone just three months to get organised for this great happening. The reason was because the Duke of Edinburgh was 'doing' Kenya a few days later and it would be convenient for him to 'do' us on the same trip. Satan was very bitter because he knew the people were not ready for full independence. The children had fully expected to come out for Christmas and had not said goodbye to their friends or to the island. I set about making arrangements to meet them in Nairobi instead, and for us all to go on one last safari, and travel home on an Italian liner.

During all our preparations for Independence Day and the Duke's visit and our own departure, we heard of President Kennedy's assassination. We were dining with the American Ambassador and he had ten telephone calls during the meal but never said what had happened until we were leaving, when he told us in an undertone. The next night a dance was being given for us by friends but Satan said we could not go if there was dancing. In the end we went but left after dinner so that the others could dance, but we certainly did not feel like it. Even our driver was mourning loudly as a fellow Catholic.

Farewell functions abounded. I was gradually getting packed up and was amazed at the number of crates. My horror at the Scout rally when I spotted a large copper tray with a deep rim being incompletely concealed by a cub in the second row can be imagined. It was difficult to plaster a delighted smile on my face when it was presented to Satan, and I spent the speeches period mentally squeezing it into box after box. But it was touching to hear some of the things said in speeches; they seemed genuinely fond of us and grateful for help given, and of course we had become fond of them too.

One day we went to the Palace and the Sultan invested Satan with the Brilliant Star of Zanzibar, Class I, quite the grandest decoration, with a broad red sash over the shoulder, a huge star like the KCMG and a neck dangler on a red ribbon. The Ministers gave us a lunch and presented us with a Persian rug from the Residency. They were a little reluctant when we had told their secret envoy beforehand that that was what we should like, as not being new and costing Government money, they felt it was not worthy. It was what we wanted though; Honeybun had had a lot of bones on it and bitten a bit off the fringe and we had had many happy times sitting round it on the terrace in the moonlight – we even saw the first Sputnik going over from there, sitting with one of the Mercury Americans who had in his pocket a piece of the silver fabric of which it was made. At the last minute it was discovered that the Sultan had done nothing about getting a present for Prince Philip. Being urged, he bought a large Arab silver coffee pot, and to Satan's horror when he presented it, he presented an identical one to Satan!

Arrangements were extremely difficult. The Zanzibaris were really already independent and the Sultan was able to have the last word on all matters. All the countries who were to be represented in Kenya thought they might as well send their chaps to Zanzibar as well, with the result that every bed in the capital must have been full. We had the Duke of Edinburgh to stay for two nights, and four of his staff, plus Duncan Sandys, the Secretary of State for the Colonies (and the villain of the piece as far as we could see). This accounted for our three spare rooms, Satan's dressing room, and the housekeeper's flat, she having left a week or two earlier under a cloud. We kept trying to discover whether Sandys' wife was accompanying him, to make room for her at functions, but a few hours before they arrived we received a signal that she was not, but his daughter was! We hurriedly made a room habitable in the tower, but it had no bathroom and the nearest was mine (which Satan was sharing) so she elected to share her father's room.

The Duke was a very easy guest. Everyone wanted to meet him but the Sultan was allotting all his time to events away from the Residency, and was not having women present anyway. The Duke had dinner with us on the evening of the ceremony itself, but had a long reception to attend first at the Palace, and then had to dash back to bath, change and eat, before changing into uniform for the ceremony at the parade ground. I managed to squeeze in a coffee party on the second morning so that a few women could meet him, otherwise I felt I might have been lynched.

Celia Sandys and I were incarcerated in the purdah tent beside the great dais for the men during the ceremony, so at least I was not subjected to the emotional sight of the Union Jack being lowered, which I had seen in Uganda. The Dowager Sultana threw back her *buibui* to reveal a daring décolletage on a spangled, gold satin dress underneath. All went well except for the Prime Minister's speech which was very long and had to be given in two languages. The Navy, the Army and the local Mobile Police (who were very smart) were in the parade and when they unfurled the flags they fired a *feu de joie* which for the first time, after numerous rehearsals, went off simultaneously. After all that we had to trail along to the Palace at 1 a.m. to watch the fireworks display over the sea, which was lovely but dragged on far too long; Celia and I were again banished to the ladies' apartments until the Duke managed to get us released.

Next day after the coffee party, the Duke went with Satan to an exhibition and had lunch at the Palace. We all swam together in the afternoon and we saw him off from the house after tea, as we had to change for our own ceremonial departure. I gather he had a pretty quiet send-off at the airport as everybody was in town to see us off.

Leaving was the saddest occasion; not only was Satan's career at an end, and a period of satisfying toil for both of us, but we strongly felt that we, representing Britain, were leaving a country insufficiently prepared for independence. The crowds lining the street this time were immense, as many people had come in from the countryside for the celebrations; again they were mainly silent, but cries such as 'Thank you' and 'Come back again' made us feel it was a more personal occasion. Satan, a very modest man, had reluctantly decided we should leave with pomp; it had not been understood when a governor elsewhere had left without, and we felt Britain must be seen to be going with head held high.

Satan was in full uniform and I in the charcoal grey linen suit that nobody saw me arrive in, and a flame flowered hat. At the quay, which is cobbled, a guard of honour of police was lined up and Satan inspected them and they played our national anthem for the last time. The Deputy Commissioner of Police was beside me and muttered: 'Very moving' and I was so moved anyway that I snarled back:

'Shut up.'

A long line of VIPs stood with their backs to the sea to shake our hands, including Arabs in tears, two previous British Residents and Lord Twining, Ministers, Duncan Sandys, and the Chief Justice and his wife with her leg in plaster from our last shelling expedition when she stood on a sting-ray. When we got to the end we could only wave to all the others who crowded round, then the band played 'Will ye no come back agen' as we went down the steps to stand in the launch out to the frigate HMS *Eskimo*. The sailors stood at attention all round the decks and she was dressed over all. We set sail through a flotilla of little yachts from the Sailing Club, and as we crossed their finishing line they rang the usual bell – we remembered that the last time that had happened to us, we were clinging to our boat which had just turned over as we crossed the line to win! It was hard to bear as the seventeen-gun salutes were exchanged from ship to shore, and Satan gave me the job of counting the explosions so that he could stop saluting in between the seventeenth and the first of the reply, and so that I should not cry. We wondered what would become of this charming island and its people.

The Navy treated us marvellously. I slept in the Captain's cabin, Satan in the First Officer's. They presumably stood up all night. They showed us a Maurice Chevalier film which was cheerful. In the morning we arrived at Mombasa harbour where the Captain incurred the wrath of the harbourmaster because he performed a grand swish to turn the ship around and anchor alongside the jetty, nearly carrying said jetty away. From all this pomp we descended in our safari gear to get into a Land-Rover with an army driver and set off for the Serengeti Game Park.

Exactly a month later, as we arrived home at Duncannon after the Tsavo Game Park with the children and the sea trip back to England, the telephone rang to say there had been a revolution in Zanzibar. The Foreign Office were in constant touch for a time, wanting to know who this person was and who that, and Satan had to go to London and help the deposed Sultan with his arrangements. Great confusion reigned as to what exactly happened. It would seem that a man called Okello, who had been a boat boy at the Sailing Club for a short time recently, had been Cuba-trained and had managed to foment the revolution. A well-planned raid in the middle of the night had given the revolutionaries possession of the Police Armoury, so the only defensive force the Government had left (for the British troops had been withdrawn in spite of the Sultan's pleas) was almost helpless, though many of them put up a good fight, and enabled the Sultan and his family to escape. It was reckoned that there had been treachery in the local Police Force, many of whom were not Zanzibaris. So many Arabs were killed, probably about 15,000, including quite a number we knew well, and the killings were very brutal. Our own Arab ADC was in England on a course but returned at once and was arrested at the airport and imprisoned. His father had been killed in front of his family, his mother went out of her mind, his wife was in a concentration camp with her four children and her teenage sister-in-law. Many Arabs were deported in overladen dhows, some of which sank. The stories we heard caused us much distress, and a film we saw months later, taken by a German airman, proved that certainly a lot of it was true: lines of prisoners guarded by armed men trooping out to the countryside, mass graves already lined with corpses of both sexes, bodies floating in the sea to which they had fled. Europeans were not in general molested and none were killed: the issue was between the Arab rulers and the African 'underdogs'.

In fact our impression when we were there was that the average man in the street was reasonably contented with his lot. People everywhere need to grumble and say the government does not know what it is doing, and of course all their circumstances were not ideal. But I do not think most of them wanted an uprising and, when it happened, I feel sure most of them were appalled, and even the revolutionaries must have been surprised to find themselves, if anything, worse off. Freedom was not what they had expected. It was an externally-engineered disaster, a great tragedy. All the work of so many dedicated people, to build the protectorate up into a country able to govern itself in the modern world, was shattered in a few hours.

I had insisted that the British Red Cross should send a Field Officer out to help the local committee which I felt was not yet ready to stand alone. She arrived before I left and my heart sank. Janet Adam was a decorative widow, upper class, and I did not expect her to be good in an emergency. In the event she was superb. Woken in the small hours to go and help with casualties in the hospital, she was later asked to drive to a shop on the outskirts of the old Stone Town and buy up all the bread they had. With one old servant she did this but on the way back was stopped by a gang of cutthroats who started on the bread that was stacked on the roof rack – they were hungry after the bloody deeds of the night. Calmly she began on the Swahili salutations she had been learning:

'Good morning.' 'How are you?' 'How is your wife?' etc.

Finally she said, 'Please don't eat this bread. It is for the hospital.'

This had no effect but when she said it was for the Red Cross they stopped, even putting half-eaten loaves back. They knew about the Red Cross because of the work of that nurse who helped the handicapped around the island. After three days Janet was brave enough to beard the new President in his office, where he sat behind his desk with nothing on it but two guns, and she told him that he must take action because there would be deaths and pestilence if the unfortunate Arabs penned in concentration camps were not fed, watered and properly accommodated. He invited her to sit on his Council and advise them what to do, and she did so for a week.

'Freedom' did not mean that the night-soil men need no longer work. Water and doctors were sent daily to Prison Island (Oh, the lovely picnics we used to have there!) where many men had been dumped with nothing to eat but the giant tortoises, and with no water. The TB patients and lepers were taken from the camps and reinstated in their previous homes. The other prisoners were sorted out and either sent to their homes or put on dhows to go to Oman. Our ADC's family were sent to Pemba, where his wife came from, and were sadly persecuted. They would be taken out at night and made to dance (they were all women) which is something they would never have done. Food was extremely short and the wife would go out into the fields looking for scraps of roots left by farmers.

Altogether it was a most terrible disaster. More than 15,000 people actually lost their lives, and many more lost their homes. Hideous brutalities were performed (for instance the welfare officer I used to visit with was forced to watch her husband and baby son of two being chopped up before they did the same to her) but no white people were harmed, though several were molested. If, as I have heard said, such shocks can bring on cancer, I would say that could have been the cause of Satan's final illness. It was a sad ending to his career.

Seven years later, after Satan had died, I went to Mauritius as a Red Cross Field Officer, and on my way took the opportunity of looking up some Arabs then living in Dar es Salaam. Satan had been beavering away about their pensions, as the British Government had said they would pay them if the Zanzibar Government failed to do so. The Arabs concerned did not communicate and I decided to go and see if the pensions were coming through: it was an excuse to see if they were all right and to show them that they were not forgotten.

One was the ADC, Issa, who had been on a course at the time of the revolution, another had been the Senior District Commissioner. The pensions had just begun to come; one of them had received his first payment. But I was saddened by the fear they lived in. The DC came and sat in the car I had been lent by the High Commissioner, with a driver, and talked drivel for thirty-five minutes. I found later he thought the driver might have been a spy. Issa would not even get into the car but later came to the High Commission and offered to show me the new university; driving slowly round and round the campus in his car, we were safe from eavesdroppers and he spoke freely of the persecution they were experiencing in all directions, lowly jobs only being available, their children not allowed to attend secondary school and so on. He was horrified at the free way, when he had come to fetch me, that the High Commissioner had spoken and questioned him with servants within earshot, and possible spies in the dark garden beyond the open windows, and was resentful that he had not been received upstairs in the airconditioned, and therefore soundproof, flat. One evening he invited me to his tiny house, and was waiting at the gate when I arrived in my borrowed car; he asked me to dismiss the driver and said he would take me back. When I entered the little house, I found it stuffed to bursting point with Zanzibaris who seemed overjoyed to see me; it was very heartwarming but, as they kept all the windows closed for privacy, it was also very bodywarming!

I had intended to stay with a South African couple, John and Lorna Cameron, who had been in Zanzibar with us and who had a flat in Dar es Salaam as well as a house in Zanzibar. Because of a postal strike I did not hear that the flat had been given up and that, if I wanted to see Lorna, I would have to go to Zanzibar where she was still working. At that time one had to give nine days' notice or go in as a day-tripper: I only had three days and I refused to go as a day-tripper. I asked Lorna to telephone the revolutionary President, Abeid Karume, who knew me quite well as he was leader of the opposition in our day, and ask for special permission. She was very much afraid but after much difficulty managed to speak to him, and as I expected he said of course I could visit. She asked if he wanted to see me – he hesitated and then asked if I wanted to see him; she naturally, in her fear, said yes. So when I arrived I was taken to the Residency, by then 'State House', to call. He was not living there but received visitors and probably had an office there. Barbed wire had sprung up on all the high garden walls and a platoon of armed men guarded each gate instead of the two ceremonial guards we used to have, and all the grass around the gates had been worn away by them.

We sat on dreadful brightly-coloured plastic sofas in the once gracious hall, with many other waiting people, but when I whispered to Lorna that I would not stay more than ten minutes she said, 'Oh you must!' and she was so upset I knew I must. However, we were not kept more than a minute and were taken up the lovely old stone staircase on an unnecessary red carpet, to coffee on the boiling hot veranda. Karume had always been entertained there, though in the evening at receptions, so received me at the top of the stairs and did likewise. He was very affable and told me of his new daughter, who I knew was born of a Parsee girl who was one of many forced into African beds because they had white skins. I asked if his people liked the high-rise flats he had had built across the golf course, and he said they loved them; I expressed surprise as English people who are taken from ground-level living usually hate high-rise flats. I could see the ballroom was filled with more plastic sofas and electric yellow edge-to-edge carpeting, and enquired what had happened to all the antique French and English furniture and Persian rugs.

'In the museum in Dar es Salaam.'

I knew this was untrue as I had just been there. I commented that he was still using ERII china and he laughed and said he had kept it to entertain me to coffee. He was not a bad man really, we had always quite liked him, a rugged fisherman, but he was put into the position of President by the revolution and had to do what he saw fit, which was unenlightened. Cameramen and journalists were covering the meeting and reported next day that we had discussed our former lives. I was very glad to leave.

I visited the nuns at the Cathedral and amongst other things was told that the flats were a disaster. The Africans who moved in had no idea about refrigerators, electric cookers and push-and-pull plumbing; they soon discovered how the plumbing worked and were very pleased, putting all their rubbish down, so quite soon it did not work. At the end of the first month they were not so pleased to get bills for electricity and water, which they ignored and the services were cut off, so their state was far worse than before. They had to go down and up stairs to fetch water from a distant tap, and to collect wood to make fires on the concrete floors (once they had burnt up all the parquet). A corner of each flat was used to relieve nature when it was too much trouble to go out, with the result that sewage seeped from floor to floor. The nuns knew, because they went to help old Christians clean their rooms each week.

We went shopping just so that I could see what was available. There seemed to be no market, but a row of State shops had sprung up. There was no rice for sale, no soap, very few vegetables, but there were cornflakes, brandy and tinned peaches at a price nobody could pay even if they wanted such things. In one shop a girl lay asleep on the counter and when I poked her and asked for rice she opened her eyes, said, 'Come back tomorrow' and went to sleep again, but I was told there had been no rice, the staple diet, for over two weeks. We met two East German women who looked at me angrily, knowing me for a stranger, and it seemed to me wondering what I was up to. The lovely old Stone Town, once so busy and filled with interesting as well as useful shops, now stood shuttered and unkempt. It was a sad day.

Very soon after the revolution, I started the Zanzibar Association, which is open to all Europeans who ever worked there, and which meets once a year in London for a meal and to exchange news; the secretary puts round a newsletter to all the members whether they can come to a meeting or not. I ran it for five years and then handed over to Joyce Dickson, Satan's ex-Private Secretary. At the time it was a great comfort to many people, especially to those serving in Zanzibar, whether actually there or on leave, at the time of the revolution, during which some had experienced unpleasant things. They felt displaced, unwanted and shocked, and this gave them a feeling of being part of something. Even when all that was over, we enjoyed meeting each other, and as the years rolled by many of the younger generation began to come, remembering their childhood time in that lovely country.

In spite of the great sadness which overcame us in the end, I would not have missed our four years in Zanzibar for anything. They were worrying times, but one felt we were all together achieving a decent goal; the fact that it turned out differently does not change the nature of those years of hard work, hard play, great satisfaction at the time, and happiness.

CHAPTER 5

Suffolk I
1964-1971

IN THE COLONIAL SERVICE the retirement age was fifty-five, though occasionally this was extended; in Satan's case, had his five-year contract as British Resident Zanzibar not been cut short by independence after four years, he would have been fifty-six. As it was, when he retired he was fifty-five and I was forty-five, so we felt there was a good deal of life before us. In fact, we had five more years together, most of which were good.

The first thing we did, however, was traumatic – we sold Duncannon. Satan had become chairman of the Civil Service Commission which entailed three days' work every two or three weeks, but it always took him away for five days because of the travelling. He envisaged other part-time jobs and wanted to do them, but did not want to spend more time away from home than necessary. Also, of course, he realised that it was hard work living at Duncannon, everything having to be carried up or down that wicked hill, no rubbish collection or milk delivery, collecting the coal himself by boat, no village woman willing to come and help me in the house, and so on. I felt as if a part of my heart had died as we toiled up the hill for the last time, and I wept as never before. Until that moment the move had been so extraordinary that one did not have time to dwell on it. We had to move the contents of the house by river, and a barge duly arrived and tied up alongside the wall; the jolly men fetched and carried and laughed and were fed all day, and then said they could not complete that day because the tide was going down and they would be stranded; so they left the beds and completed the next morning.

We had found a good house in Suffolk, having looked in areas within easy reach of London and near at least one lot of good friends. Satan knew and favoured East Anglia, having spent holidays at the coast as a child, and John and Gwyneth Phillips (she was Julia's godmother) lived at Stowmarket not too far from our village of Earl Soham. Moat House stood on top of the 'hill' going down to the village; we laughed at calling it a hill but soon got used to the flatter landscape. We had six acres of blackcurrants but they had black spot and had to be rooted out; we let the two fields to an adjacent farmer, one as arable and one as pasture, which much improved our view. There was an orchard and barns, a large garden and a pond which was part of the moat. The house itself was L-shaped, one wing being Tudor and the other early nineteenth-century. We had five bedrooms and three bathrooms, an enormous kitchen, three good reception rooms and a small study for Satan. There was a cottage next to it, in which we housed an old shepherd and his wife who were turned out of their house opposite by their employer, when his wife was killed hunting and he wanted to move house. They were offered an inferior cottage in the village but preferred to come to us. 'Cooker' Calver and his missis were a boon to us; he became our gardener and our mentor (once we mastered his dialect and became used to his 'boogers'), and Mrs Calver, who had been a lady's maid long years before to a literary lady who lived at Moat House, although she would not be employed by us, simply could not keep her hands off. If I went out without doing the washing-up, I would probably come home to find it done; she looked after our animals and the house when we were away; and she became a very dear friend.

So we began our new life. It was a busy one. Julia was at the Godolphin School in Salisbury and William at Canford not far south of it, and they had to be transported to and from each term and at half-term, and we visited at least twice a term and took them out. We both became involved in local affairs, being particularly welcome because we were comparatively young and jobless, and because a busy Army couple were emigrating to Canada and bequeathed to us most gladly their village responsibilities. Thus Satan became the Church Treasurer and a parish councillor and had to take Bingo sessions in the village hall! I became a Rural District councillor for a while but found it to be a useless body by that time. I became President of the WI and Director, and later President, of the area Red Cross which covered Woodbridge, Framlingham, Saxmundham, Leiston and Aldeburgh, and thirty-five surrounding villages. It was very tame work after Red Cross work overseas but helped to form the backbone of the organisation. I also kept a list of blood donors in the area and called them up for six-monthly sessions; and started a club for disabled people called the February Club.

We made new friends and the family began to gather in the area. Pam and Archie bought a house at Grundisburgh for their retirement and in the meantime came there for holidays. Penelope bought a cottage at Framlingham three miles away and got a job at the College. Val and Mervyn Cowie came to stay and became interested and eventually also settled in the area.

We had lovely holidays with the children fast growing up. Twice we went skiing together to Kössen, a little known place in Austria. William won his bronze medal in ten days and Julia gained reasonable proficiency, but Satan and I were really too old; the second year he did not ski and I elected to return to the nursery school, having been frightened out of my wits by the second year school. But it was enormous fun and the family was still a unit. We went to Malta for a summer holiday and nearly bought a house on Gozo.

William travelled out (at seventeen) by hitchhiking, which we forbade a furious Julia to do. She and I took him to the other side of Ipswich one rainy morning and left him there. We sneaked up a side road to see how he got on and we reckoned it was our extrasensory perception which made him put his canvas bag between his feet to protect it a bit as he stood in the downpour in an army forage cap and a depressing plastic mackintosh of Satan's. He was taken up by a milk lorry which we blessed whole-heartedly, and later he was lucky enough to get a Rolls-Royce being driven by a driver to Milan; unhappily William had to wait at Dover for his friend Johnnie, who was also welcome but got there too late and the Rolls-Royce went on without them. After many vicissitudes they reached Milan and could get no further because the laws against hitchhiking in Italy were fierce. They did the rest of the journey by train, third-class, in sizzling heat, packed tight among the shopping mommas. In Sicily they slept the night on the police station steps. When we met them off the ferry in Malta I saw a look on William's face which said: 'Mummy! Food! Comfort! Soap!'

A great adventure happened to us that holiday. In a rocky bay we were swimming with two other teenage boys and a girl, when they discovered an underwater cave leading out of another cave. As I swam into the outer cave, William popped up wild with excitement to tell me about it and to encourage me to go down and see. I was not keen but, when I realised Julia had done it, I felt I had to. It was only about ten feet underwater but along under the rock so it was very frightening, and when I got there only Johnnie was left. The roof was about a foot over our heads and the only light came in from below, from the outer cave. I clung shamelessly to Johnnie crying, 'Don't leave me, I can't breathe!'

I do believe the area was short of oxygen after all those people had been there, and I was breathless too with fear. Johnnie was wonderful and persuaded me that I could get the deep breath needed to dive back again or I should still be there.

Satan had three overseas assignments during this period: to Ghana, to Antigua on a Boundaries Commission, and to the Gilberts on an economics advisory commission. He was away three months at a time and I got on with painting the house inside, with the gardening, and with the storing of produce. He was very ill in the Gilberts, being found crawling along a corridor to find help in the middle of the night, but I never really got to the bottom of it.

We had a good interlude when Satan and I stayed with the Dick Goodwins in Bielefeld where he was the 1st British Corps Commander. The mansion itself was a Nazi gin king's palace. We had the Gloucester Suite, so called since the ducal pair stayed in it; a mirror-lined bedroom (very disconcerting as I found the first day – prancing in from the bathroom with nothing on, I was confronted by six nudes waving suspender belts), a sitting room with balcony and deckchairs, and a dressing room. The place crawled with German maids and British batmen. Satan, however, was not well and had suspected cancer. On our last night we went to the Canadian Regiment's celebration of Canada Day, Beating Retreat and all – it was lovely seeing them in traditional British uniforms, kilts too, playing our tunes and 'God Save The Queen' – they obviously felt very close to us. I sat next to a German colonel and THAT was a funny feeling.

Our last holiday together was to Menorca, and this time Satan did buy a cottage. We were staying with Anna, who had a villa over a lovely little creek, with a stupendous view of a rocky cliff and Arab tower, and after a few days she returned (much the worse for wear and laden down with bottles!) to Sweden, leaving us in possession. The cottage we found was a mile or two away inland, and was a 'farmhouse' but the land had gone; it was quite charming and impractical for us to buy really, but you live and learn. We were delighted with it.

Satan had not been very well for some time and once or twice on this holiday was extremely unwell. Our village doctor, Charles, a great friend, had even thought whatever it was might be in the mind, and I had had that thought myself. When we got back he began on a course of antibiotics but they seemed to precipitate his illness and he began vomiting. We had four dreadful months; twice he went to hospital in Ipswich and there they operated on him. They warned me it might be cancer of the pancreas, but after the operation (during which I remained in the hospital) the surgeon told me it was 'nothing sinister', which was unforgivable: it WAS sinister, so he should at least have been able to say he could not find the cause. Satan came home determined to get better but became steadily worse. I insisted on a second opinion but all they did was take him to a hospital at West Hammersmith, miles from anywhere, which I think now was probably for incurables. Still nobody told us, in spite of Satan actually asking several times if it was cancer. On Christmas Day we had our dinner in the middle of the day, with Ann and Satan's mother who were staying; then the 'children', now nineteen and seventeen, and I drove over to the hospital, nearly four hours, with presents and good cheer. Poor Satan, he tried so hard but he was clearly in a bad way with further symptoms which mystified me. His bed was in an extraordinary alcove like a cupboard and we three had to stand in a row beside the bed.

When we got home, Granny had been taken ill. I knew she had cancer of the colon and I did not call Charles till eight in the morning as he had a wooden leg and one did not call him out lightly. When he had seen Granny I told him about Satan's new symptoms and asked him:

'What IS the matter with him?' and he said:

'My dear girl, didn't you know? He has cancer like his mother.'

I drove straight back to the hospital to bring him home but they would not let me take him; they had tests to do, they said. But what persuaded me was that he would come in an ambulance and I would be fresh to greet him when he arrived. I realised he was dying and wanted that to happen at home, and I realised too that I would have to tell him. His ambulance was delayed for hours in London because of a journey the Queen was making to Sandringham, and I nearly went out of my mind trying to find out where he was. Finally he arrived, looking dead already on a stretcher, but he said to me:

'Please thank the Red Cross man for me.'

Julia was skiing in Austria for a week; I had decided to let her go and not tell her the bad news beforehand, as the doctor had said Satan had about three months to live. In fact he had three weeks. He thought as ever that he was being sent home to convalesce so set himself grimly to the task. Lowering himself with my help into the bath the next night he said fiercely:

'What did that bloody man in London tell you?' and when I at last told him he said:

'This is cancer? My God, what a relief.'

He had guessed that it was, but they had denied it; now that he knew, he knew he would die; he need not struggle and bear this pain indefinitely. He did not leave his bedroom again but almost cheerfully waited for the end. Friends came to be with him the day I went to Harwich to meet Julia, and they said he gave them courage. Julia seemed to me like a brilliant catherine wheel as we drove home, telling me excitedly of all her doings. I had cruelly to cut her down with the news, and she wept, but thereafter was a great strength to us both. For the few days that were left she spent a lot of time lying on my bed next to him, chatting or watching TV and being companionable. William had been at Sandhurst for a year, and came home for one weekend at that time, when he and Satan talked about a sailing trip as if they were going to make it. When I knew the end was near I sent for him again but Satan was in a merciful coma by the time he arrived. The rest of it is either too dear to share or I was too dazed to take it in. Friends and relatives took over and arranged the funeral in the tiny village church. I had not thought of saying family flowers only, and the church overflowed most joyously with colour, which was transferred to billow over his grave. So many people who loved him came, and others wrote me wonderful letters which often revealed things about him that I had not known, thus enriching me further.

*   *   *

It was a bleak time that ensued, though busy of course with business and decisions. The solicitor advised me to sell Moat House and live in a cottage we had recently bought in Aldeburgh, and also to sell the Menorcan cottage – I

William at Sandhurst, 1970.

did neither. I sold the ocean-going yacht Satan had bought the previous summer, and which we had never had time to take to sea. He had been going to sea with friends to learn the ropes of channel-crossing and English waters for several years, and this was one of his dreams that did not come true. I could not manage the boat with both the young away so much. The Aldeburgh cottage was furnished and let, and I stayed on at Moat House for two years, with the devoted Calvers at hand.

Being a widow must be different for each one, not only because they are different people but depending upon the age they are widowed. The hurt must be most intense when one is young, yet recovery should be quicker; when one is old one is half expecting it but the loss of one's long-term companion, with no prospect of a new life of any kind ahead, must be hard indeed to bear. I was fifty and was certainly not expecting it. Our working life was over but we had begun on a new one together. I felt utterly lost. I had been part of a unit that no longer existed so what was I now? I had basked in Satan's love and become used to myself as seen through his biased eyes, but with him gone I was reflected in a thousand eyes, all seeing me differently, and I no longer knew myself. I had to grow into a new person.

So much happened in those two years. First of all came the death of Satan's mother, in the Cottage Hospital in Aldeburgh, only three months after he died, during which time I had a lot of visiting and care to do, and her grief to cope with. Only another three months passed, and my beloved labrador, Jill, went too. Dogs are such close companions, giving their love and utter trust so freely, that I find their death is sometimes a greater loss than some human deaths; in this case, we had both lost Satan and she was a great comfort to me. We had adopted her after the death of her master, and she had become a great friend, too, to old Honeybun; Honeybun had been flown from Zanzibar and undergone quarantine most stoically, and emerged into a new world. She was rather alarmed by country life and was sure that all these rabbits were the leopards her mother had warned her about (in fact one of her siblings was taken by a tiny Zanzibarian leopard when they were still with the mother). Jill cheerfully disabused her of such fancies, and taught her to work a hedge with her, one on each side, in a most workmanlike way. Two walks a day with them had helped me to keep my balance.

Basil's wife Doreen, too, was ill and I feared the worst, though kept telling myself I was being morbid because of my loss. I had their three children to stay several times, disturbed because of the upset in their lives and their father's distress. Hers was a particularly painful and ghastly cancer and it was a relief not only for her when she died that December. The care of the children, and the comforting of Basil as far as one was able, did help to keep my mind off my own troubles.

The May after Satan's death I went to Menorca with the Phillipses to furnish and generally see to the cottage we had bought there. We drove down, as Satan and the young and I had done the year before, and crossed from Barcelona on the overnight ferry. Driving aboard that ferry was heart-stopping up two planks! The cottage was difficult to furnish because of the restrictions on the amount of money one was allowed to take, but John and I used to go 'totting' to the dump every day with a load of tins and bottles we were clearing from the garden, and I would pounce on quite good items of furniture there which I transported gleefully back to the cottage.

William graduated from Sandhurst and to my horror was posted to Northern Ireland in the Royal Anglian Regiment, 1st Battalion. Julia was to take a secretarial course in Cambridge in two languages, utterly refusing to go to university.

In August she left school and persuaded me to take her and no fewer than nine of her friends to Menorca. I took Penelope, too. There was an annexe to the cottage which she and I shared, which had the only bathroom in the place at that time. We arranged for the girls to sleep upstairs and the boys down, taking it in turns to sleep on the floor because there were not enough beds, and I believe it was a good clean time! The girls were all eighteen and the boys twenty and there were two sets of brother and sister. They hired two little Seats and would drive off with one in each car sticking up through the roof. Penelope and I hired a moped, a great heavy fat thing which Penelope could not manage so she rode pillion. The village was much entertained when I rode up and down with the teacher riding pillion; good wives stood knitting at their gates and the men tried not to look interested from their doorsteps. The only difficulty was I had to kick start it before Penelope got on or her leg was in the way, and then I had to keep the engine going while lowering the machine sideways far enough for her to get her little leg over. We mastered the technique in the end.

When Julia finished her course she set off instantly for Menorca with two other girls in a second-hand Mini they had clubbed together to buy – Julia had £100 from savings I had made for her from Family Allowances over the years; (William too had spent his on a car but an MG Sports which gave endless trouble and was always letting him down, but it was the 'image'). I could hardly believe how much stuff the girls packed into that diminutive vehicle, with me contributing useful kitchen equipment, and at the last minute Julia came staggering out with a box of books. When I remonstrated she said:

'Well, if we haven't got boys, we must have books.'

They returned a week early because their money ran out and they were hungry. However, Julia announced that she was in love with a Menorcan and was returning to live in our cottage. She was of age and I could not stop her; all I could do was to go too and make sure the cottage was fit to live in in the winter. I knew that at that time, feeling her wings, she would not stay if I settled in too; I had to let her go. An absolutely dreary three months ensued when Julia took on jobs of utter unsuitability, according to my book, mostly at night, and I did battle with Spanish authorities for permissions, for electricity, for heating etc.

Christmas Day was light relief. The family of Julia's boyfriend invited us to lunch. The father ran a jewellery factory and I quite approved of the friendship which was heavily chaperoned. The young man had younger siblings who were always present in their drawing room, and the grandmother lived on the ground floor and supervised the hall. He would not have dreamed of taking her to a nightclub or a disco. Christmas lunch bore signs of an old English influence. We ate sole first with absolutely no sauce or garnish. Then a huge turkey was put on the table and Señora attacked it across its breastbone with a colossal knife. Sprouts and potatoes were served by a little maid but not a drop of gravy. Things livened up a bit when an aunt, who had broken a leg and had it in plaster, caught fire under the table from the charcoal burner it is customary to have to keep warm; because of the plaster she did not notice until she was truly ablaze. The last course was sticky iced cakes in various shapes

Julia in Mauritius, 1972.

and colours. Conversation was sticky too, as their English was not good and we were learning Spanish; I still am but Julia became bilingual.

She had grown into a beautiful girl and I was very loath to leave her alone in Menorca but there seemed nothing else to do. I felt doubly bereft as, on top of losing Satan, both the young had flown the nest. William in Northern Ireland was having a pretty grisly time as a platoon commander but at least it was real soldiering, and although he grumbled a lot, he was doubtless aware that he was becoming a man sooner than many of his contemporaries. Sandhurst had been tough enough; he was one of the last required to stay there two years. An incident he told me of in his first term always stuck in my mind. He shared a room with a Kenyan called Okello (coincidentally like the leader of the Zanzibar revolution), who suffered terribly from the cold; he smelt abominably before long as he refused to strip in order to change his underclothes. William made it his business to do it for him. Then, in a particularly cold November when snow lay on the ground, they were ordered in pairs to dig themselves a trench long enough to lie down in and deep enough to stand up in, and there to live for three days. William being 6'3", their trench was longer and deeper than most and he had to do all the digging. They were given rations and a primus stove, and were required to go on patrol every so often. Okello just resigned himself to death and would do nothing. William was unable to make him go on patrol, thus getting his circulation going, or to eat or drink, and in the end had to report him for fear he should die. The colonel came and insisted on Okello coming out and walking with him, and told William in the meantime to heat him some soup; forced to drink it, Okello threw up, and the authorities decided that this boy was unable to stay the course and he was sent home. On other occasions the men had to dive through a culvert fully clothed, a sergeant above waiting to drag them through if they failed to emerge; and the one I should have hated most was crawling through a tunnel one behind the other, so little headroom that William, being so big, could not crawl but had to wriggle, his head near the boots of the man ahead, the next man pressing up behind.

He had rowed for Canford, and Sandhurst wanted him to row for them, but he went in for the pentathlon, doing very well: riding, shooting, swimming, running and fencing. He became a very good orienteerer. He had hated his preparatory school, being really too young to have been torn from his family and being a rather gentle child; Canford, he was surprised to find, he enjoyed. He achieved two A levels with great slogging, and failed a third which he tried for again at Sandhurst but really did not have the time. He was a keen sportsman and academic work was a necessary evil. I do not think one could say he enjoyed Sandhurst, but it was a great challenge and he always rose to challenges. The first of note was when he wrote from school aged eight:

'I have got the school skiping (sic) record, I have done 1,361 skips.'

We noticed at once an improvement in what he spelt as his 'Fortnight Liorder' in classwork, which had been extremely disappointing before that. When this fell sharply about two years later, we looked at one another and felt sure somebody had beaten the 'skiping' record. Sure enough, after several weeks we were told that it had been stolen from him but now he had got it back. Once more his classwork improved. Years later as a lieutenant in Cyprus, he trained several Army teams of three each to run the thirty miles up Mount Olympus and the thirty miles back, competing against police teams, UK, Greek and Turkish Army teams. He was just determined the British Army was going to win and they did, first, second and third prizes. His own team came first, in spite of one of his three spraining an ankle and having to be carried by the others; when the second man could no longer manage to run and also help support the third, William carried the man for the last few miles.

In Londonderry at a ball he met a girl for whom he fell; he danced with her throughout the evening, and took her home, and fell into his own bed in a happy daze. Next day he was appalled to find he could not remember her surname, nor the name of the road where she lived. He therefore read through the telephone directory, confident that he would recognise the name when he saw it, and he did, but as it was Starritt he had a great many names to get through! Lyndsay was reading French at Coleraine University and was to go on to do a teacher training course.

Basil was slowly getting his act together. He bought a shop and post office with an old house and garden at Alderton, about twenty miles from both Pam and me. He was sixty-two and it was tough to have to earn a living still, and bring up his family single-handed, but this is what he did. Neither he nor I would have wanted to live together, though we loved one another dearly, and although his establishment was supremely disorganised, the children had their father, and he was a remarkable and erudite man. I went over a great deal to help at first but gradually the children took over on the whole.

Now somebody who knew me well suggested that I should become a Red Cross Field Officer. It was an inspired suggestion and I knew at once I should like to be one, as I had met several when working in Africa and knew the sort of work they did. I applied to the British Red Cross and to my delight they took me on and gave me a job in Mauritius for a year.

William came over to visit me before I went, bringing with him Lyndsay Starritt, with whom I could tell he was very much in love and she with him. When they went back to Londonderry he asked her father (ex-Chief Constable of Londonderry) for her hand, which took the old boy aback. When he told me, I said I could not go away for a year without coming over to meet her parents, and to meet Lyndsay again in her role of fiancée. It was rapidly arranged: William said the family insisted I should stay with them. Poor things, the parents were in England and arrived in Belfast on the plane before mine; they hung about for eight hours to meet my plane and we drove back together to their house. This was a tiny three-bedroomed house on an estate, spotlessly clean to such a degree that I thought the sheets must be new, the drawers in my room newly lined, but surely the cooker and the fridge could not be new also? I had yet to learn what fanatically clean people they were, perhaps a Protestant reaction to the easy-going Catholics locally, perhaps a family thing, perhaps even Lyndsay's thing, for it was she who made everything ready for my visit, as she lived at home. She was at Coleraine University, and the parents had only agreed to the engagement on condition that she should complete her degree first, and then take a year's course in teacher training. They would have agreed to anything. I went off to Mauritius then, happy that they would not be getting married before I got back, and that Julia would probably not become bored with Menorca before then. In fact Julia stayed there for five years, but William and Lyndsay married in the summer, at very short notice, and neither Julia nor I were able to get there in time. William was old-fashioned and did not believe in sex before marriage; he had three weeks' leave and she had three months, and they felt they could wait no longer. But it was sad for my family as none of us were there.

CHAPTER 6

Mauritius, Rodrigues, Réunion, Madagascar 1971-1972

M Y BRIEF IN Mauritius was to get the Red Cross there made independent, i.e. a member directly of the International Red Cross and no longer part of the British Red Cross; the country had become independent and it was important that the Society should be too. This entailed seeing that the Society was working along the right lines and was viable, and getting a Bill passed in their Parliament, recognising that they were independent of the Government and answerable only to the International Red Cross. That was the difficult bit.

The year I had there was a very good recipe for learning to be independent again myself. I worked hard and played hard and enjoyed it all enormously. Nothing there reminded me of the sad time I had been through; nobody had known Satan; they might ask if I was widowed or divorced, but that was that. Julia came and stayed for a couple of months, and my sister Pam's daughter Alison also came for a holiday. A little house was found for me which had been a stable in the grounds of a well-to-do Seychellois in Beau Bassin, an area where on the whole Europeans did not live. He, however, had married a very beautiful coloured girl and this is where they lived with their four children. He collected antiques and when he had too many he decorated and furnished the stable; then he did not know what to do with it so both he and I were delighted to be, as it were, put together. It consisted of one room with a kitchen in a cupboard, a bedroom and a staircase up to a 'gallery' where I had Julia and Alison sleeping; and there was a bathroom. I had a small car with 'Red Cross' emblazoned on the sides, and a desk in the Red Cross office in Curepipe.

I found the organisation was running very well, and quite according to the rules. It needed a source of income and I was not happy about the level of nutrition in the island. The one instruction headquarters had given me was not to feed the people, but it was their greatest need! It was due in large part to poverty but also to the people not recognising the value of the foods available to them. They did not fish, and they considered that guavas and pawpaws, which grew wild around their huts, were bad for their coughs (and pawpaw is so rich in vitamin C). If they ever had a chicken to eat, Father was given first go and ate his fill, handing the rest to the children. The mother was lucky to get any, but she did not know that boiling the carcase would result in a nourishing basis for soup. I therefore embarked on a health and hygiene programme which included nutrition, and wrote a simple booklet on the subject for Red Cross workers to use. I also persuaded two hotels to supply soup kitchens outside their premises with their kitchen waste, one not including pork (for the Muslims) and one not including beef (for the Hindus). Other hotels sent their waste to piggeries. I felt that organising this was not contrary to instructions and it was not using Red Cross funds.

To make the Society viable I suggested a Nearly New Shop on the lines of an Army Thrift Shop, one of which there was on the island. I found out how it was run and told the Indian Red Cross ladies; that was all I had to do. They grabbed the idea from me instantly and before long had three such shops going, everyone swapping saris furiously. They disliked being seen in the same sari too often, so for those short of sisters to swap with, these shops were a godsend.

Getting the Bill through Parliament was the real headache. The Government wanted to take delivery of the dried milk which was sent from UNICEF, but we knew that it would then be unlikely to reach the poor for whom it was intended; somehow it would find its way on to the black market and those who could pay would benefit. In any case, the rules of International Red Cross are that they are an independent body working for the benefit of the needy. I finished all the legal work and prepared the documents for signing but those I had to meet were adept at vanishing whenever I was nearing my goal. In the end I had literally to sit on the doorstep of a Crown Counsel (luckily he had no back door) to get one signature, and then to visit the Minister of Health, at home with flu, and to sit on his bed and persuade him to sign. And this was several months after my tour ended; I had had my leave, and stopped off for a week in Mauritius on my way to the South Pacific, specifically to get these precious signatures.

I found Mauritius a most fascinating place. Originally it had been unpopulated and the Dutch were the first to arrive in the sixteenth century, but abandoned it as being too difficult to colonise. Then the French came in the eighteenth century, bringing African slaves and planting sugar, and making the place a Department of France. During the Napoleonic wars the British felt they must take Mauritius, although they did not really want it. They abolished slavery which brought on a crisis in the sugar plantations, so they imported Indian labour which was eventually to decide the future of the island, for they multiplied so busily that they became an overwhelming majority. The British pronounced that English should be the official language and that the Governor should be British, otherwise life soon settled back into its accustomed ways. I found when I attended my first Red Cross meeting, slightly apprehensive about my rusty French, that although the meeting was entirely conducted in French, the secretary was taking the minutes in English. I relaxed, feeling that I could ask her afterwards about anything I had not understood. Not so! She could not speak English at all, she only understood and wrote it. There were quite a number of English settler families on the island but the flavour was French, to the extent that even English surnames were rendered in French form, 'Larcher' for instance being pronounced 'Larshay'.

The Indian population was vast and one wondered where they all managed to live, as most of the land was agricultural (sugar mostly). It is dotted with attractive, sudden little mountains in extraordinary formations, which I enjoyed climbing with the Navy or Special Force. The beaches were wonderful; one day I saw two French boys drive a shocking-blue beach buggy at seventy mph along the shore, towing a superb skier on a surf-board. Where in the world today could one find such a run of beach with nobody ON it? I also learned to waterski properly; I had had a few tries in Malta but was not proficient. However, I went too far and tried to mono-ski, and unluckily for me the ski was old and split when I managed to achieve my aim, and I was precipitated with terrific force on my head – down, down it seemed for ever. I was winded and when I came up all I could do was grab my bathing dress from round my ankles and float until rescued. This accident resulted in a neck injury and the aggravation of my old riding injury in the back. I spent weeks in traction in hospital where Julia tended me wonderfully, and friends revelled round my bed in the evenings with whisky and baskets of fruit.

When I left hospital I was kindly invited to stay with the Larchers, he a sugar baron and she the owner of several antique shops. It was interesting indeed to see their way of life. Their old wooden bungalow was vast and dark and richly furnished, the gardens dark too, with huge trees. Servants abounded and were part of the establishment; they and their families lived and died on the compound, caring for and being cared for by the family. Not only were there house servants and gardeners, but a carpenter, a plumber, a mechanic and so on. Pam Larcher, with high blood pressure, started the day lying in a gorgeous carved four-poster, correspondence she was dealing with lying all over it, phoning, shrieking to servants at the ends of the house who cheerfully shrieked back, doors open in all directions, her husband Jean and me passing through in anything from night attire to Red Cross uniform to city pinstripe, in order to get to the only bathroom. All sorts of people were received in her bedroom; one day I found an American professor stretched out on the daybed with a cushion over his face, waiting for a lull when he could ask who was coming to dinner to see if he wanted to come. Half an hour later and she'd be receiving in the bath – but not him perhaps!

Much alcohol was consumed and entertaining done. They also had a seaside bungalow for weekends. Pam was English, he French, and you never knew which language they would choose to speak in.

One of the most interesting facts about the island concerned the Chinese. All the children went to the same schools, English, French, Creoles (French/African mixes), Indians, Chinese, and Africans. Monotonously first in everything and winners of all the scholarships were the Chinese, in spite of their crowded living conditions. Next would usually come the Europeans from their privileged homes and educated backgrounds, not valuing their scholastic opportunities. Next came the Indians, who lived in the same sort of crowded conditions as the Chinese, who valued education like the Chinese, but who were just not so clever. Finally the Creoles and the Africans were at the bottom – the French blood did not seem to help and even those who lived in the comparative luxury of European compounds could not compete. In the world outside school, the Indians were excellent at figures and trade, and being in the majority of two thirds of the population they formed the Government; so all ministers were Indian but significantly all permanent secretaries, who did the work and knew the answers, were Chinese. In my experience of them, in countries other than their own, I see them as having the best brains, being very industrious, keeping very much within their own communities, and being content with their lot, never striving to take over or dabble in politics, never rioting or complaining.

During this year in Mauritius I also visited the island of Rodrigues, about 350 miles away but a 'part' of Mauritius. The ten days I spent there were strenuous but of enormous interest. At that time there was no airport, though they were beginning to build one, so one went by the only outside contact, a rusty, old, monthly steamer, if the sea was navigable; on my visit the steamer was fourteen days late. It was loaded with goods for the island, a relief doctor and a missionary, among others who needed to go.

The island is nine by five miles but teems with life and the usual Government officers. They have dreadful cyclones so they had Red Cross there, the only voluntary organisation. I trundled round the island by Land-Rover visiting the nine schools, each with six to eight hundred children, the hospital, the community centre, and the airport in-the-making (what a labour) out of coral. There was a cocktail party, a lunch and an allnight dance which was a wow. There were too many men so there was no nonsense about trying to keep a female to yourself – anyone was free to ask you to dance whether he knew you or not; etiquette demanded that he left you stranded in the middle of the floor when the music stopped, to show he was only interested in having somebody to dance with. The community was so small that if you had a party everyone came, invitation or not.

The people were very healthy and lived very much easier lives, I felt, than

those on the main island because they had more room, and most worked on
the land, but they did suffer severely from the cyclones. There was one family
with a persistent gene that produced bald children, and a wig had been sent via
me for one of the adolescent girls. It was a great success; I had thought it
would be terribly hot to wear but everyone was so keen to have a go that
certainly while I was there nobody had a chance to get too hot in it.

Two young ornithologists were visiting, a Kenyan and a Scot, looking for
two birds peculiar to Rodrigues, one of which was supposed to be extinct.
During their last two days they found two nests, so were cockahoop. I played a
card game called Hearts with them and the young agricultural officer Jacques
Brown. He was a great character. His grandparents were English and he spoke
English properly but was a French Mauritian, educated in Rhodesia and at
California University. He was virtually King of Rodrigues. The real king was
an elderly Creole magistrate who lived in the Residency but Jacques never
agreed with him and always won, and built roads and bridges, took a census,
started a farm school, knew everything about the place and everyone turned to
him. He was, into the bargain, charming, musical, he painted, had good books
and good food, and played chess. He was not as much as thirty. He returned to
Mauritius on the same trip with me, Julia arrived the next day and he duly fell
for her, but to my chagrin she was not interested. The last I heard of him he
had become a monk.

On the return trip the ship was loaded with the island's exports: onions,
goats, cows, chickens, pigs etc. It worried me to distraction because of the poor
animals. Cows were swung up on straps over the hold, sometimes long
minutes while space was cleared for them; goats were slung in unceremoni-
ously, several from a basket, and you wondered how on earth none were
damaged (none were). Fowl of all kinds were crammed into cages on deck and
I spent my time moving them out of the sun; I learned that they were
crammed like that so that they could not break their legs if the cages were
mishandled. But worst of all were the pigs: they were parcelled up individually
in banana leaves, just their snouts projecting, and were stacked four or five
deep in two rows back to back, one lot pointing out to sea, one in-board, and
when you went by they cried out for help most piteously. In thirty-six hours
they were not given food or water, but were sprayed once or twice to cool
them, and at journey's end they were rolled along the quay to their transport. I
really wept over them. Jacques and I and the Captain argued furiously about
improving ways of transporting these poor creatures. Apparently they had to
travel live because the recipients wished to see them slaughtered according to
their customs. My idea that they should have abattoirs in Rodrigues and
transport them refrigerated was not greeted as the answer; a refrigerated ship
had been used once but nobody would accept the meat, and nobody cared

enough to spend money on building the necessary abattoirs and providing the approved supervision in Rodrigues itself.

A visit to the Seychelles did not do much for the Red Cross. I really learned the meaning of the phrase 'laid back' when I was there. The Red Cross existed, oh yes, but I could discover nothing that they did. The French director and his very intelligent doctor wife, who had been a member of the previous government, were hard put to it to amuse me. They took me to a 'cocktail' and to a dance (not fundraising) and arranged lunch for me with the Governor, Humphrey Greatbatch. I had to insist on visiting the hospitals and going round with the Health Visitor to see what the needs were.

It was a much hotter place than Mauritius because it is a large granite mountain with a little ledge running round it bearing a road, and the houses hook on where they can. The beaches are gorgeous, all sand with nothing sharp or horrid, the sea clear and going deep at a civilised angle, with a few great granite boulders here and there, easily seen through the clear water – the beaches fringed with breadfruit trees, mangoes and palms. The people are a wonderful mix from European to negro and all stations in between in all classes. French is the main language.

Julia's arrival in Mauritius was a great event in my life. I had quite a time getting her out of the airport as she arrived unvaccinated and without the compulsory return ticket so was very nearly returned on the same plane. She looked marvellous, her hair a gorgeous sun-bleached gold. It was the day of the Red Cross Ball in which I was, of course, heavily involved. She was 'into' hot pants which were really not quite the thing in Mauritius, however stunning she looked in them. Her 'wardrobe' could be described as tired and unsuitable, and my clothes, needless to say, she would not look at. In the end I allowed her to appear in the only thing she had that did not look as if she'd slept in it for a week, unsuitable though I felt it was: hot pants and a bra and a long skirt split to the waist, white with grey giraffes printed all over it. She took the floor with the son of the Red Cross president and they won the competition for the national dance, the Sega, which she had never done before! However, her experience as a go-go girl dancing on tables in Menorca, whooshing the long yellow hair about, did help.

Next day she started dressmaking all over my stable.

Alison arrived a month later beautifully equipped with all the right clothes. They shared the 'hayloft' in my stables which I had equipped with beds and nets and we all got on surprisingly well, relying heavily on our sense of humour. I protested that for health reasons they should turn out stale food from the fridge and occasionally empty the rubbish bin, and this saying was so hysterically funny to them that it went down in the family lingo. There is even a photograph of Alison sitting in a bathing suit at the edge of the sea, legs stretched out before her, in extremis because there was no cover on the beach, and it is labelled 'for health reasons'.

Meeting Alison had been a marathon, too. Julia and I had been to two drinks parties and out to dinner so would not have been feeling like meeting a plane at 6 a.m. in any case. Into the bargain Julia had a fall and banged her head and when she got home left the front door open accidentally. When I got home I met a furious watchman who said she had done this and his dogs had got in and stolen from the fridge, also open, and subsequently it had leaked water all over the floor. Then came a phone call at 5 a.m. saying the plane was coming in at six, so after a couple of hours' sleep or so we had to rush off, very part worn. At the airport there was a vague statement that the plane would come in between 6 a.m. and 9 a.m. which meant one could not go away. One was not allowed inside the building and there were milling crowds of Indians, the sun already high. When an announcement was made that it was due at 9 a.m. we repaired to a beach about ten miles away where we swam in our pants with our arms nicely crossed over our chests. We had breakfast there with friends, half an hour's snooze, and back at 8 a.m. to the airport, in case it was early. We sat in the car with all the doors open and cooked our hangovers. I have rarely seen so many people together. I had to go to the loo and it was indescribable; only one was Asian and people did not know how to use the others, the floor was under urine and there was faeces on the seats. I used the Asian one as it was cleaner, putting my handbag on top of the high cistern. Then it began to rain. By then we were on the roof watching the arrival and got drenched; Julia without a bra looked indecent and had to do the crossed arms act. Our hair hung dankly and we were pressed in among the Indians. We kept saying:

'There she is!'

'Where?'

'There, in green (or white, or blue).'

'No, it can't be.'

'Gosh, she's got fat!'

'No, that's her in that funny hat.'

'She wouldn't wear a HAT.' And so on.

Finally, when we did see her, we knew her at once. She headed for the customs shed and we for the stairs. Fifteen minutes of terror ensued: I was sure somebody would fall and there would be a massacre, children were almost underfoot and everyone was shoving and a lot of lunatics were trying to go UP for some reason, others just sheltering from the rain as the stairs were under cover. Down below we stood and steamed in the sun, now out again, for half an hour while the police allowed cars through a narrow lane in the crowd and one was not allowed to kiss one's dear one there for fear of holding things up. She duly struggled through, having beaten down the customs officer from £4 to £3.

I had given up having a maid as two had stolen most of my jewellery and one left to have a baby. With both girls coming I had felt we could manage. My job was polishing the floor as I found that an exercise the osteopath gave me was just the action the locals used in polishing the floor: you gripped half a coconut husk in your toes and furiously pushed it about with round actions of the leg.

We had wonderful laughs over Alison being 'The Englishwoman Abroad'. She could not stand creepies and there was a spider (according to her a tarantula) which was after her. She made nightly prowls to make sure he was not near her bed and one night actually hit him, but when she got into bed there he was before her, clearly rather ill, taking shelter by her pillow...Ants I managed to teach her were good but, of course, cockroaches I could not. Dear little lizards gave her fits and when we would tease her about our little shrew she nearly took off. We taught her how to use a snorkel in shallow water over sand, then we took her to a deeper place with coral and much of interest. She went over the side of the boat in my equipment, laughing and excited, and was back in two minutes flat looking white and shaky. She had not seen anything move but did not like what she could see. We took her to see fire-walking and the festival when people stick narrow skewers right through one cheek and out the other, through their lips, and threaded across their chests, apparently feeling no pain. This did not worry her.

Meanwhile, work was rather like swimming in treacle. One never knew when the telephones were going to work and spent hours on them when they did. Interviews took ages because people talked and talked and then did not do what they said they would do until one had been through the performance again and even again. Meetings never took less than two hours. I was trying to get a course for Welfare Officers committed to paper, as London wanted a prototype course for undeveloped countries. I lent all my notes to the local Welfare Officer-in-Chief to add in her Mauritian specialities, and she lost the lot over Christmas. This was a bitter disappointment as I did not have time to start over again.

The American professor friend of Pam Larcher became dangerously ill; he was a professor teaching at the Mauritian University. He had sub-acute pericarditis and left ventricular failure. When I visited him in hospital I was appalled to find that all and sundry were allowed to visit for indefinite periods and he was exhausted. Six students all at once when his temperature was 104 degrees was bad enough, but one woman could not be stopped visiting for an hour every day, leaving him like chewed string. I decided it was my Red Cross duty to mount guard outside his door until he was put into an oxygen tent.

The Chinese doctor kept saying he was better. I asked the Principal of the University, a Frenchman, to cable the professor's brother but later discovered he only sent a letter, and that was after the post office closed for the weekend. I then persuaded the American Ambassador to cable the State Department and ask them to contact his twin sister; that bore fruit and she duly arrived. The hospital staff did their best but it was simply not good enough and arrangements were made to get the man to South Africa. An acute resuscitation expert arrived from England to escort him but was so young (uneducated?) that he thought he was in the Mediterranean. I obtained a visa for the professor for South Africa because nobody else had, and I had to take him to the airport at 4 a.m. because they had not laid on an ambulance. Then I found that they had not cabled his brother who was to have met him in London. The inefficiency which abounded in that island was in this case lethal, and the professor died on the operating table.

Alison had gone and Julia had found a temporary job with Pam Larcher helping in one of her shops and learning the ropes and dreaming of opening one herself. But in the end she left the island a few days before I did. A lot of us went to see her off, helping carry her hand luggage which was a huge Menorcan shopping basket filled with Mauritian handicrafts of great weight which she expected to sell at vast profit in Menorca, plus an airbag containing her worldly goods, almost as heavy. I could not imagine how she could carry them across to the plane and, when she boarded up the steps, the muscles of her legs all the way up to the inevitable hot pants were bulging.

I organised a dress show as a fundraising exercise but also to publicise the embroideries I was fostering among poor Indian women. They could do the work and the designs were their own, but they needed materials and outlets. I designed the clothes for the show and still have two of the garments I modelled myself in the popular role of 'the older model': a tobacco brown evening dress with a V of amber embroidery from neck to waist, and an amber trouser suit with flared sleeves and legs and brown embroidery on their cuffs. The Governor-General and the Prime Minister came so I was quite nervous about it all, and my party of eleven were primed to cheer madly whenever I appeared. I hope that little industry is still in existence.

An invitation to a lunch party at Government House when a Japanese dignitary was being entertained was much enlivened when he found himself obliged to introduce himself around the gathering. Very correctly he stationed himself in front of each person, put his hands together and bowed, saying clearly, 'Fuck you' each time.

Presumably he spelt it Fuku.

One mad exercise I remember was taking twenty little orphan boys on board a submarine; I had two people to help and sailors too, but the boys were like driver ants swarming over everything, and cries of '*Ne touchez rien de TOUT*' had no effect whatsoever.

Everything seemed guaranteed to jam the works if touched but I have never seen such abandoned male confusion. In the torpedo room a bucket hung on one torpedo and an airbag on another, somebody's pants were soaking in the bucket, everybody's shore-going suits were hanging in plastic bags, a box of tomatoes lay on the floor and dirty teacups were everywhere. They put on a film in a room twelve feet square in which, unbelievably, eighteen men slept in bunks three deep. Twenty-three of us and three sailors (one pickled) were jammed in, back to back and belly to belly and they dished out such crazy refreshments as Coca Cola and ice-cream and squashy cakes so that I was soon weeping for Kleenex; this the drunk summoned on the intercom and the driver ants swarmed all over me to get one piece each. They were so deprived of possessions that they were frantic to HAVE something.

I made a survey through the Youth Clubs to find who and where were the children who did not go to school, and why. If they went to school they received free milk, bread and cheese every day. I also found out where the handicapped ones were who could not go to school and those who could not pay the bus fares. Visiting the schools was quite alarming: there might be 600 in one school between the ages of six and eleven, all from one village, in another 800 going in two shifts, and in a few years they would all be breeding, and family planning had not yet got off the ground. I hope that the figures and conclusions I gave to the Government were of help in their decisions.

When I left Mauritius I flew with Pam Larcher to Réunion, a 'department' of France, and stayed there with French friends of hers for four days. They lived high on a mountain with a swimming pool that seemed to be on the edge of the world, with woods and orchards falling away below. Réunion is a remarkable place, being mostly mountains, sometimes rising straight out of the sea, but elsewhere with a small ledge of plains. Where the rock rises from the sea, they have industriously carved a highway out of the rock, and tunnelled a railway twelve kilometres long through it. Three quarters of the population is white, and all colours look most prosperous as France seems to pour money in. It was fascinating in the mountains to see completely white people living like natives. Apparently two hundred years ago there was an economic crisis when the slaves were freed, and the ruined Frenchmen, rather than be seen to work on equal terms by and with their ex-slaves, retreated to farm in the mountains. Their French has deteriorated into an old-fashioned Creole, their children run about naked in the mud round their hovels, no one wears shoes, and their fair or red hair and blue eyes give you quite a shock with their sun-tanned faces. They have hardly intermarried but keep themselves aloof in the heights. Very little seems to be known of what culture, if any, they have preserved. They are supposed to go to school till they are fourteen but it is not enforced and is often too far for the children to go.

An extraordinary happening had occurred just before we got there and I found out when I was taken round the hospital and encountered a very sick man suffering from radiation sickness. He was one of these hill Frenchmen and had been walking on a distant mountain when he saw a curious round flying object land not far away. As he approached it, two figures which had emerged, hastily re-embarked and the UFO took off. He went to inspect the ground where it had been and found a round depression of some size. After an unspecified time, after he got home, he began to be so sick that the family decided they must take him to the hospital where I saw him. The radiation sickness was so severe he was not expected to live. He and his people knew nothing about UFOs.

On I flew alone to Madagascar where I stayed with the British High Commissioner Tim Crosthwait and his wife Anne. He had been the first British High Commissioner in Zanzibar after we left, when, the country being independent, a British Resident would have been inappropriate. Flying over the country was fascinating as it was so different from anything I had seen before. There were a profusion of moated hamlets each one with its own church, and a great deal of forest. The Protestant missionaries had arrived first, but when the Catholics arrived they worked hard to get a foothold wherever their 'rivals' were. The people are of Melanesian origin and have very sweet gentle faces. They all wear straw hats, even tiny babies. Their houses are tall and French-looking, though are made of rose-coloured mud and have mellow tiled roofs with a slight curve upwards at the eaves. Inside they belie their civilised exteriors, being mainly devoid of furniture and having bare mud walls. The kitchens are upstairs as there are no chimneys and they thus avoid kippering those who are sleeping. The High Commission house was on a 5,000-foot plateau netted with serpentine hills and valleys where they grow rice; it is ludicrous to see men and boys apparently fishing in the fields because, if the rice is high, you cannot see the water. The roads were appalling, tarmac with huge potholes, and the driving was to match. Extra hazards were the charcoal carts, drawn by two oxen, looking like little Boer wagons with rounded tops, which were strung out down the roads into the towns; at night they unyoked and camped at the roadside.

On my first morning there I was woken by a bang on the door which I guessed was a servant with my tea.

'Come in!' I said, but nobody came.

Instead I heard Tim shout:

'Good news! Karume's been assassinated!'

Karume was the president thrown up by the Zanzibar revolution and I was not really thrilled by the news as I had quite liked him when I knew him as Leader of the Opposition and did not feel any of it had been his fault.

In Madagascar I met another Mauritian who, like others I had met had, I reckon, been let down by the British. He had worked with the SOE in the war and had been dropped over France to work with the Maquis – the French of such men was a great asset. Even though they have strong French accents, they consider themselves fiercely British, but with the coming of Mauritian independence they lost their British passports; Britain would not allow them to remain British if they insisted on retaining Mauritian nationality as well. The French allowed them to become French and to retain the Mauritian nationality which was essential for them if they were to go on living in the country. I see that immigration has to be restricted but these men had given up eight years of their lives to fight for us, risking losing those lives as so many of their brothers did. They were justifiably bitter.

William had been having a horrid time in Northern Ireland, but it was certainly real life. The snipers were out to get you. One night he led his platoon at the double down a lane in pursuit and a roll of barbed wire had been hurled down, with horrid resulting lacerations for him. Another time a stone caught him on the elbow and he always thereafter had pain when he was writing. The worst part was the feeling of being at war with one's own people, and they could be so awful. Once one of his men on sentry duty was ribbed by two fifteen year-old-girls with vile language and even with obscene handling; he could do nothing but swear at them in return. William was bearded in his office by the father of one of the girls, who said his daughter had been sworn at by the soldier and he wanted an apology. He was most abusive and there was nothing to be done but apologise in the absence of witnesses. He said he could hardly believe some of the gruelling gunfights they had in the City.

He was present at Bloody Sunday that year, and I well recall his record of events. His regiment was in the throes of handing over to the Parachute Regiment but had not actually shown them yet how they would enter a trouble area, skirmishing alternately down opposite sides of a road and covering each other. Furthermore, the Royal Anglians knew all the likely places where a sniper might be, but the Parachute boys did not. In the event the Paras approached a troublesome crowd in a square, marching in a block which no sniper could resist. William was on duty at a road block and heard the first shots which he recognised as being from a Thompson's machine gun, not in use by the army. The Paras, not knowing where the shots came from, shot into the crowd and killed thirteen people. At William's road block a young man was brought, shot across the chest, in charge of a corporal in a requisitioned car. They looked through the boy's pockets (he was about seventeen) and found a nail bomb. He was moaning that he wished he had not joined the march and he would never do it again.

'No,' said the corporal nastily, 'You won't never do it again because you're going to die.'

But he did not die and he gave evidence in court and said that William's lot had planted the nail bomb on him at the road block.

The last party I went to in Mauritius was fairly incredible. It was for Brigitte Bardot and Curt Jurgens. The drive and steps of the Whites' house were lined with 'slaves' wearing long loincloths and bearing flaming torches. Everything matched that idea and it was rather scandalous that so much money should have been spent on a party among a starving populace. Mauritius had helped me very much; I doubt whether I should have 'recovered' so quickly at home. As it was it took twelve years before I felt ready to marry again.

A good friend, widowed two years after I was, apparently found the following dreary letter some comfort and kept it, together with another I was able to write after three years:

> It is a bit depressing when people tell you it takes about two years to get over the death of one's spouse and then to find it does, just about! One feels one should never get over it but the saying that life must go on is so true. The open wound heals over, the scar is left, and occasional twinges of pain, but in spite of the fact that one doesn't operate in the old way, one finds a new way. I reckon I can face the future now. Getting away amongst strangers has helped; I found them looking at me as a complete person, new to them, and in responding to them I began to grow again. At home I was regarded as the bit that was left of our marriage, as poor Patricia.

I did find, though, that it was necessary to discipline myself not to think about Satan. To this day, when I do, the tears well to the surface, so the healing is only skin deep.

CHAPTER 7

The South Pacific 1972-1975

THE SOUTH PACIFIC was indeed another world, completely different from anything else I had ever experienced: a tough assignment in a beautiful setting.

I had had a good leave, staying briefly with William and Lyndsay in Cyprus and with Julia in Menorca. I had reported to Red Cross headquarters to get my new briefing, which was to find and train local people to do my job. Whilst there I had a hysterical interlude with a *Daily Telegraph* photographer; I had not been wearing uniform and the only one in the building that was at all suitable had to be safety-pinned up the back to make it fit, and the skirt pinned low on my hips under the jacket to make it long enough. This tireless man eventually persuaded me to walk down Grosvenor Square like this, saying 'Nobody will know you', which was perfectly true, and that was the picture he chose to print. You would never have guessed.

My new territory was enormous: the Solomon Islands, the New Hebrides, and the Gilbert and Ellice Islands, myriads of small islands covering an area a thousand miles from top to bottom, and all with different cultures. I was based in Honiara, the capital of the Solomons, where I had a little house on stilts, and made sorties of several months to the other two groups each year. I was also asked to visit Tonga, Brunei, Australia and New Zealand and had to go via Fiji on most of the trips, so it was the most interesting, exciting and rewarding time.

Before attempting to find people to do my work, I had to decide what the work should be. In Mauritius, which was working well, it had been finding a means to make them viable, and promoting the teaching of health, hygiene and proper use of available foods, malnutrition being their biggest problem. In the Pacific there was plenty of food; coconuts fell off the trees, fruit trees grew wild, and every family had an allotment where they grew vegetables. Also they were great fishermen, and kept pigs and chickens. To start with, therefore, I went on an investigative tour.

The Solomons
Travelling here was often by very small plane, which I loved as I would sit next to the pilot and enjoy the panoramic views, particularly of the incredibly beautiful blues and greens of the sea, or by diesel-engined cargo boat which

was not easy. The airstrips were often very frightening; land being at a premium, ingenuity was the middle name of the engineers who designed them and they were as short as they could be, with perhaps woodland at one end and a coral cliff at the other, and it was wonderful what skilful use the pilots made of them. Others were simply an open space, a field, with a thatched shelter in the middle, known as the airport building, but with no personnel, and no label. The pilot would find a shady spot to leave a hamper marked perhaps 'Mrs M's meat' and one hoped she would get it before the ants. At one such benighted spot the pilot leapt out and ran round to the luggage compartment, only to find he had taken my case out at the last stop. As I was staying several days on that island and would not be able to buy so much as a toothbrush, there was nothing for it but he had to go back half an hour's flight and fetch it.

On the cargo boat there would be only one cabin with up to five bunks occupied by whoever had a ticket, be they nuns or policemen, doctors or tax collectors, but hardly ever European. Once a small pink pig insisted on sharing with me. One never undressed, and washing on board would have been at the communal sink in the cabin where the crew washed fish, so one hastened ashore to find a washing place every morning.

The people are shortish, stocky people called Melanesians, with skins varying from reddish to black and with soft woolly hair, which can be anything from black to blond. It is a remarkable sight to see a very dark man with yellow hair and it is a very particular ethnic difference which these people have, nothing to do with mixed blood. Children are frequently blond, with silky wavy hair which later darkens and becomes woolly; some of the adult blondness is due to rinsing with lime to cope with the wild life. The feel of their hair is quite different to African hair, which is wiry.

They live simple agricultural and fishing lives. Their houses and most of their possessions are made from palm-trees: canoes from the wood, houses from the leaves, rope from coconut fibre and so on. Before the Christian missionaries came in the nineteenth century, they were pagans, headhunters and cannibals, and many of them took a lot of converting. They could not be said to have stopped these practices till well into the twentieth century. I still came across the odd treasured skull in someone's house, though nowadays it is just as likely to be in a European souvenir-hunter's house. The Australians used to indulge in what was called blackbirding: getting labour from the islands by fair means or foul, to work in their settlements, and this made life even more difficult for the missionaries who, to the people, were just more white men who were not to be trusted, and I still felt the result of this practice in the great reserve of the people towards me. The men thus taken were told that they would earn good money in Australia and be able to return rich. In fact they spent all they earned on living and were never able to save up their return fares, so as far as their families were concerned they had just disappeared.

I do not know how many languages are spoken in The Solomons, but probably hundreds. On Guadalcanal, for instance, where the mountains sloped down to the sea in steep ridges, the people on one side of a ridge spoke a different language from those on the other side. They could understand each other but they would not understand those who lived beyond the ridge after that one. This relieved me of the need to learn a new language. A smattering of pidgin helped and there was always somebody who could act as interpreter, for better or worse.

Travelling was more than exciting. Sometimes I flew to an island if there was an airstrip, and stayed there for up to a week, getting about on foot or in Land-Rovers or lorries, or in little motorboats or dugout canoes, or pillion on motorbikes. Once I spent nine hours in a dugout canoe in bad weather, sitting in a puddle and trying to resist the percussion as the canoe went slap-slap into the waves. I would stay with missionaries, or with a local family in a palm leaf hut; occasionally I slept in a clinic where there was a bed for cases waiting to be taken by sea to hospital.

There were several man-made islands, built long years ago off-shore as being good defensive positions, painstakingly made of coral rocks and covered with congested huts. On one of these I saw feather money being made: this was an entirely local and ceremonial currency used for such things as bride price. The nine-inch sticks were covered, sadly enough, with the feathers of brilliantly coloured tiny birds, of red and white and black.

A number of beaches were called Red Beach in memory of some terrible action during World War II between the Americans and the Japanese. Many rusty relics of ships and weapons could still be seen. The local people had been wonderfully brave and loyal to the English left amongst them, hiding and supporting them for long periods. When I visited the island of Munda, a party of Japanese were there searching for the graves of their own people and I found myself sharing a very small 'guest house' run by a mixed-race woman. Her English father had settled there, having two local wives and twenty children, who tended to intermarry with the young of a similar family on an adjacent island. I caused much dismay when I arrived, as the Japanese were lounging around in their underpants. They dashed away and reappeared in cheesecloth trousers which did not really make much difference. They gave a party that evening which I felt I had to go to at their insistence. We sat on the grass overlooking the sea, with banana leaves for plates, and were served with mounds of rice, fish, fruit and vegetables. I found myself the centre of many a photograph taken with two different Japanese posing either side of me each time – oh well, let's hope it helped international relations.

Going ashore at these remote places was usually a job. At the first port of call of the day I would be taken off by a village maiden to a waterfall, a spring or a stream of great beauty, where the girls would be splashing and screaming and jumping off boulders, and the older ones would be doing their washing. The men used the same place but at different times and would call out as they approached. Loos were a problem. The one on the ship was to be avoided if possible. On shore if there was one at all, it would probably be on stilts in the sea, approached up a slippery log, doorless and facing the land. I accompanied a consignment of concrete loo platforms (a hole with foot imprints on either side) to one village where I had to instruct the people how to make a loo. First they had to choose a suitable place, and dig a very large and deep hole, which had to be larger than finally required because the man digging it had to be able to move in it. This did not appeal to them as a good idea, and I was not surprised on my next visit to find that nothing had been done.

I would demonstrate mouth-to-mouth resuscitation on the blow-up plastic body (Andy) I brought with me. This would cause dismay at first, then mirth, and finally deep interest when they understood what it was all about. Those who agreed to have a go could do it perfectly at their first try, unlike the people with whom I trained at Red Cross headquarters in London! So I felt pretty confident that those who were too shy to try would be able to do the job in an emergency. My act had a great rival when I travelled with the dentist. He had a Victorian foot-operated drill and he would operate in the school, sitting astride the end of a bench with the prostrate victim's head in his lap, the populace hanging over the walls watching entranced.

One island had been settled by Polynesians and as soon as we had anchored, quite far out, we were boarded by several chaps in G-strings who had swum out with gifts of whole hands of bananas and the like. The chief's brother was ill and we were to take him to hospital. With the doctor, I was invited to their meeting house, a huge leaf building with an entrance so low you had to crawl in. Once inside you went on crawling as it was considered rude to stand in the presence of the seated chief. A skirt is very difficult to crawl in. I distinguished myself when I left, crawling backwards, by aiming at a weak place in the wall which was letting in the light, instead of at the doorway, and by getting mildly stuck, to the great enjoyment of the company.

Perhaps the most interesting island, though sinister, was Tanna. I was warned not to wear my uniform here as the people have a cargo cult which has a red cross as its emblem, and they believe wonderful planeloads of fridges and other such items will one day arrive, probably all based on Red Cross relief planes in the war. Rough red wooden crosses dot the island, and martial events take place in the name of John Frum, whoever he may be. There is a volcano up which I was escorted by teenage girls to make sure I took not even a stone from the sacred surface. I lay on the edge and peered down into the bubbling red interior. It does occasionally throw up a careless handful and somebody had recently been killed, they told me later. The only water on the island comes up in springs along the beach at low tide; the people themselves manage with very little and wild horses which live on the central plateau never come to drink. This I saw for myself when a doctor I was staying with rode home after a hard day's journeying and just left his horse tied to a tree. When I reminded him about watering it, he said it never drank and presumably extracted from fresh grasses what moisture it needed. It seemed a gloomy place, partly because of successive tragedies: a wife overcome by gas fumes in the shower had died, another European committed suicide, and then a plane crashed on coming in and a young woman was beheaded and other people badly injured. But the wild horses were sheer delight to see, galloping over a plain with their manes and tails streaming. I was specially privileged because I sat alone under a tree while some other people went to have a closer look at a herd, which became alarmed and stampeded down past my tree.

Many are the interesting anecdotes I could tell of my travels, but one I think I must record. I was asked at one island to take on board a woman with gangrene of both feet, probably due to diabetes, and take her to hospital. I radioed the hospital for advice as to whether I should divert the ship or take her on the tour and deliver her a week or so later; I was very worried about her condition. However, they passed the buck firmly back, telling me I must decide, and reminding me that if I diverted the ship the expense incurred might jeopardise the lives say, of a mother and twins in difficulty later on, who would not be helped. I decided not to divert. The clinic on the island had absolutely no drugs, as the assistant in charge had failed to re-order in time; all he could do was lend me a bedpan, which was invaluable, apart from its real use, as a swab tray and for bedbathing the patient, as there was no suitable receptacle on board – the one bucket looked as if an elephant had trodden on it.

I had some aspirin which I could administer as painkillers but that was about it. She had been found by the medical assistant trying to walk twenty-five kilometres to her village, and had been brought in by canoe. Her husband carried her on his back to the wharf, from whence she crawled on board and collapsed into the bunk below mine. When the pain was not too bad she sat up, naked to the waist, smoking her pipe. At one stop she had a number of visitors who clearly held her in deep respect. When we ran out of water, everyone went ashore to get their own supply and I went with the bedpan. Cockroaches abounded, making a soft whooshing noise as they disappeared whenever one opened a locker. The rats lay low till after dark when they could be heard scampering joyfully around the decks.

There was a cyclone warning, too late for us, as we were already in open sea, practically rotating. The men formed a chain to get the thirteen women and children, all going to hospital, off the decks and into the cabin; one was a mental patient. I had been lying on my bunk (as there was nowhere to sit), and became stuck there for thirteen and a half hours. The bunk had no sides to stop me falling out and the mattress kept slipping and I had to cling to one of the two suspension chains to stop myself landing amongst the bodies below.

The poor woman died six months later.

The Queen visited Honiara while I was there, on board the *Britannia*, accompanied by the Duke, Lord Mountbatten, Princess Anne and her husband. Terrific exhibitions and demonstrations were laid on for her benefit and to the delight of the populace. I organised a display of First Aid using only local materials such as banana leaves, lianas, and palm-tree products of all kinds. Unfortunately it poured with rain and the vast green area where everything was staged became a morass in which I for one was paddling barefoot as shoes were simply sucked off. I was demonstrating resuscitation on 'Andy' which was very popular, but the only member of the Royal Family I saw there was the doughty Princess Anne.

I was surprised to be sent an invitation to a reception on board. As it was at 9.30 p.m. I dined first at an hotel with a bank manager who was also a guest. To enter the hotel he had to wear a jacket and tie; but the invitations to the *Britannia* had stipulated 'Island Dress' and we were all much confused. The islanders were annoyed: were they expected to come in grass skirts? They ignored the bidding and had glorious suits and dresses made for the event. The European men normally wore evening-dress trousers, white open-necked shirts and cummerbunds, so decided that that was what they should wear. The ladies wore long dresses but no gloves. Dismay reigned when the Queen greeted us with tiara, diamonds, gloves and a magnificent gown, and the royal men wore white ties. They eventually realised what had happened and tactfully, and doubtless thankfully, retired to remove their dinner jackets and white ties. Everyone loved seeing the Queen in all her glory; she was different.

I was told I was to meet the Duke, who of course had stayed three nights with us in Zanzibar, but although I stood where I was told, the first person I met was the Queen. She was superb as she went around our circle, enquiring what people did and making apt remarks, laughing and appearing to enjoy herself. I was then removed and had a brief encounter with the Duke, but was then accosted by Lord Mountbatten, who had also stayed with us in Zanzibar and recognised me, and we had a long and interesting interlude. I was struck by the attention to detail and the necessary homework they must all do for these events.

I never succeeded in training a Field Officer in the Solomons. The man they suggested I should train had so little common sense he could never have been

Girls showing their dowries of shells to the Queen on the Solomon Islands.

left to organise anything. I was warned fairly soon, as he arranged to take me to a village he said needed a visit, and he walked me twenty-three miles, crossing crocodile-infested river mouths and relying on coconuts for sustenance. The boat he said would pick us up on the return trip never materialised. The second man I found myself, and he was shaping up quite nicely when he developed a brain tumour. The third was a bright enough young man but, when he married, he resigned because he said he could not go on tour and leave his wife. It was difficult to find literate men or women who fitted the job and were willing to take the low wages offered, because there were so many better opportunities. When I left another Englishwoman took over.

The New Hebrides

This territory, a condominium of French and English, and usually known as the Pandemonium, was a place where there was never a chance of my finding a local Field Officer, as there were so very few people with enough education. The whole place was rather a muddle from my viewpoint. Government departments were divided between the French and English, so that the French might have Agriculture and the English Public Works. Schools were both, but it was interesting to find that the English schools were more popular because a small fee was paid and the people felt they therefore had more say in what went on. Currency was bewilderingly both: one could pay for something in French francs and have English shillings in change, or even worse, in both. I found it hopeless to know if I had been given the right change. The Red Cross had both English and French branches, and although I tried to liaise with the French one, it was tricky as feeling ran a little high amongst the Europeans who lived there.

Wherever I went I enquired for handicapped people, but far fewer than one would expect were ever produced. I am sure some really badly deformed babies would have been allowed to die at birth: one man told me that if his older sister happened to be ill when his mother had a new baby, the baby would be sacrificed, and that a baby born without legs would be considered to have had bad ju-ju put on it by ghosts and would be killed. But people coped so well with disabilities that most of those we would label disabled were not considered so in these isolated, necessarily self-sufficient, islands. For instance, one day when I was waiting for my plane in the usual thatched shelter, a personable young man and his pretty half-American wife came bumping over the field on a motorbike and manhandled a large box into the shelter. It was only later that I noticed, as he leant against a post, that he had no feet and was walking on his ankles. I chided the Red Cross representative who was seeing me off, that he had not told me of this handicapped man.

'Him? *He's* not handicapped!' was the reply. 'He's the richest man on the island,' and he recounted the various businesses the man was involved in, how he could climb palm trees and handle a boat – in fact on a later occasion I saw him hauling a boat up over a pebble beach. Consequently, a year later when a woman asked me to send her little son to New Zealand to get artificial feet, I thought long and hard and decided not to. The child was two years old and toddling about quite happily on his ankles; if he had been fitted with feet he would have had to keep returning for bigger ones as he grew, and the expense would have been enormous. It was clear that he was going to adapt just as that man had.

There were seven cases I saw who appeared to be thalidomide babies, though I was unable to prove it. They were all born to nurses who might have been able to take the drug in samples sent to the hospital, which had no record of ever receiving any. Had proof been available, the Chief Justice was prepared to apply for help internationally from the drug company. We were able to help six of these children but the mother of the seventh would not allow him off her back, where she had carried him for seven years, in spite of having borne two more children since.

The most rewarding case was a girl who was born with no legs at all and no arms from the elbow. Her family cared for her in a dark hut. We were able to send her to Fiji where a New Zealander ran a school for the handicapped and made artificial aids. When I saw her two years later at the school during the holidays, she was helping in the kitchen, tearing cabbage leaves off with her

A Big Namba beating a drum on Malekula.

upper arm bones. It had been decided not to give her artificial arms because she was so deft with the two bones in her two upper arms, and the only thing she complained about was not being able to thread a needle; a knitting machine was being bought for her, however. Her body was sitting in a kind of bowl with artificial legs emerging from two holes, and she could walk on flat surfaces. I have never seen such utter happiness as shone out of her face.

On one occasion my arrangements went seriously wrong on Malekula. The District Commissioner was away and his wife saw no reason why I should not make the planned day trip across the island in a lorry to another village. I was accompanied by the driver and a policeman who was going to arrest a murderer. There had been very heavy rains and before long the policeman and I were plastered with mud, due to our repeated efforts to push the Land-Rover up difficult stretches of the narrow dirt road. The truck slithered along very slowly until it finally ended in a ditch with a broken axle. We were more than halfway by then, so we walked the remaining six miles. I carried my flipflops as they were too slippery to walk in and the policeman had his boots hanging round his neck anyway. Outside the village the murderer sat on a big stone, patiently waiting by himself for the policeman.

When I had finished my work in the village, I did not fancy the long walk back and, with the help of a passing Greek in a motorboat, made an alternative plan which he radioed back to the DC's wife. I would be dropped off by him at a Rest House on an island further south, and could canoe across a bay to the airport two days later to catch my plane; would she please put my luggage on that plane? An outrigger came out to meet the motorboat and I affected a very dodgy transfer. I was duly taken to the rest house which had no caretaker and was devoid of every necessity except a rickety bed and a tired sheet. I walked a mile to the store and was able to buy soap and a tin of bully beef and some biscuits, but my only luggage was 'Andy' and I could not even buy a toothbrush or anything to read. I washed my clothes and, while they dried, draped myself in the rough-dried sheet and meditated on the peaceful view. The next day I did teach artificial respiration to a very small group of women and children, but all the men had gone off for an extended fishing trip. On the following day when I had to catch the plane, it took me two hours to find a reluctant elderly man to paddle me across the wide bay, an alarming performance as I sat high on a thwart across the outrigger and the huge waves came at us sideways on. We were only halfway across when the plane came over and, although the man did his best and even carried 'Andy' when we landed and we ran the mile or so to the airstrip, the plane took off before we got there, taking my luggage with it. I was lucky to find a group of young Australians who were carrying out some kind of survey, and I was invited to sleep in the very grand house they were occupying, which was the French délégué's house; he had left on the plane so I gladly slept in his sheets on a comfortable bed after the horrors of the rest house. Until the next plane a couple of days later, I earned my keep by cooking for the Australians and teaching them some elementary recipes and First Aid.

On one island which had a very strong tradition of cannibalism in the past, I had an amusing adventure. I taught a group of women how to immobilise a person who had fallen from a palm tree and broken his back, a fairly frequent occurrence, after which they would have to be transported to hospital, probably by canoe. We used all local materials and when I had shown them how to do it, I called for another 'victim' and a volunteer to have a go. Nobody wanted to be the victim, so I lay down and they produced a keen volunteer. She did it beautifully, I could not bat an eyelid by the time she had finished, and then they all stood back and laughed. No doubt we all had the same thought, but I decided I had to laugh too.

There are so many memories, amusing, amazing, touching and instructive. Here are a few: in a remote rest house was a copy of *Little Lord Fauntleroy* and a 1949 *Punch*; children played with spears and shields rather than with guns as in Europe; twins born when I was visiting a hospital were named Redso and

Bunjee jumping in the New Hebrides, 'The Pentecost Jump'.

Crosso, and another unfortunate child in another hospital was baptised Lady Mooring; on one trip I was given a lift sitting on the floor of a truck with thirty-four other women because my car would not go through a ford; London Headquarters might have been interested to see me at a dance being fairly decorously shoved round the floor by a black man wearing only an oily rag back and front, strings and cowries round his neck and his face painted with lime. The red and green parrots and big white ones, beautiful butterflies, ground cuckolds (big birds that climb trees and glide down but cannot fly), lovely flowering shrubs, all made walking on tour a joy. Not so pleasant was wading across crocodile-infested creeks or trying to balance on logs over them, and seeing nasty things like a crab with all its legs cut off, which had been waiting since the night before to be cooked. I saw megapodes, large black chicken-like birds, which lay their enormous eggs in the sand. I saw men casting themselves off a towering edifice of branches and lianas, tied by the leg with fibre ropes each tailored to its man so that he was brought up sharp just before he hit the ground. (Was this the origin of bungee jumping?) I stayed with missionaries, native clergy, isolated nurses, traders of all kinds, and in huts made available to me, all with varying 'comforts'. I ate breadfruit, mussels,

Conches for summoning people.

coconuts, chicken in many guises, rice, rice, rice, cassava, and *laplap* which I found particularly hard to bear as it was a heavy paste served in huge slabs and made of manioc, sweet potato, coconut and banana and having a very strange taste. I remember many wonderful swims with goggles for looking at the strange fish, once somewhat alarmingly, when on my own, meeting seven colossal manta rays, harmless creatures I knew, nevertheless daunting for their very size. (In the Solomons I was unable to swim in the sea because the sharks there were dangerous, probably due to a tradition of eating human flesh since so much had been available to them in the war.) I have memories too of the sort of sandy, palm-fringed beaches you see in tourist brochures but only here were they unoccupied.

The huts in the New Hebrides are made of leaf in parquet patterns and not up on stilts as in the Solomons. At one island I went with the locals in a great tin tub of a boat with a bar across the middle which we held on to while standing up, and were towed out to a ship which called monthly and sold tinned foods, flippers, aspirins, combs, tin openers, etc. and exchanged gas cylinders and other necessities. Along one strip of New Hebridean coast the water supply was dead simple: a visible pipe with a tap in each village. A conch shell was used to call the people together when I wanted to speak to them and demonstrate, and presumably at other times too; at one place there was one beside the electric generator for use when a workman was needed.

Landing at one island was disastrous as our dinghy overturned in the surf. I came up spluttering to find the redoubtable boatman holding me firmly by the wrist, while 'Andy' was held on his shoulder by his other hand and he held the boat off us with his knee. When the visit was over, our clothes dried on our bodies, returning through the surf was exciting, though the boatman was skilled at knowing the right moment to take the plunge.

The island of Futuna was extraordinary as the entire coast was a cliff and to get to the village one had to climb up a bamboo ladder with huge gaps between the steps; I tried to hide my trepidation as a teenager ahead of me zoomed up carrying my suitcase on her shoulder. I fear I drew the line at visiting another village which necessitated edging along a twelve-inch ledge for quite a distance. The people just laughed and edged along it to the first village to meet me.

One particularly lovely visit was to a girls' school on its own little island. The headmistress was a Polynesian and had blue tattoos all over her forehead and from her knees to her waist (so she informed me, and in her short skirt a lot were visible). She gave the girls the afternoon off in honour of my visit and they escorted me round their island along the beach, finding shells, swimming when the spirit moved them, swinging easily in familiar trees. The standard of education there was particularly high, their charismatic head having been educated herself in New Zealand.

The Gilbert and Ellice Islands

These people were again quite different from all the others, short, stocky and immensely strong, far less affected by white men historically because the islands are so far away and so small. The land is almost non-existent! The capital, Tarawa, is a horse-shaped atoll surrounded by a lagoon and coral reef. A more or less proper road drifts along one half of the horseshoe, with buildings built here and there where there is enough sand to build on. A few mangoes and bananas are grown and there is even a 'golf course' contrived by the British fanatics. The other half of the horseshoe is dotted with tiny villages linked by a dusty path, along which I meandered with a group of twelve disciples, eleven men and a girl, teaching and learning for a week, while searching for handicapped people. Otherwise in the capital I travelled on the back of a motorbike or, if lucky, was given a lift or lent a bicycle: there were three taxis but, if they were in working order, one was lucky if the driver was not drunk. So I did quite a lot of walking.

It was not easy to tour the other islands, but when I did I went in an erstwhile pleasure cruiser from Europe, in which young Gilbertese were trained as stewards. This meant that I had a luxurious first-class cabin to myself, excellent food and almost immaculate service. But here again the hazard was getting ashore. The islands are all atolls, and the sea inside the coral reefs is shallow so that sometimes the ship had to anchor very far out and one went in by flat-bottomed boats as far as possible and then waded. One day when we were rather late returning, the tide had gone out and left the two ferries stranded on the sand. They were extremely heavy and had to be pushed over rollers made of palm branches, my job being to pick up one of the ones a boat had just gone over and run round to the front and place it for further use. The ship was so far out we could not see its lights and the ferries kept each other nervously in sight with torches until the battery of one expired; then we had to shout. On land we used motorbikes or bicycles, the latter being very hard work on the sandy soil, the former rather painful for me sitting pillion behind enormous men or women.

On occasions when I had to spend a night on tour, I would be offered a hut to myself as a rule, with a platform to sleep on made of the spines of palm leaves, and very sharp they are too: you found a possible position and stayed in it all night rather than turn over. One night I slept in a *maneaba*, the village meeting place, a very large thatched area with no walls, just the odd upright timber, and the floor was made of loose coral stones, which a thin mat did little to make more acceptable. However, they had taken the trouble to rig up a clean mosquito net in one corner which afforded me privacy from interested villagers. Breakfast with my disciples on these occasions was an eye-opener; three brightly coloured washing-up bowls full of hard-boiled eggs, green coconuts and dough balls made of manioc were demolished with vigour by my party, in less time than it takes to tell about it.

I learned how useless it was to give a radio to a blind man, as I did, because according to custom, he would gladly give it to the first person who admired it. Another interesting thing I learned was learnt rather gruesomely; they brought a woman to me who had a wound to her skull made by her husband taking a swing at her with a machete. I did what I could and made arrangements for her to be taken to hospital, and she later, as an ex-nurse herself, became part of a scheme that my trainee Field Officer brought to my notice: he knew, which I did not, that a Government regulation decreed that if a village had a nurse living in it, even retired or half-trained, they could build themselves a lock-up cupboard and apply to Government for items to stock it, such as bandages, antiseptic, aspirins, forceps, a kidney dish and so on, and the nurse would administer it. Another good idea of his was to get a group to go round singing to raise money to provide food for the relatives of people in hospital, who had accompanied the sick people from other islands, and after a time had no means of support.

Here, too, were Red Beaches in memory of some terrible action during World War II between the Americans and the Japanese. One such on Betio, near Tarawa, was the scene of carnage when American ships unloaded their soldiers far out, where the shallow water began, and they had to wade over the reef to the beach. Unable to run and exposed for a long time, they made easy targets for the defending Japanese.

After my first tour of the whole territory (1,000 miles as the crow flies from one end to the other, with hundreds of islands, only a few of which I could ever hope to visit), I decided that the work was clearly the teaching of hygiene and health, in colleges and schools, and in villages in a more elementary way on tour, as well as the discovering of disabled people to see what could be done to help them. Eventually I made a list of all the deaf people I encountered, which revealed a great number, due to 'coral ear' contracted in childhood from swimming in the sea. My aim was a deaf school which my successor got off the ground. It was all so different from Mauritius where so many people lived in such congested conditions, the land being owned and farmed by great landowners, and the main need beyond the teaching being coping with malnutrition. In the Pacific the islanders had plenty of room and everyone had his own 'garden', usually some way from the village, which he tended to provide for his family. They fished in the sea and bred pigs and chickens, and the coconuts fell off the trees. Malnutrition was not heard of, First Aid was urgent because the hospitals were few and far between, and if anyone needed to go to one he would have to go by canoe. Apart from drowning, for which I taught artificial respiration, the most frequent casualties were people who had fallen out of palm trees and broken their backs, so I would teach them how to handle and immobilise the patient before the dreaded canoe journey to hospital.

In all the territories then, I did quite a lot of teaching in Teacher Training and Theological Colleges, as well as in schools at different levels. I rewrote booklets which were in difficult English and had them translated into pidgin. (Pidgin, which I only toyed with, is a fascinating language and I always remember two amusing adaptations: a helicopter was 'Mixmaster belong Jesus Klais' and the feathers in the Governor's helmet were 'Grass belong arse belong cockerackel'.) I gave several radio talks and wrote First Aid stories which were translated into pidgin for radio. I also wrote an accident prevention leaflet which was translated, and made up a sample Home Medicine Chest which the Red Cross reproduced and sold cheaply. I tidied up the Blood Transfusion Service.

Other Islands

On one of my round trips my plane came down in Nauru overnight. This is an independent island and was not part of my territory. It is a phosphate island and the mining of the phosphates, which are close to the surface, has left the land looking quite extraordinary; an eleven-mile road runs round the coast where the people live, and the centre of the island is a mass of jagged peaks of coral rock left by the removal of the phosphates in between. My hostess and I overslept and I missed my plane and was stuck for a week until the next one came. Filled with guilt, I flung myself into talks at schools and a course for the police; this was quite a laugh as they are such enormous people that my triangular bandages simply would not go round any part of them. They solved the problem by persuading their senior officer, who was half-Norwegian and not so big, to be my patient. A nun at one of the seventeen schools asked me to talk about the evils of taking drugs because one of her pupils, a boy of fifteen, had died of doing so. I apologised that I did not know enough about it, but she was undaunted:

'They will take more notice of you,' she said, 'because you are an outsider.' So she educated me about the art of sniffing and injecting and just taking pills, and the results, and I duly gave the required talk.

Tonga was also not part of my territory but I was asked by Red Cross headquarters to visit there for two weeks to help them sort out some difficulties. The Tongan Princess was very helpful towards Red Cross and there was an English colonel in command of the army who had been influential in organising them but now wanted to hand over. The Royal family were only slightly bigger than the biggest Tongan I met, and I quailed when told that the King did physical jerks every day on the first floor of his rickety wooden palace. The Crown Prince provided some excitement while I was there. He was to go on a picnic which the Colonel had laid on by boat to show me more of the country, but in the night there was a terrific explosion in the forest which held everything up. Apparently the Prince had bribed or bullied the Petty Officer in charge of ammunition to let him have a quantity of explosive so that he could make a big bang, and the Colonel was extremely angry with him, the Prince being by way of an officer in the army. When the lecture was over, the crestfallen Prince simply said:

'Do you allow me to come on the picnic?' and the Colonel had not the heart to say no.

One evening I was taken out to dinner by a police officer I had known in Zanzibar, to a night club, and as we were leaving a woman, in a group I took to be prostitutes leaning on a bar in the foyer, blew smoke into my face. I was pretty annoyed and told my friend when we got outside, and he told me they were transvestites and they were giving a lot of trouble. It was rather surprising as Tonga is a very religious country. One of the most lovely things was to hear the singing at an ordinary church service, every voice an instrument of great beauty, and so many parts, but no books and no music. Horses were ridden bareback through the streets, taxis looked like ice-cream carts, everyone wore mats or bits of crochet-work or basketwork round their waists on top of their clothes, the men in *valas* (skirts), the women in long skirts with short dresses on top. The men wore their hair 'short back and sides', the women's hung loose or was put up in buns.

One day I was taken to a church service which turned out to be a real exercise in patience, as the pastor preached in Tongan for a whole hour. Afterwards we went to a lunch laid on by students. There must have been at least fourteen suckling pigs, also whole fish and crabs, huge taro roots and beef wrapped in leaves. At each place was a delicious dish of raw fish marinated in coconut milk. We were expected to eat at least half of what was served, but there were plenty of people waiting outside to take our places.

I found it impossible to buy anything to read when staying in the capital of the northern group of Tongan islands. One bookshop said:

'Oh yes, an exercise book? Oh, a reading book. Yes, we have an encyclopaedia.' The other shop had a dictionary. Altogether I found it a delightful country, romantic, sleepy, dirty, with dignified, gay, courteous people with their own absolutely adequate culture.

Again, Brunei was not part of my territory but headquarters asked me to go there to see how they were progressing as they had not had a British Field Officer for some years. I spent a month there, finding it utterly unlike any other country I had worked in. To start with, there seemed to be no want. I commented one day to an Indian who was showing me around:

'There seems very little agriculture going on.'

He replied gravely:

'It is difficult, because so often when you dig you strike oil.'

If one man in an extended family had a job, it was enough to keep them all going. It was impossible to get domestic help as they were all too affluent; domestics had to be imported. The lovely engraved silver which used to be Brunei's speciality was hardly made any more, and I was lucky to find a small second-hand tray.

Red Cross had lapsed sadly, with all the goodwill in the world. I had a sleepless night after a demonstration of First Aid put on for my benefit; people who could do faultless roller hand bandages did not know how to stop bleeding. Two seven-year-old boys performed a parody of artificial respiration and heart compression on another seven-year-old. I gave a course in First Aid to twenty teachers, as well as short courses in several schools. I found qualified teachers in an Airport Fire Brigade officer and two nurses who were all willing to carry on with teaching and seeing that people kept up to date. I recommended to headquarters that a British Field Officer should be sent out to train a local one and to set things going again on the right lines.

Whilst there I visited a longhouse in Sarawak just over the border. Half an hour in a fairly ropey sort of covered dinghy/canoe with an 850 hp motor which swept us along at 55-60 mph, then half an hour in a car and we were in another world. The village was on stilts about twelve feet high. A covered veranda about 150 yards long was the main street and thirty-nine large rooms opened off it, each housing a family, altogether about 400 people. Each room had a beautiful cock tethered by the door with a tin of food nailed to the wall, dogs and cats of all ages were everywhere, children abounded. These people still had smoked skulls hanging up and used blow pipes and home-made guns for hunting. Babies hung in pieces of cloth on hooks and springs from the rafters. One young woman wearing national dress (topless, with quite small breasts) said she had ten children. All the tinies were being breastfed supplemented by bottles.

The best memory I have of Brunei is of a horseshoe-shaped building with a statue of Winston Churchill in the middle of the open area in the middle. One half of the building was the most lovely aquarium, the other a memorial to Churchill: a replica of the room he was born in, models of him playing with his soldiers in the nursery, writing outside his tent on the N.W. Frontier, working in his dugout under the Houses of Parliament in the war, while the sounds and flashes of an air raid go on in the sky; photographs; his decorations; hats and hats and hats! Suits and overalls; his paintings; his books; even his voice.

I cannot leave the South Pacific without mentioning its memorable golf courses. In Honiara there was quite a good one, with sand 'greens' and horrible bunkers; one woman I played with there was Japanese and she was so happy to be able to play, because in Japan land was so precious and golf links so few that women were not allowed to play. On the great island of Malaita opposite Guadalcanal the course was devised on a field below a cliff; the first tee and the last hole were up on the cliff which made it a very testing course. Quite a memorable one was on a small island where no open space could be given, but the intrepid British golfers stationed there played in a coconut plantation, the grass kept short by cows; bunkers were not required, the hazards being cows and trees. On Tarawa in the Gilberts I was not even aware I was standing on the course until my partner pointed out, by my foot, the red stump which indicated the first tee, on the beach; here one drove over the only road and a clump of bushes in the direction one was told the 'brown' was; having attained the 'brown', one took a short plank and smoothed the path one hoped one's ball would take in the soft thick sand to the hole.

★ ★ ★

All in all I look back on my travels in the South Pacific with great pleasure in the differences they presented, the amusement, the difficulties, together with the helpfulness and humour volunteered by the people, the sunshine and the peace. I know it is not always peaceful and they do have appalling weather and great afflictions at times, but my memories are fascinating and happy ones.

CHAPTER 8

Katmandu to London by bus 1975

FINALLY IN 1975 I began my journey home. The Red Cross had sent me the money for the air fare home, but I elected to spend it on travelling by bus, which took three months and was a great adventure.

Singapore

I flew here and spent a few days at a YWCA hostel. The city I found exhausting, teeming with people and uninhibited traffic, often three-lane in the middle of the town, and going at speed; the two taxis I took had no hands on their speedometers. There were often no pavements, but there were wicked open drains, full of horror and erratically edged; we saw an old man covered in blood being fished out of one, together with his bicycle. The local paper said there had been ninety-four road accidents the day before, including two deaths. However, the streets were very clean due to stringent fines, and full of slender young people, often with lovely faces, dressed in clean bright jeans. 74 per cent of the population are Chinese, 14 per cent Malay. Only Malays received free primary education but few went on to secondary because, I was told, they were lazy.

I visited various places of interest but the only ones to leave a lasting impression were the Aquarium and above all the Jurong Bird Park, where there is a valley completely netted over; the brilliant birds can zoom about freely and one walks around over little bridges and along paths below.

I called on the Red Cross and had a long talk with the Secretary General, a Mrs Chong, which was full of interest. She gave me lunch high up in the first skyscraper I had ever been in, and I was horrified when I went unsuspectingly to a window to look at the view.

Bangkok

The plane served free champagne, and the meal was quite delicious – prawn cocktail, chicken, éclairs, wine and coffee – and I was presented with an orchid. In Bangkok I stayed with friends in the Hong Kong and Shanghai Bank who lived in the utmost luxury, better than any Government House! In this city, too, the traffic was appalling, dangerous and two-lane; the pavements were jagged and there was a lot of rubbish. A pedestrian had to creep and dodge and run like hell to cross the street, and in desperation twice I held up the traffic. I once inadvisedly took a bus, which was crammed full inside and out; a child sitting on a seat was screaming because my leg was jammed against his, but I just could not move it. People ate in the streets, clustered round vendors with little roofed carts; they barbecue things on the pavement – corn, bananas, fish of all sorts. People jogged along with baskets on poles across their shoulders. It was all very picturesque, a mixture of the old and the modern.

I had a dying friend to visit, which I did daily; he was the artist who had taught me to paint in Zanzibar. I visited the house of one Jim Thompson, an architect who disappeared one night when staying with friends in Malaysia in 1966 and was never seen again. He had revived the silk industry in Thailand and made it the success it is now. His house was full of objets d'art, paintings, tapestries, silks, carvings, statuettes, porcelain and a most beautiful stone Buddha of the sixth century which stood in his garden overlooking a *klong* (canal).

Early one morning I took a boat to the Floating Market, up a tributary of the river, lined with houses, factories and warehouses built over the water. The water was thick and filthy; everything happened in it. I saw a dead dog floating, children diving, women washing clothes and themselves, people brushing their teeth, and all sorts of ordure and rubbish being thrown in. One prayed not to fall in. There were factories for flax, timber, soysauce, and great water jars. Every house had a shrine to house the tree spirits and others which were on the site. Nuns in white and Buddhist monks in orange abounded; young men before marriage are expected to be monks for three months, to teach them discipline and restraint. What a good idea! Temples were studded with gold and broken china and tiling and enamels. At the market there were boats everywhere with car engines fixed on the back and eight-to ten-foot pipes sticking out with propellers on the end, serving as rudders. Women as well as men drove them, peddling vegetables and fruit of all kinds, and calling at houses.

A visit to the Rose Gardens outside the city was interesting, the countryside was not, being flat with very few trees and little grass, concrete factories and wooden shacks. At the gardens one was taken to a bamboo building with an arena and seats stacked up round it, to watch cock-fighting, bull-fighting, sword-fighting, bamboo and finger dances, a mock wedding, and Thai boxing (with the feet). Outside one saw folk-dancing, and elephants at work rolling logs in and out of water. Their strength and skill were remarkable; if a log did not fall right, the elephant would tidy it up without being told.

One day I was taken to see the bridge over the River Kwai and the railway which cost the lives of 15,000 Europeans and 100,000 other races during the war. The graveyards were heartrending, thousands of identical little slabs each representing a mother's son, and mostly so young. The gardens round were beautifully cared for. A nearby Japanese memorial was for those 'who helped to build this railway and died of illness whilst doing so.' The bridge was single track and the bridge was very ropey; we were told that the prisoners used rotten wood whenever they could. A little way downriver were limestone caves, each housing a golden Buddha. The people buy thin squares of gold leaf which they smack on to the figures, which in consequence look a bit leprous as the bits don't stick properly.

Nepal

The Roof of the World! I was met at Katmandu by a Mrs Joshi, a Red Cross contact, and taken to my hotel. The room was clean but totally unheated, there was a bathroom, but the water ran so slowly that it would have been cold by the time one had enough, and anyway there was no plug.

I was entranced by the city, which was so utterly different from any other place I had been. They were about to have a coronation so everybody was busy making the processional route look smart. A widening of the road, which was made of crumbly red brick, produced clouds of dust everywhere. People clung in improbable places laying on paint: one man was painting the roof of a temple with a rope round his waist and another on a higher roof was dangling the paintpot for him so that he had a hand free for hanging on. People were digging holes for bunting poles.

In the centre of the old town muddy courtyards were surrounded by tenement blocks with heavily carved window frames and people hanging out of them to watch the life below. Individual rooms on the ground floor that I could see into were like cupboards and may have been shops or living rooms. Door steps did not exist but there was a wooden ledge which you had to step over. Grass grew on roofs. Golden temples and shrines glistened. People carried bamboo poles over their shoulders with baskets of rubbish or of produce; others had heavy loads in baskets on their backs slung with straps round their foreheads. Women wore long skirts and shawls, men wore riding breeches and shirts with stand-up collars and sometimes jackets and little round hats; children wore padded jackets but mostly no pants or shoes. Washing hung everywhere high up on ropes across the street. Gorgeous vegetables were on sale, tangerines and apples, coconuts and dates. Troops with their colours sat in heaps about a great parade ground, bicycle taxis tooted, ragged children begged or played marbles.

One travelled about in bicycle taxis, the cyclist being in front, a form of transport I became used to throughout India, too. Walking was hazardous as the streets were filthy, not only with rubbish but also with faeces, and some back streets were clearly just used as lavatories. The streets themselves were often of red brick with parquet designs, very beautiful, sometimes great irregular blocks of stone.

On my first day I encountered a traffic accident, and hanging fiercely onto my bag all the time, I gave First Aid to an unconscious young man. Onlookers said they would look after his bicycle when he was taken away in a kind of ambulance, and I hoped they would be doing so on his behalf.

I visited a Hindu temple in a very beautiful valley but, alas, everyone was making sacrifices of goats, chickens, rabbits, ducks – it was very upsetting as the poor creatures were queuing to be killed and must have known by the smells what was coming. But the people believed they were doing the animals a kindness because, if they are sacrificed, they go on to a higher form of life; the people benefit too by helping the animals to be sacrificed.

I went on an elephant trek to watch for tigers from here and it was very exciting. I had never ridden on an elephant before and it is an extraordinary lurching experience. The animals are so intelligent that if they have to pass rather close under a branch they know it will knock you off their backs, so they break it off as they go. They are like enormous great nannies and give one a feeling of great confidence. They took us to a camp by a river and round the campfire that night we were told what was going to happen. We had to go to sleep fully clothed, and when a tiger came to the kill (which was a poor live goat tied up in a lit clearing), one of the hunters would come and whisper to us to follow him. Forbidden to speak, we tiptoed through the jungle to a spot where we had to leave our shoes, and then went barefoot along a swept sandy path to a hide which had several lookout windows on to the scene below. Then one of the party made a rude noise and I have never known any creature move so fast as the tiger which had arrived and killed the goat. He vanished. I went on peering through my window until I heard the hunter saying 'Let's go.' When we reached the shoes, mine were not there, but he led me to another spot and there they were. What had happened was that my party of five had been called to leave the hide and I had not heard, so the other party of six came in and I had left with them. I was thus the last to come into the camp and everyone fell upon me saying:

'Well, it must have been YOU!'

We went on the River Rapti in dugouts, with a man and a boy paddling, and saw Brahmin duck, cormorants, herons, spotted deer and langur monkeys and lots of whirlpools. We had bush walks and were taught to recognise the prints and droppings of various animals and other signs of their presence. We visited Tiger Tops, the well-advertised place to stay, but reckoned we preferred our camp.

When we returned to the enormous barren plain where the plane had come to pick us up, we waited, in the leaf hut which was the airport, for the other elephants to arrive. The last, carrying the luggage, came tearing along in a lovely flowing movement. She knelt down near the throbbing plane while they unloaded her, then she hurried over to her friends across a ditch, trumpeting and making shrill noises, and one of them answered, touching her mouth with her trunk – quite a discussion it seemed about the hurry, and did you want a drink, dear?

Back at Katmandu I embarked on a week of concentrated sightseeing – palaces and stupas and other temples. Just roaming the town was fascinating. Everything was beautiful but tatty; gilding and carving, faeces in the street, the red brick streets and great irregular pavements of stone. There was a Tibetan refugee camp for 10,000 who had come over in 1959 after a revolt against the Chinese communists who had taken over their country. I particularly remember the little open-air school for two-year-olds, toddling about in very thick coats with a lama in charge. The women wove carpets and combed and spun wool, and made handcrafts to earn their keep. They all hoped to go home one day and refused to become Nepalese.

I consumed borscht at the Yak and Yeti Hotel, run by White Russians to whom I had an introduction. I drove out of town to the ancient city of Patan, where the original language of Newali is spoken – elsewhere it is Nepali which is close to Urdu. I saw a chanting man chained to a post and guarded by a policeman; he was a lunatic and this was the only way they had to restrain such people. I also saw a child chained to a post in a school, but did not discover why. I went to a religious festival where monkeys pressed in on every happening and people picnicked and threw paper about and sucked lollies.

Twenty elderly Japanese came to stay at my hotel and I was thankful when they left; they lunged about the passages with their flies undone, mumbling in carrying tones. One day I found an English girl in the hall, a drug addict in terrible distress, as she had lost her money and her papers and did not know what to do; after enquiries she was taken off by somebody from the British Embassy. The hotel restaurant was unbelievable. Nothing arrived hot and most tasted of nothing. Boiled eggs came without eggcups and were very runny. Tea after much education did come hot, but the hot water did not, and they once forgot the teapot lid and another time the cups. One soon learned to have meals, except for breakfast, elsewhere. One evening I was invited to the British Embassy where the 'small chop' was so generous I did not have to have a meal; it was all very pleasant and civilised but one could hardly believe one was in the middle of Katmandu.

I was taken to Red Cross headquarters to see what they were doing. They had nine ambulances and a large number of cars throughout the country. Their main work was coping with disasters: floods, famines and fires, of which they had many. They were the legal guardians of the refugees and were toying with a welfare plan, though this seemed a little vague. They were also organising a blood transfusion scheme.

Then I set off with my group for the three-month journey, which in 1975 was not as often undertaken as it probably is now, and we were able to go through Afghanistan and Iran which one could not do in 1978 and for many years onwards. The first day, driving down the mountains into India, we were in a small bus driven by a Sikh, who knew the heart-stopping curves of the precipitous road by heart. The hillsides were covered with brilliant rhododendrons and azaleas growing wild. There was only one other English person in the group, a very tall youth of eighteen called Richard. There were two Danish women but they soon left us, feeling no doubt that it was not their scene. There was a couple from Pitcairn Island, the rest were from Australia and New Zealand, mostly teachers, one an Austrian doctor which was rather a good thing. All but one of the women were much younger than I, so we were often considered a pair, which I found rather trying as she was by no means a soul mate. At first we always shared a room but her snoring kept me awake and a younger woman, who said nothing kept her awake, took over from me. I usually shared thereafter with an Australian teacher who had had polio and was incredibly plucky in how she kept up with everything. But frequently we had to share with a third or even a fourth, and the first night in Birganj there were five of us in a room with nothing in it but excruciating beds and one nail in the wall by mine, on which I hung my shirt and then put on a clean one in the morning and left the other behind. It had been a bad night with mosquitoes thundering up and down and men outside apparently beating steaks – we could not think of anything else to account for the noise. Shrill dogs barked. Somebody endlessly filled a container with water outside our window. Elena snored. I had a sleeping bag so at least was warm but the others were not. A fire engine was called out. At 5 a.m. was the call to prayer.

The proper coach called for us in the morning, driven by an Irish man of twenty-five, Bernie, a dauntless fellow indeed, with an untidy head of golden hair and a moustache. He was incredibly tough with lorry drivers who would come hurtling down the middle of the road on the narrow strip of tarmac, heavily laden and with their lights on, hoping to frighten allcomers off into the dust. He would give them half the road and then lean out and yell at them. His flaxen hair won him a lot of points but I was always afraid he would overdo it and the lorry would be overturned like many we saw along the way.

Margrit, our guide, who was a German, made the whole trip both interesting and enjoyable. She worked very hard and knew most of the ins and outs. For instance, before we even started she told us that in India you were expected to pay your hotel in foreign currency and, if there was change, it came in rupees which you were not allowed to take out of the country. She therefore took the correct number of American dollars from us which would cover our expenses in India. She often gave talks on the bus about what we were going to see or about the country we were entering, though the tannoy was not very good. She decreed that we should move around the bus each day so that no one pair hogged the front seats, and we actually moved around quite a bit having interesting conversations and even, when the scenery was perhaps a completely flat desert, playing games such as Scrabble.

Everything was very squalid and dirty. The towns swarmed with people and the roads were blocked with bullock carts and rickshaws. One hotel had a notice saying 'Rooms available complete with bed and attached latrine'. The countryside was heavily cultivated: tobacco, rice, wheat, maize, lentils, bananas, mangoes. We passed carpets of scarlet chillies drying in the sun.

The hotel at Patna, our next stop, was an improvement on the last one – it had to be, but was ramshackle and rambling. Hotels varied enormously. Some were quite ordinary and acceptable, others quite extraordinary, one culture trying unsuccessfully to satisfy another. Gone are the days of the Raj when white men were masters and Indians were servants with pride in their masters, themselves, and their work. There are so many people and jobs have to be shared, so everyone is desperate and scrambling for anything going.

At Benares we were taken to the holy river Ganges, though to me it looked pretty unholy, a dirty mud colour and everything happening in it: people washing themselves and their clothes, peeing in it, drinking it; dead holy men and children under five are weighted and thrown in, though everyone else gets burnt on the high flight of steps by which one descended to the river. Monkeys abounded and, being sacred, were allowed to do what they liked, and you had to take care as they were quite vicious. Cows, too, are holy and, although not vicious, can be an awful nuisance, eating what they like at vendors' stalls, even the paper bags, and lying down in the road obstructing the traffic.

On our next leg we went to Khajuraho, which was at that time a little known group of temples of the ninth to eleventh centuries, set in a lovely park of flowering trees and shrubs. The temples are covered inside and out with carvings of people doing all sorts of domestic things, like combing their hair, writing letters, painting their toenails, talking, but above all many extraordinary erotic scenes. A group of giggling Indian men made it difficult to examine these graceful and beautiful things. It was the first pleasant scene we had seen in India.

The country we drove through was fairly barren but there were some pretty mud villages, some walled, grand old palaces and forts on hill tops – and then we came to Agra and the Taj Mahal. Although I had seen it as a teenager, I was glad to see it again as it truly is one of the wonders of the world. It is made of white marble inlaid with semi-precious stones. Half the Koran is inlaid in black round the doorways, which are very high, and as the writing gets higher the inlay gets bigger so that it all looks the same size from the ground. It was built, as a tomb for a much-loved wife, by Shah Jehan, who intended to build a black one for himself on the other side of the river, but his son overthrew and imprisoned him and murdered all his brothers so as to rule himself. Charming boy.

In the very nice hotel in Agra I had cause to dig up some of my teenage Hindustani when speaking to a waiter. He was transported with nostalgic delight: here was a memsahib! It was often clear that such people remembered the British with affection and longing for the good old days when, for instance, you did not have to share your job with three other people, working in shifts. But now they were lucky to have a job at all. We also went to see the Fort where Shah Jehan was imprisoned and where his son Akbar lived. It is immense with lawns and spectacular buildings, harem courtyards for 400 concubines, under-floor heating, a huge judgment hall. Another of Akbar's forts was Fatehpur Sikri, a red sandstone city where justice was sometimes meted out by the criminal being trampled by an elephant; if the elephant refused, the criminal went free.

We came to a river where a large bridge had been swept away in the last monsoon, and a pontoon bridge was in use. Bernie decreed that we should all walk over and he bravely brought up the rear in the bus. We had 'bush stops' mid-morning throughout the trip, which could be hilarious. Men went off to one side of the bus and women the other, but for one girl this was not enough – she had to have a bush. This could be difficult on desert plains but she would plod off to find a fold in the land that might conceal her, and we were continually held up because she was missing. In India particularly, people were everywhere; we would stop to picnic somewhere remote and miraculously people would appear to stare at us. I soon became aware that some of our women were offensively dressed as far as the locals were concerned, wearing tight jeans and tops, with bare arms, but it was difficult to get this across.

In Delhi I thought the most memorable building was the Qutab Minar, a Muslim tower of terrific height and very decorative. One is allowed up to the first balcony only because of the suicide rate from the other two, but I had no wish to go any further and feared I might involuntarily commit suicide myself. After climbing 350 steps, one felt a bit shaky anyway and the rail round the parapet only came halfway up my thighs, the parapet being so narrow two people could only just pass one another. Nearby was the iron pillar described by Erich von Daniken in *Chariot of the Gods* as being made (probably by aliens!) of iron and something unidentifiable which prevents it rusting. *Son et lumière* in the Red Fort was a great occasion. We sat in a garden opposite the Hall of

Justice and the Shah's Pleasure Palace, with the Pearl Mosque on our left; the full moon hung over us half the night most effectively. The sound was excellent: good voices, good English, and one heard troops marching, horses galloping (in one instance the messenger galloped up and one nearly SAW him), women weeping or laughing, people being massacred, harem dancing and singing, the call to prayer, even Gandhi and Nehru speaking. The lighting was varied and good and it was a most excellent production.

It was a 300-mile journey to Amritsar all in one day. We got lost in Ludhiana and it was quite a feat getting the bus through the narrow streets, under a low bridge, and round large roundabouts in small places. There seemed to be an infinite capacity for making slums, everything crowded and squalid, cows everywhere eating whatever they fancied. We saw one completely naked man standing by the roadside, holy or mad we did not know. We noticed how dung heaps made by local ladies had changed from elegant slim cowpats arranged in herringbone patterns to much fatter pats in rugged cones – thus do cultures vary!

The Golden Temple at Amritsar is the Sikh holy place, their Mecca, and has been, since I was there, the scene of much violence. It is not architecturally very splendid but is covered inside and out with copper-gilt and semi-precious stones, and is set in a lake. People were stripping and washing in the lake, some were bustling across the path to the temple, throwing coins into the lake, and handing in food offerings; half would be retained for the communal feeding kitchen and half blessed and returned. We all had to cover our heads and remove our shoes and we sensed the spirit of real reverence and holiness.

We visited the Jallianwallabagh where the massacre by British troops of an illegal assembly occurred. It is a large well-kept garden in a ring of houses and only one narrow exit between two of them, in front of which the soldiers stood and fired. They said the crowd was defenceless but even in the museum painting their swords were lying all over the place as they died. A large notice in two languages explained rather one-sidedly how it all happened. General Dyer was undoubtedly wrong to fire to kill but he had some provocation to fire, as assemblies were at that moment banned because of civil troubles.

I had a date in Amritsar, which turned into an adventure, with an Indian teacher I had met in Brunei, who had said he would be on leave at his father's rectory here, and would be delighted if I would visit them. We arrived after dark so I thought I must contact them that night as they would be expecting me and the next day we would be sight-seeing. Telephoning failed; the exchange said they had no phone but kindly told me how to find the house. I hailed a bicycle rickshaw which had a slippery seat tipped at such an angle it was difficult to stay in. The man pedalled furiously round four sides of a large square, then at a tangent down a dark alley, by which time I was sure I was going to be mugged. When I found we were going up a road we had already been down I remonstrated but he only threw frantic glances over his shoulder and gibbered. Finally by yelling '*Bus!*' (meaning 'Stop!') a number of times I got him to stop, and I got out to ask an educated-looking man with a motorbike if he could tell the man where I wanted to go. He spoke to him and then said:

'Madam, he is simple. I suggest you give him fifty paise and I will take you to your destination.'

I was so relieved I hopped on to the back of his motorbike and only when we were zooming along did it occur to me that I might have jumped from the frying pan into the fire. However, he was a real old-fashioned gentleman (the sort we have unfortunately grown out of) and took me to the rectory and waited to see that I was received. It was a ramshackle building in a muddy yard, complete with cow, and I was most joyously welcomed by my friend Michael, his brother, his father, and two small boys, all in their nightwear. Michael had been to my hotel but, not seeing the bus, concluded we had not come. They managed to rake up some tea and cakes and the little boys served. The old man said he only had a congregation of four because there were so many churches in the town! It was not a very satisfactory evening but I was glad I went. They found me a safe rickshaw for the return journey and told me what to pay.

We never reached Kashmir because we encountered a particularly large landslide which it was obvious would not be cleared for a couple of days. We did wait for some hours, hoping. I, at least, had been to Kashmir in my teens but the others were very disappointed. Some of us walked to a village about a mile away where we found a little man making his fortune churning out the most delicious puff pastries, so we sat and had tea there, beside an open drain, enjoying seeing the life going on around us. Some people were smoking hookah pipes; one lovely old man with a henna-ed beard wore shoes with turned-up toes. Eventually it was decided to return the five-hour journey to Jammu and occupy the beds designated for a coach tour stuck on the far side of the landslide among 400 or so other vehicles. It was a hairy drive, as so many vehicles had no lights, one side of us was a precipice all the way, two lorries were locked together on a bridge and had to be sidled round, and then a new hole had appeared in the road and the demarcating stones did not quite take in the hole so we nearly went in. A bush stop was enlivened by a lorry passing us which did have its lights on. Poor Bernie really earned his pay that day.

Pakistan
It took hours to get through the two checkpoints at the border, being searched by magnificent representatives of the armed forces on both sides, and going

through customs. The 200 yards between the two checkpoints was thronged with coolies carrying loads on their heads because lorries were not allowed through, so cargoes had to be transported to the line, taken over by coolies from the other side, and reloaded on to other vehicles. I was accosted by an Indian with a British passport who wanted to deliver a dormobile to the other side, and he wanted me to drive it! Bernie advised me it was probably carrying drugs.

We had an interesting drive into NW Frontier territory, rocky, barren, inhospitable, and it is difficult to see men and animals moving on the hillsides as they blend into it so, people all being garbed in shades of mud. Churchill received his initiation into war here in the 1890s and a picket post is named large and clear after him: a stone box perched on the hill above a fort. We went up through the Malakand Pass, at one point edging round two more lorries locked in mortal combat on the inner side of the road. The Attock Bridge, built by the British in 1880, has turreted gates at each end which made the approach for our long bus only just possible; many bridges are set at an angle to the road so that attackers cannot easily charge.

We stayed five nights in Lahore and were lucky to be able to attend a military tattoo which was quite magnificent. The armed forces all had spectacular uniforms, some being mounted on beautiful horses and camels, others marching faultlessly. They were followed by really entertaining clowns and other circus artistes, by poor dancing bears and other performing animals.

Three of us one day took a tonga (a two-wheeled horse-drawn vehicle) through the town, when the unfortunate horse collapsed. Down went the shafts, up went the back of the tonga, so that I and another woman were lying on our backs with our feet in the air. We were not surprised about the horse, just desperately sorry for him; they all looked near to death anyway.

From a huddled village at the top of the Pass we dropped down into the cosy little valley of Swat, surrounded by the rugged, sometimes snowcapped, mountains of the Hindu Kush, rice and wheat and mustard flourishing on the plain through which a handy little river runs. We ran through several awful-looking villages and then, surprisingly, stopped in one with an impressive hotel in a garden of sweet-smelling flowers. Here I went for a walk with Richard, and attracted a horde of ill-mannered youngsters, one of whom threw a handful of gravel which hit me on the back of the head: he was surprised and frightened when I rounded on him and roared! We struck off left and downhill through the town – fantastic – just paths and rough steps between the mud houses, all jumbled together, definitely not tourist country so all the more attractive. They were living as they have lived for centuries, no mod cons at all.

Afghanistan

We went through the Khyber Pass, so well-known to us because of the Afghan Wars and the terrible retreat from Kabul of our army and many civilians; only one out of 15,000 got back, and a few women and children were taken captive. The scenery is lovely through the mountains. We saw the crests of the regiments who fought here picked out on the rocks. A railway line now runs through with forty-four tunnels, and beside our road was the camel track along which trudged past a camel train of Kuchis, a tribe which had wintered in the plains and were coming up to their summer homes with their flocks. There were tiny children who could not keep up the pace, hens, baby camels and puppies, all sitting on camel humps. We saw a bus with people on top and hanging on behind, and a taxi with thirteen people hanging on outside and, when it stopped, twelve more got out from inside. This made us realise what utter luxury we were travelling in, even if we had not thought so till then.

At the customs post we were held up a long time on the Afghan side; they seemed to be looking for drugs. A Mercedes was being very thoroughly examined, with two very suave, shining types inside; a crippled youth on crutches had given up and was being carried by a friend; bearded patriarchs strode along at the head of parties of purdah women and small children; police in faded uniforms chased with sticks people who tried to nip across before their time.

In Afghanistan there was evidence of a lot of foreign aid coming in: hydro-electric schemes from the Germans, a modern road thanks to the Americans and there was another road going north built by the Russians, which must have been a great help when they were at war later on. The Russians had reclaimed a desert valley and planted 23,000 acres of cereals, sesame and sunflower seeds, sugar cane, citrus, figs and olives. The Chinese had made a lake and stocked it with carp. On a great gateway which gave the history of the area an allusion was made to the British as 'our well-matched and respected foes who parted in friendship.'

We passed through two gorges. The mountains of bare rock high on each side were very close and so high that, when you were at the bottom by the tumbling river, you only caught a glimpse of sunlight at the top. The road winds up incredibly steeply, 4,000 feet in a few minutes to above the snowline, emerging on to the snow-covered plateau where Kabul lies.

The old city of Kabul was a sea of mud and dirty snow swept into heaps. People pushed and hurried and bumped you. Every male over the age of about twelve carried a gun of some kind, mostly ancient rifles. The shops looked attractive but the goods were shoddy. A man sitting on a Persian carpet was selling ear-pickers of an astonishing assortment of kinds, another sold a puff on native water pipes or single cigarettes. Some sold second-hand shoes or repaired what you had on. Lapis lazuli was the thing to buy here as it is mined in Afghanistan and I bought a savage great ring for a song. The museum was filled with lovely things from all over the world, found on the Old Silk Road, which started (or ended) here and on which we were to travel until we reached Istanbul. I mourn all the beauty destroyed by the Taleban in the year 2001 when they sacked this museum and blew up the great Buddhas in the mountains. The people were very varied, Uzbeks and Turkomans, Afghans and Hazaras and descendants of the Greeks and Persians. The language generally spoken is Farsi, as in Iran, but there were many others being spoken, too. Men sold great baskets of peeled cooked beetroots like huge carrots, mixed with ditto carrots and turnips, looking quite tempting. They keep them wet to look their best. Others sold baskets of different nuts, strings of figs, lots of different raisins.

Walking in the old town was a messy business and it was overcast and very cold. The streets are not paved and swept snow is piled in a ridge down the middle, while you paddle in at least an inch of black sludge; in one place a man with a pick was breaking up the ice beneath that. There were salt shops where great blocks of grey salt were stacked and a chap would be patiently hand grinding it on a millstone with a little pick and grinder, and it looked quite white in the bags. Funny cuts of meat hung up in one row and a bloody man heaved carcasses out of a cart with a poor horse that looked as if it might be the next victim.

In contrast to the old town the streets of the modern town are wide and there are gardens, but it has no real charm. Old snow here is swept into dirty heaps in the side streets which are muddy. People sell things on the pavements. Men lurk inside shops and pop out like spiders to lure you in as soon as you hesitate. Donkeys are everywhere, just visible under great saddlebags of pomegranates or oranges or carrots or something, poor little things.

We had a nice-looking hotel but nothing worked. We were continually ringing for help. The bedside lights did not work: they brought bulbs. There was no hot water: they came and tinkered and said it would come in a few hours but it didn't. There was no water in the bedside thermoses: they brought some. There were no bath towels: oh yes there were, on top of the wardrobe; there was only one and no hand towel: sorry, no more, they had gone to the laundry. It was fairly typical of this part of the world but it looked so grand that we had hoped it would be better.

We had awful trouble with Helena, my elderly friend, at every customs post. She was travelling to England to visit her son, who, it seemed, collected weapons, so Helena kept on buying cutlasses and heaven knows what, till one day in Kabul she bought a handgun. She had no ammunition for it and it was, in fact, an antique but still it was a gun and we were all afraid of her being caught with it, as we should all have been in trouble. At customs points there onwards, when the inspectors boarded the bus and demanded to see inside bags here and there, we all collaborated by shuffling her bag of weaponry along to and fro under the seats. It was horribly exciting.

On the road we passed quite a number of nomads and at one place stopped and communed with the people who had pitched their hand-woven, much patched, black tents. One tent was full of lambs, and they had a camel and a brown sheep outside. Their dogs have cropped ears so that there is no tooth-hold for a wolf; they cut them off when they are puppies and feed them to the others. The women were very much afraid of us and, at another tent, Margrit, who had given one woman some sweets, had her hair pulled by another and the evil eye cast upon her, while another threw a handful of earth at her. They were doubtless frightened because their men were not around and really one would have been more surprised if we had been welcomed.

Kandahar seemed very uninteresting to us except for our accommodation. Tiny rooms with basketwork walls and three sagging *charpoys* were the norm and the wash-place was for all. This was a central room with urinal and plugless basin, and four dungeons off it holding a shower and three loos, one Asiatic and two skits on European, with boxes for used paper. We hardly washed, just cleaned our teeth, and hurried on to Herat.

The brown countryside was now dotted with mud huts which had domed roofs, because it was difficult to find wood for flat roofs. There were sometimes mud enclosures a foot high with mihrab*-shaped alcoves where travellers could pray and we often saw them at it. Once, miles from anywhere, we saw a woman carrying a baby, with a three-year-old at her heels. Buses were brilliant, painted and covered with clinking adornments, and having apt mottoes written over the cab such as 'Live and let live'. A windmill for grinding corn was a tall, mud edifice with three wings making two channels for wind. It was apparently very fertile country, growing cotton, rice, wheat, pistachios, melons and grapes, but at this time of year there was nothing of that to see.

At Herat they fire an 1802 British gun at noon. There are four minarets left of the fifteenth century mosque built by Sharuk, the son of Tamurlane the Mongol, who destroyed Herat, but Sharuk's son built it again. This mosque was covered in blue and green tiling, quite a lot still remaining. Sharuk's wife was Chinese and quite a girl; we saw her mausoleum with three domes, one outside the other. She was a builder of monuments and a schemer, and when her husband died in Teheran her grandson, whom she had insisted should accompany her to Teheran for fear he should grab the throne from her in her

---

*A mihrab is a niche in a mosque showing the direction of Mecca.

absence, simply took over and stripped her of all her possessions and made her walk (at seventy) from Teheran to Herat behind the coffin; she was murdered ten years later. We watched tiles being made which was rather fascinating. They make the mosaic with different coloured glazed pieces specially chipped out for their position; they are inserted face down in the design and have to fit exactly, then concrete is poured over the backs and holds them together.

Iran

One of the most interesting things was the qanats – these are a 2,000-year-old underground irrigation system. The water comes hundreds of miles from mountain springs in man-made tunnels and every now and then there is a mound with a shaft and steps in it, going down to the water; thus much land is farmed which otherwise would have been desert. The Shah had done wonders for his country, I thought, so it was sad when he was deposed. He had turned over most of his land to be sold gradually on favourable terms to the workers, and persuaded other landowners to do the same. He invested money in industries, built roads, built up the army.

Getting a taxi in Teheran was an education. You had to stand in the road and hail the taxi and as it slowed down you shouted where you wanted to go; if it was going that way it stopped and in you got. But getting in was a business, as there would be other passengers and any amount of varied luggage. These would be dropped off here and there and others taken on. You would be dropped at the nearest point to your destination and have to make your way there on foot. I was not staying in an hotel with the others, but with an Armenian friend of Basil's, so I had to go through this performance, which was kindly explained to me in the hotel by one of the guests who found me trying to identify either a taxi rank or Basil's friend in the phone book.

The Armenians lived behind an extremely high wall and one had to go through a security system at the gate and also at the front door, such was the fear they continually lived in. They took me to the Armenian church where everyone milled around as they chose while the service was going on; even those at the altar seemed to go off for coffee or something from time to time. Extended family called to make my acquaintance and they were a charming lot, well-educated.

I saw carpets being made that might take three women two years to make. Children, too, were employed in carpet-making and recently a great fuss has been made in our press about this activity in Pakistan. The people in these countries feel that it is right that a child should do what he can to help his family and indeed some of them would not survive without the little contributed by the children. Another point is that it keeps them off the street and out of the sort of trouble so many other youngsters get up to. We saw a camel underground, which was only there to show tourists how linseed oil used to be made; he would walk round and round operating two grindstones which crushed the seeds. In another room were two enormous tree trunks, with weights one end, and two men would jump on it from a height to express the oil. Now it is done by engine and pulley.

We shopped in a lovely covered mall, which is the traditional kind of shopping centre of the Middle East, to protect shoppers from the heat. The variety of things sold here was wonderful and so different: jewellery and carpets, tapestries and spices, exotic fruit and vegetables, and extraordinary cuts of meat one could not recognise. One day I saw a soldier go up to a policeman on point duty in the middle of the road and kiss him – it made my day. The town was filled with lovely yellow forsythia bushes, solid with bloom and no leaves, also japonica. Down the centre of the main street was a promenade with small pools and fountains every few yards.

There are many wonders to be seen in Iran, perhaps the best being the Crown Jewels, with unbelievably enormous precious stones, though sometimes a very primitive setting. Persepolis, a town built 2,500 years ago by Darius the Achaemenian when the Persian Empire was born, only stood intact for thirty years because Alexander the Great defeated Darius and sacked the city; what is left are remnants of a great stone palace with columns and grand flights of steps and wonderful relief carvings and sculpted beasts.

One day we ate at an eating house where they served *chelow* kebab: grilled meat, rice with butter and yoghurt and raw onions – very good. It was all the more enjoyable for watching the other customers, particularly one Persian I could hardly take my eyes off. He had a huge heap of rice and meat before him and he behaved as if it was a competition – his spoon would be piled with rice, he would stuff it in and as soon as he could load another spoonful, he would cram that and two or three more in, his cheeks would bulge, his jaws working, his eyes starting, then he would lean across his companion and grab the water jug, pour out and rapidly drink two glasses and then start again, sometimes putting his hand flat against his mouth to keep it all in. Rice surrounded his plate. When it had all gone he collapsed sideways on the table. At another table a father with two small children ordered three heaps of rice and meat. They did not eat quite so voraciously but it still looked like a competition and they kept at it furiously till not a grain was left, when they rushed out like all the others – it must be the way to behave!

One day we went to a resort on the Caspian Sea which was very Victorian in atmosphere. People were taking pony rides along the sands, or going for rides in rowing boats. We ate grilled sturgeon out of the Caspian and drank their very good bottled beer. The cost of caviar was rising because of the pollution of the waters by Russian factories belching waste and oil into it further north.

I loved visiting Isfahan because my mother was brought up there. She may have lived in the Armenian quarter, which was walled, as she used to talk of walking on the walls. The Armenian woman I had stayed with in Teheran said she had lived in Isfahan as a child and her mother would not take her shopping in the main town 'or the Muslims will kill you!' Apparently when they *did* go shopping they would go in a band of about sixty, because they were so afraid; the Muslims would throw things and shout rude rhymes. When there was trouble they would retreat inside the walls and shut the great gates.

Turkey
Getting into Turkey was quite a marathon. To start the day the phone rang and I answered it:
    'Hello,' said a honeyed voice. 'Good Morning, it is 6 o'clock.'
    'No it isn't,' I said rudely, 'it's 6.20!'
    The voice collapsed weakly, breathing 'yes' – it was our 6 a.m. call.
    We drove to the border, where Mount Ararat and Little Mount Ararat were to our right, snow-coated almost to their bases. The border posts on both sides were deep in mud. We all went off to use the communal loos and get our shoes muddy. A couple of storks were nesting in a tree: one would fly off to get more sticks and a rather hopeless ruffled one was left in charge, fussing about – immediately a cloud of sparrows would descend to steal bits of the nest.
    The coach had not gone more than a mile through awful slime when we became stuck in a traffic jam which rapidly piled up behind us. We moved a few inches in five hours but otherwise just sat. We got out and found a dry patch on the verge to sit and have our picnic lunches, a lower mud track below us and below that the plain, patched with water, stretching away towards Mount Ararat. Rumour had it that the jam reached ahead ten kilometres and that some vehicles had been stuck for twenty-four hours. Most were lorries, some with huge trailers. The law was every man for himself. A few jeeps and private cars risked the soggy plain and chose to attack the slope near us, so many an interesting skid and bog-down enlivened our wait. At 5 p.m. the Muslims lined up on the edge of the road to pray, some spreading handkerchiefs to kneel on. A mullah with water managed to wash, but others smeared earth symbolically on their hands, faces and necks. One lovely sight was a woman with her *chador* (purdah garment) spread like a cormorant's wings between her and the line of vehicles, and in her shadow on the other side a man relieved himself, water pot and all, taking quite a time – her husband? We never knew as they walked away in opposite directions. Two of the nice big local dogs with cropped ears, and a puppy trailing behind, came walking briskly over the plain from Mount Ararat. They are quite like furry golden labradors with curled tails. Lorry drivers kept losing their patience and

overtaking if the road cleared, which resulted in head-on confrontations with
the line coming the other way.

In the end some of our men went ahead and unsnarled a few things and said
that drivers who did not overtake were so incensed with those who did that if
the latter came to grief nobody helped them. About 6 p.m. we began to move
and passed several appalling sights, showing what crazy risks people take. We
stopped after dark in a tiny village for an unscheduled meal. The villagers
really got cracking at this unexpected bonus, not a woman to be seen but
young boys dashed in and out fetching extra chairs and tables and glasses of tea
from a nearby teahouse. Old men came in clutching eight or nine loaves to
their unattractive jerseys with their filthy hands, others went and bought
glasses and cutlery from the local shop. A male crowd gathered outside the
window, including several characters straight out of *The Godfather*, wearing ties
and cloth caps and old-fashioned overcoats carefully buttoned up. The
representatives of the establishment occasionally opened the doors and shouted
'shoo' in Turkish but they soon gathered again. The proprietor sat next to
Peter, the English accountant, with an English grammar and tried very hard to
make contact.

'What is your profession?'

Peter settled for being a banker as he could not get 'accountant' over.

'Is that your mother?' This was me, as I was sitting next to Peter and he was
sure I must be somebody's mother. Peter eventually made him understand I
worked for the Red Cross and was travelling alone, but that was difficult too.
They served us with very good soup in enamel bowls rather like babies'
potties, followed by raw onions and tiny meatballs the size of truffles and lots
of bread. I bought oranges across the road. Then we took to the road again,
sleeping if we could. It was rugged hilly country and Bernie could not speed;
starting at 7.30 a.m. he completed the 400 miles about 1.45 a.m. next day. The
hotel was good and the people were up, and I had a good hot bath before
turning in.

Next day the roads were clear but we drove through snow-covered country,
up to 7,000 feet. First impressions were good, though the people were clearly
poorer than in Iran, but the peasants here had built themselves dry-stone
houses with either flat roofs or red-tiled, with stone walls around. The sheep
were long-legged and mostly brown; horses and carts abounded and the horses
looked well cared for. In the towns the 'modern' buildings looked older than
Iran's, though Atatürk only took over in 1923, about the same time as Shah
Reza. Women in national dress wear a lot of red, laced bodices and dirndl skirts
and head scarves, and one wore green knickerbockers to below her skirt, with
red and orange stockings – I didn't see any *chadors*, but lots of storks, one
nesting on top of a telegraph pole. Turkish arches are inverted Vs, (not curved

and pointed ones), which are not so pretty. The dogs have ears. They use horse ploughs. Schoolchildren wore black smocks and white collars.

We stopped at a caravanserai, the Sultanhani, a Seljuk edifice of the thirteenth century and quite remarkable. It was built completely of stone with groups of pillars decorating the huge outside walls, an enormous archway and a square courtyard inside with a large square mosque in the middle. Round the square were decorative arches and arcades, one side having rooms which were shops, big, with high, vaulted ceilings and very little light. On the far side there was a huge hall with two rows of pillars where the travellers slept. A flight of steps in the courtyard led to the roof and people could sleep on the walls and roofs too.

We drove through Kayseri which is Caesarea, to Urgup where I went to bed feeling rather poorly. Fritz, the Austrian doctor, had been a boon on this trip, knowing which drugs we all needed which could usually be bought easily in the open market. Nothing would have stopped me going to the Goreme Valley, though, to see the caves hollowed out by the Christians in the eighth to thirteenth centuries, which was called Cappadocia then. There were monasteries, nunneries, and churches, all very small and painted throughout with colours still bright and intact where Muslims had not defaced them. One picture I enjoyed was of the Nativity, with Joseph looking absolutely fed up, his back to the scene, his head on his hand, his eyes reluctantly swivelling round to see. Nearby is the Underground City which is under a village, and each house has a kind of disguised trapdoor in the floor, so that when persecution was imminent the people vanished below. The formations in the valley are extraordinary. 'Fairy chimneys' are formed by erosion of the soft sandstone, often leaving a little hat of darker rock on top. The Christians hollowed rooms out and apparently, once hollowed, they did not fall in. Some of the caves were still being lived in and one fairy chimney had the loudspeakers on top that the modern muezzin uses!

I was struggling a bit at this stage and did not go to a disco with the others, where apparently some pretty wild Turkish dancing carried on – a cross between Russian and Greek, very virile, and according to my room-mate the dancers had erections! Our party were drinking wine and *raki*, the local form of anis, and felt very unwell the next day. The standard of hotels in Turkey was better than anything we had so far experienced, and the whole feeling of the country was a mix between Asian and European. But the plumbing, though different, was not a lot better. In one hotel when I pulled the plug in my bath, the water poured briskly out of a special hole at the side of the bath all over the floor. After a moment of panic I put the plug back and found that the water then just seeped away. In Dyarbakir, feeling very clever, I put my own plug in the handbasin, and filled it with water and to my horror the whole thing came away from the wall, never having been so unreasonably treated before. On the whole the plumbing in all these countries had to be seen (and smelt) to be believed.

In the countryside the women were still wearing yashmaks though not purdah garments; however, they contrived to look quite shapeless. The carts have wooden wheels and metal rims and must be bone-shattering to ride in, quite unpadded. A lot of opium is grown, for medicine and for export, as the people are not addicts. The United States asked the Turkish Government to restrict its growth and the Turks, with an eye to arms, agreed and 'only' issued 150 licences that year – the year before they had issued seventy-five! People hoard it in underground stores and smuggle it and the trade thrives.

Pammakale was lovely, a spa with calceous water pouring over a hillside to form ice-white solid cascades with shallow pools atop. It has been a resort for centuries. The Phrygians are thought to have built the first town, the Romans built another, though it was peopled with Greeks – each time it was wrecked by earthquakes. I was quite ill here and the others were marvellous to me, rallying round with my luggage, bringing me flowers from an expedition, and bringing me food.

At Izmir we had a ghost with diarrhoea, or so it seemed; the chain pulled of its own volition about ten times an hour, though of course was never up to pulling when you wanted it to. Fritz put me on a good drug which helped so that I was able to see Ephesus. We approached Ephesus along a lovely cypress-lined road, with grassy sides where donkeys and horses grazed; families in colourful local dress worked in the fields and we saw gypsies with old-fashioned barrel roofs on their carts.

We visited what is thought to have been the Virgin Mary's house and it seems more than likely that it was. Jesus had put her in the care of St John, who later lived and died in Ephesus. A German nun who had never been out of Germany had visions and stigmata and described the place where Mary lived: she said you could see Ephesus and Samos at the same time and this is apparently the only place where you can. In 1891 when people came to investigate, they found Christians who had made a pilgrimage there annually, as their ancestors had, to the house they believed to be Mary's. Now it is a little church and the room near the altar is said to have been her bedroom. Below the house are springs of holy water which cure people. The view is gorgeous, through trees and between hills to the sea, everything covered with daisies, and it has not been spoiled by being a tourist attraction.

Ephesus is composed of three towns, the third being the famous one. They kept moving it because of the river silting up and attracting malarial mosquitoes. This third one was built by the Greeks and was clearly quite a place. Several streets have been excavated, all of marble like the buildings. The first street led downhill and we saw the Council Hall, a five-storey house, fountains, a temple, a brothel, a lavatory (with rows of marble seats with nice 'keyholes' in, a drain with running water for washing in front, and one underneath), baths, one hot, one tepid and one cold, and a theatre. At a crossroads one came to another lovely straight street lined with columns. On one side there was an enormous agora, or market place, below, and at the end a simply splendid auditorium in a wonderful state, to hold 30,000 people, dressing rooms and all intact. At right angles to that another street called 'Arcadian' led past the agora to where the sea used to be, and had gymnasiums and churches and four pillars which used to have the figures of Matthew, Mark, Luke and John on top. St Paul was here and the people rioted about him in the agora and then ran over the road to the amphitheatre to hold a protest meeting, while St Paul was popped into prison some way off on a mountain-top for safety. The country round here was full of olive trees studding the hills to the very summits.

I could go on and on about the things we saw but my most vivid memory is of my Turkish bath in Istanbul. Nobody would come with me but I was determined to have one, though it was so difficult to find one for women that I nearly gave up. Eventually I found one, and was received by a woman who could speak a little French so we were able to communicate. She gave me a key to a cupboard for my clothes and tried to persuade me to take off my knickers but failed. She provided me with some clogs which were needed to prevent slipping on the wet marble floors. The circular 'bath' room was huge, and domed like a mosque, with coloured 'lights' in the ceiling. A great round marble slab occupied the centre of the room, surrounded by pillars and a gulley for water. On the other side of the gulley, steps went up to silver bowls in the walls, every other one gushing hot water from dolphin taps. A beautiful woman was lying on the slab being pummelled by the most colossal woman, who also appeared to be naked, but when she stood up I saw she had a tiny pair of black pants on, into which she scooped her stomach, and this seems to have been uniform. A similar woman grabbed hold of me, removed my pants without a by-your-leave, and soaping me all over, turned me on the slab like a wet fish, deftly preventing my sliding away altogether by grabbing my wrist. When the massage was over, she sat on the steps with me between her thighs and to my dismay took what appeared to be a brick and with it washed my hair. One certainly felt clean afterwards. A flock of schoolgirls came in twittering while I was there, and were told to be quiet. An old lady nearby was busy catching the wildlife in her furrier parts, whilst another was doing her washing. So many people have no running water at home that these baths are a godsend. I walked back to the hotel clean, bedraggled, and carrying my wet pants. That doorkeeper had been quite right.

Istanbul kept us busy for five days and we could have spent far longer there.

The Topkapi Palace, built in the fifteenth century, held so many treasures. There were painted ceilings, tortoiseshell and mother-of-pearl inlay on the doors, tiled walls in soft colours, niches with mattresses and cushions, huge copper fireplaces with hoods, and rather inferior carpets, but above all what I believe are still called the Crown Jewels, although the country is now a republic: enormous emeralds and a really lovely, huge, drop diamond, set in smaller diamonds, a jewelled dagger with three of the biggest emeralds, rings and turban ornaments and all sorts of nonsense. One room was full of past sultans' old clothes, one set having been worn by a sultan at the time of his murder and being stained by his blood, another in lovely condition had been worn by a sultan on his deathbed in 1481! Lots of the clothes were padded so they were probably never washed and it is miraculous to think they have survived so long. There was an armoury, an embroidery room with wonderful things exquisitely finely sewn in gold and silver and delicate colours, and a porcelain room. One sacred room held a casket containing Muhammad's mantle, another contained hairs from his beard. There was, rather surprisingly, a hand of St John in an arm-and-hand shaped case, and a piece of his cranium. We wandered in the harem, and saw a room which had a fountain bubbling noisily out of the wall so that the sultan could talk secretly there. In one room were two raised sleeping apartments, one on each side, for two wives as sometimes the sultan changed wives several times in the night.

An expedition up the Bosphorus was a must. It cost so little that we were stunned to discover by experience that it took six hours. It was pleasant, a bit cold, chugging from stop to stop. Bootblacks tried to polish your shoes and other chaps to sell you tiny glasses of tea or 'sandervich'. An old man, rather poorly dressed but speaking good English, talked to us part of the way. He had been a schoolboy when the battles were fought at Gallipoli – we had visited the beaches at Gallipoli and wondered how our soldiers had ever hoped to scale those cliffs. We saw the rows and rows of war graves, most beautifully tended, and the wall with the names of thousands of men who never even got a burial. One of our party found human remains in the bushes which we presumed were wartime relics.

Greece

I am not going into details here as almost everyone has been to Greece or read about it. Suffice it to say we did a pretty good tour of all the main tourist spots, Mycenae in my opinion being one of the most interesting; Delphi, too. Meteora did rather vie for first place, with its monasteries perched on peaks, one of which we visited, with beautiful medieval frescoes. Hair-raising paths and steps led one up, with horrifying sheer drops to be passed. Everything needed is hauled up by ropes and in some cases people are, too, in baskets.

A personal experience in Athens was an evening at a nightclub, to which I went because I wanted to see Greek dancing, but did not understand that we were going to take part ourselves. It was rather like Turkish and Russian dancing but more energetic than it looked. The wild flowers everywhere at this time of year were so lovely, huge red poppies, wild mustard, big yellow daisies. We passed a place on the road where a bandit used to waylay travellers and force them to wash his feet before he pushed them over the cliff. We passed where Hercules killed a lion.

One night I was taken out to dinner by friends of Basil's, and it was interesting to hear their views on the political situation. Gloomy. They were clearly not sure of the new regime, which was moderate right, as opposed to the military extreme right which they had suffered for seven years; even Athens was ruined by indiscriminate building being allowed; political prisoners were tortured, not tried, and conditions in the prisons were indescribable.

Beyond Delphi we drove through the most luxuriant olive groves in Greece, thick with trees. The Judas-trees were out, absolutely loaded with pink blossom and no leaves, and there was lilac. There were many donkeys about and the village life seemed delightfully old-fashioned and rural. The only blight was the number of memorials along the road to people who had gone over the edge.

Yugoslavia

First stop Skopje, which is a fairly modern town, as the old buildings were nearly all destroyed by earthquakes in AD 518 and 1963. Only the rather beautiful fortress on a hill has survived, together with a few minarets and mosques. I had a single room to myself, what a treat, with a bathroom, but the water was lukewarm. The service was incredibly slow and bad, the food lukewarm, nobody to help with baggage and so on. Agriculture was more efficient; barefoot men and boys with horse ploughs produced neat furrows. Women wore baggy Turkish trousers, and the houses were square and one-storeyed.

We entered mountainous country, travelling through steep and narrow gorges with a turquoise blue river tearing along far below as if it was cold. The engineering feat of that road was wonderful. It had been cut out of the sheer rock face and we went through sixty-eight tunnels. Above us was a single-track railway which had been similarly hacked out. A bush stop here was difficult, as we had to swarm up a hill and hope nobody was actually looking, as cover was sparse. Wild violets and heartsease and daisies graced the green sward where we picnicked by the river in the sun, hills before and behind with little cots dotted about and a graceful railway bridge high above.

The drive to Dubrovnik was a treat. We drove first across a lake which is

Albanian one end and Yugoslav the other. People were fishing in pointed canoes like the Solomon Islands ones. Trees and reeds grew out of the water. We drove up and over the rugged mountains down to the blue sea below. It was so very beautiful, with little stone villages and red roofs and cone-shaped haystacks with poles sticking out of the tops. Our hotel that night was six miles outside Dubrovnik, a real hotel with hot water and reasonable food, a swimming pool and nightingales singing for hours below.

Dubrovnik really is the most delectable little town, the walls complete, strong and high and thick. There seems no rhyme or reason to the outline of the town but it is beautiful in its asymmetry. We walked round the walls, which was quite exhausting as there were so many steps, but one could not miss it. It is flanked by waist-high walls and one could look down one side to the sea, blue-green and calm, with the odd little fishing boat, and on the other side lay the town where the houses were often higher than the wall. The view was of people's washing, geraniums and cats, and a little gate in the wall where they could get out on to the rocks above the sea. One looked down further on over the waving sea of pink and brown roofs and caught glimpses down long narrow-stepped alleys. We saw women in black with headkerchiefs and children in long red stockings and smocks, and an old man in blue mending red nets beside a vine in his yard. Down in the town itself one gets the impression of grandeur which one did not get by just looking at the rooftops. The streets are all paved with marble-like stone, smooth and polished with age; cars in general are not allowed, only the odd lorry, ambulance or taxi. One main street, wide and gracious, goes straight across the centre from the Pile Gate to the harbour, with a great fountain like a ball by the gate. There were a great many churches, and the cathedral is distinguished by having the head, leg and arm of St Blaize in a box surmounted by a crown, and a piece of the true cross, which one felt it really might be. In general the architecture is fifteenth century in solid stone.

The people seemed to belong to two distinct ethnic groups, one group tall and handsome in rather a craggy way, with big noses, and the other smaller and running to roundness. I asked a girl in a bookshop as tactfully as possible and she said at once that the tall ones were Croatians and Dalmatians, and the small ones Serbs. There is no love lost between them, she said, which we have all learned since. One of our Australians (the girl who worried so about the bush stops) was an ethnic Serb but noticed that, when she said so, the Croatians stopped being friendly.

Next day we went on another lovely coastal drive, with big islands appearing, one of which was Kocula where Marco Polo was born, and where Kenneth and I went many years later. We saw purple-blue irises, convolvulus, firs and cypresses and olives, and a hairy road with no edging at all. We paid a very fleeting visit to Split and I was glad later on in my life to be able to see it again.

Italy

We were copped for speeding in Yugoslavia and Bernie was furious – he had been going two kph too fast. In Italy the atmosphere was much more relaxed; the border official just flipped an eye at a few passports, waved his hand, said 'Arrivederci' and departed. Arriving in dear old Venice was disappointing, in an area filled with shipping and cranes, factories and motorways, and Bernie backed the bus into a ghastly, milling bus park; we all got out and humped our bags about fifteen minutes to our hotel, where I shared a third-floor room with two others. But the shuttered window looked down on to a wistaria-covered trellis and a little open-air restaurant.

I had last come here with Satan in November 1962 when there were very few people about; now it was a seething mass, which rather spoilt things. We walked a great deal in the enchanting, narrow side streets opening every now and then into a pretty square with maybe a church and a *trattoria*, or some swings and shops. We went under arches and across humped bridges over little canals, down which we would glimpse views of parked gondolas, canoes, waterboats, washing, archways, ornamented doors and filthy water. We saw many of the sights and I actually climbed up the campanile and had a good view all round. There is an angel up there who turns his back to the sea if it is going to be bad weather, and faces it if it is going to be good.

The population was shrinking rapidly: in 1951 it had been 55,000 but now it was 11,000. The lovely mosaic floors of St Mark's were very uneven due to the fact that Venice is sinking. Many houses had been abandoned and in many others people could no longer live on the ground floor. At high tide water seeped up between the paving stones. The Australians on our bus were surprised to see so many tall, fair Italians because the Italian immigrants they have at home are short and fat, presumably people from the south where agriculture is tough and the people poor.

One evening when I was walking around with one of the girls, we were picked up by a naval Petty Officer who wanted to practise his English, which he did furiously, while he marched us round pointing out things of special interest. He pointed out that two of the columns on the first floor of the Doge's Palace were painted yellow instead of white. This was because, when the Doge condemned a prisoner, he would come out and pronounce sentence to the people from this balcony, and if it was a heavy sentence of twenty or more years he would stand between the yellow columns. On the Bridge of Sighs there is a hole in the corner of the floor to let the blood drip through into the canal, as some of the prisoners were executed on the bridge itself. If a prisoner was put on the ground floor of the prison on the other side of the bridge, he soon died because the water rose in the winter and he fell ill and probably drowned because he could not stand up for long.

Germany

On we pressed through Treviso and Cortina, where the Winter Olympics had been held in (I think) 1956. It was lovely scenery with high sudden mountains with quite a lot of snow about, and chalets with wooden balconies overhanging. It is fascinating to see the differences between countries within a few miles, but then one can see such differences even between counties in England. In Italy everything seemed so artistic, if sometimes shabby; in Germany everything was very solid and well cared for. We did not go on the autobahn but on the old road, as it is prettier, and as we approached the Bremner Pass we were on a carriageway high on concrete stilts above the old, originally Roman (and probably earlier) road winding along by the river. We travelled over the terribly high Europa Bridge and then in to Innsbruck, a solid-looking town of four-storeyed houses of responsible-looking proportions with no-nonsense rectangular windows and arched ones on the ground floor. We drank beer and ate sausage and discovered who had any German connections: Oggie's mother was Austrian and she found herself living in Yugoslavia after the war changed boundaries; Margrit, our guide, said her father was north German but her mother was a Slav; Diana's mother's people were German Jews, but she was brought up Christian; my grandmother was Hungarian but her area (Transylvania) would now be Austrian. It was one of the pleasures of the trip to find out the backgrounds of the other travellers in a way one never does on an ordinary journey. Three months living together through all sorts of misadventures, illnesses when we all supported each other, and delights shared, brought a mixed bag of humans surprisingly close.

Another pleasure for me was the way my family rallied and wrote to every address I had given them, so that I received mail in Katmandu, Delhi, Lahore, Teheran, Istanbul and Innsbruck, and did not feel out of touch with them. I knew about Pam's new teeth which she described with her usual humour, about how Julia was getting on with painting the Menorcan cottage, about William's change of plans. I was cheered to hear that Basil thought that, of his three children, Tom was the one looking forward most to my return, as he had said so, and also that Tom found he missed his mother more than before. Also I felt that Basil seemed to have progressed in his thinking, because he welcomed me as the woman in their lives, whereas before he had, I think, been jealous that I might take Doreen's place.

In Innsbruck we visited the mausoleum of Maximilian I, which boasted fourteen over-life-sized bronzes of his relatives and ancestors, including King

Arthur of England! One of the bronzes clearly depicted a homosexual, striking an elegant pose in a new suit of armour. There was a museum of folklore, with costumes and domestic implements, furniture, porcelain stoves, pottery, pewter, copperware and so on. Another museum was of religious art, where there were lovely details such as a chap being boiled, having his eyes put out, his entrails wound out, and his nails having horrid things stuck under them, but he looked remarkably unconcerned. They also had prehistoric and Roman remains. The old town had houses built into the original walls and the famous golden roof gleamed over all. It was built in 1500 by Maximilian I and in 1899 the Emperor of the time put the gold medallions all over it because he was fed up with his reputation for meanness.

The drive of 300 miles to Heidelberg was very dull on a great autobahn, where we felt so cut off from the countryside. I walked for about two hours through the old city of Heidelberg and up a steep cobbled ramp to an originally Romanesque castle with rounded arches and heavy round towers. In the eighteenth century a baroque palace was built inside it with hundreds of windows. It had wonderful views of the Danube and the wooded hills the other side, and people were able to enjoy these views while exercising their children and dogs in what was now a public park.

We reached Ghent in Belgium where, to our surprise, we were housed in a splendid hotel. We had a terrific last dinner together, in a gallery looking down on the main restaurant where Queen Fabiola was dining; we had all been hard put to it to look respectable after three months on the move. One of our company had organised an entertainment, to which we all contributed what we could; I recited a poem about the journey which I had composed and which went down well. Ian, the organiser, announced imaginary things found on the bus: a baby donkey in the heavy luggage locker (aimed at Biddy from Norfolk Island who was crazy about donkeys), a heavily drugged belly dancer, a Yugoslav waiter, and so on. He also sang to the tune of 'A Partridge in a Pear Tree' all the things Margrit was supposed to have bought and put in a side locker, ten Persian carpets, nine golden bracelets and so on, which was very good. Harry got up, we supposed to perform, but announced that he was going to marry the cousin who was meeting him in London, so a hail of congratulations ensued. Awards were given for all sorts of mad things like the Donald Campbell Memorial Shield for the European Land Speed Record to Bernie, and the Self-Defence Award to Virginia for routing Iranian Bottom Pinchers. In fact a good time was had by all.

England
Up at 5 a.m. to catch the 8 a.m. ferry, we had a cold, wet crossing, much of which I spent buying duty-free things. Driving up to London I saw primroses

and bluebells, which the Aussies had never seen and we had not seen on the continent, and I was so thrilled by the gardens, but the others did not seem to notice them. Finally we arrived at Mayfair Place, near Berkeley Square, in all our disarray, and I was met by Alison and Michael, which was really nice. They grabbed my luggage and stowed it in a large car and swept me off to Richmond where they lived, through the park with the deer, and I felt I was still sightseeing.

The whole trip had been the experience of a lifetime and I have never regretted a moment of it. It whetted my appetite to get back and 'do' some of these countries in more depth but the only one I managed to get back to was Turkey, though I did go to quite a few different ones.

CHAPTER 9

Suffolk II 1975 Onwards

Aldeburgh

PROBABLY THIS will be my last world! I have never lived so long in one place and a very pleasant place it is to live in. When I returned from the Far East I had to have a small operation and Julia gave up living in Menorca and came home to see me through it. In the event she stayed with me for two years and left when she got married.

I sold Moat House and the Menorcan farmhouse and lived in a tiny cottage in Aldeburgh's High Street. I found employment with the Aldeburgh Festival and was within walking distance of my office. Julia's dog became mine and also worked there. Booby was a great character, a rough-haired golden terrier of indeterminate lineage, though I was assured he was a Menorcan hedgehog-hunter. When he first came he was a ladykiller and after three months of his whimpering and shivering about the ladies of the town, I had him 'altered'. He took this in his stride, simply switching from ladies to dustbins, and escaping whenever possible to do the rounds. Otherwise, he was my constant companion for ten years.

I joined the Festival as a typist, as that was all they had to offer at the time. I ended up, after doing all sorts of jobs, doing their local fundraising, which I had said was the one thing I would not do. In fact, it was good fun and allowed scope for the imagination. The nicest bit was the two walks I organised every Festival, when many concert-goers were glad to get off their behinds. Two hundred people in four coaches, with two guides per coach, would be divided into parties of twenty-five and spaced out, as nobody would want to walk in a crowd. Lunch would be provided and eaten at some chosen place of interest or charm. The very first one was along the Sailors' Path to Snape. Somebody had seen Druids behaving oddly in a Norfolk field and that started me off. I, too, had Druids in a distant field, behaving oddly; a nightingale sang (on a tape in a bush) at an unusual and worrying time for the bird-watchers; a satyr (in a very hot suit hired from the Royal Opera Company) chased a nymph through a wood; shepherds and maidens (from the primary school) disported themselves on a knoll, having had their rather basic, ringing language curbed; and Titania and Bottom wandered entwined, until they attracted the fascinated attention of a herd of cows. This walk, 'Midsummer Madness', was so popular that in future I often had a little nonsense on a walk, but not always, to keep them guessing.

We did another along the Sailors' Path as it is such a lovely walk; this was 'Snape Safari' and had Darkest Africa overtones: the General Manager's Secretary was boiled in a cauldron by dancing cannibals, a copy of *Fox's Book of Martyrs* lying on our path; two papier mâché giraffes' heads peered at us over a hedge, kept aloft by broomsticks held by staggering students in a high wind; a gorilla (me) sat on a low branch reading *The Times* upside down – I wore a very hot hired suit which none of the students would wear, and had paid a visit to Colchester Zoo to study voice and gesture; and a papier mâché hippo wallowed in the waters near the Maltings as they approached.

Other walks included birdwatching at Minsmere, a wander around Woodbridge and another round Southwold; one in Norwich where we heard a recital in the cathedral and visited the Sainsbury Centre; we trudged through forests and over heaths; we visited the poet Edward Fitzgerald's grave at Boulge, and the great moated Helmingham Hall with its extensive gardens; we walked across country when the wild lupins were out, and two hundred of us took to small craft on Thorpeness Mere with hilarious results; we walked across the fields at Dedham the way Constable would have walked to school, this on his anniversary in 1987.

These are some of the glorious walks we did, rain or shine, often accompanied by a couple with a cat, and by several dogs. Each one had some amusing little incident. Norman Scarfe, the historian, would give a talk, often from a pulpit, and would get so carried away by the vast information he had to impart that I had to equip myself with a whistle with which to threaten him when he had doubled his quota of time. We would liaise beforehand, maybe he asking if there was a good walk taking in some interesting building, or me asking if there was an interesting building near a certain lovely walk. One house at Claydon was so full of wonderful modern objets d'art that enquiry was made of the owner how on earth he insured all these things; he admitted it had been so difficult that he had bought an insurance company!

For thirteen years I organised these walks, and also other events at the Concert Hall at different times of the year: a Maltings Market selling all manner of things made in East Anglia from wrought iron to exquisite artificial flowers; a Craft Fair at which the artists were actually at work; a Flower Festival; an Auction of Promises; a Sotheby's dinner, and so on. I ran a lottery for a few years but that was too much work for little return, about £1,000 per annum, so I let it run down. A souvenir counter at every concert was also a lot of work, ordering and taking stock as well as manning it, but it meant I went to all the concerts.

In the process of selling the Menorcan property for me, Julia met the man she married, who luckily came from East Anglia so they live not very far away. John Hughes works for a meat company and at the time travelled round all the piggeries in the area. Over the years he has become a director of the company which has merged with another and become one of the biggest in the country. He and Julia bought a very old farmhouse near Cambridge which they have slowly improved and enlarged. The reason they chose it was because it had a row of pigsties in the yard and John could not resist. They did fatten young pigs for a time and I shall not forget the day when a consignment arrived in a lorry when John was away. The lone driver, bent double in the two-tiered vehicle, drove the pigs down the ramp to where Julia and John's mother and I held hurdles directing the flow into the sties. The trouble was that they would turn round halfway down and go back into the lorry. John's mother, a farmer's widow, soon sized up the situation and magnificently grabbed pigs by anything that stuck out and directed them forcefully the way they should go.

During these years I took several holidays abroad: with Patricia Gunning to Malta and to Crete, and alone to Sicily and Israel, which was the most interesting. Having thought of it as the Holy Land, I was suddenly made aware that it was not just the Christian Holy Land, but the Jewish and the Muslim too, and that politics about the homeland the Jews were making of the country were paramount. Women in khaki and people with guns and rather a dour approach to tourists emphasised the point. The Christian side of things was a little disappointing, as one found it hard to believe all the things one was told as to where Jesus was crucified, where entombed, and so on, though all in all it was good to have seen His country for oneself. All I saw of Palestine was one day, looking across the border from sophisticated, modern militant Israel, I could see an age-old landscape with a peasant and his laden donkey trudging along an unmade road, and another in his white robe working a field behind his ox and his simple harrow.

Religion has played a large part in my life. It began with going to Sunday School in Eastbourne, pretty willingly as we were given nice pictures to stick in a special book, and if you missed a Sunday it spoiled the story. When Irma left us with Nanny, church-going was stepped up and we went twice on Sunday and three times during the week to Foursquare Gospel revivalist meetings. In India religion, I fear, did not impinge. Then the Belgian convent made up for it and I was forced into the outer trappings of devoutness. It did nothing for me. When I lived alone in London it never occurred to me to go to church or say prayers, though I quite enjoyed the familiarity of going to church in some rural place when staying with friends or relations. It was only when the children began to ask questions that I began to ask questions myself. I had considered myself, unthinkingly, a Christian. My divorce had been a devastating experience, not only because of hurting Charles but also because I

Sir Kenneth Maddocks, my third husband, inspecting Fijian police.

was breaking my vows, and now that I had children I was automatically teaching them Christian values and Bible stories.

We were in Nigeria and I was incredibly lucky. Shopping in what was known as 'The Cold Store' one day I saw a twiddly stand of paperbacks, a most unusual sight, so of course went to see what was on offer. There I found C.S. Lewis's *Mere Christianity* which was exactly what I needed at that point, heaven-sent in fact. From that day I began to go to church again, having decided with a friend who was facing the same problem that that should be the place where we would find the light. Of course, there was no blinding flash but over the years my faith has been strengthened by this and by that: the wonderful pitter-patter of bare feet in a Solomon Islands church as the faithful poured in and crammed the benches, the love of God which shines out of some of one's friends, something in a newspaper article, occasionally even something in a sermon! Little things that build up. A discipline of daily prayer has helped. I have never doubted the existence of God – that has not been my problem. <u>That</u> is trying to keep up to His standard and overcome the fearful shortcomings in my nature. Tough going.

Twelve years after Satan's death, life took an unexpected turn and I got married again. I met Kenneth Maddocks at a commemoration lunch at the Chelsea Royal Hospital, to which we had both been invited by the Raymers, who had also been in Nigeria. Kenneth had been in the Colonial Service in

Kenneth and me on the Alde River.

Northern Nigeria and had risen to be Deputy Governor of the North at the time that Satan was the same in the West, and they had met several times.

When he was young and in the Tiv Division, which he toured on a bicycle, he made a map of the whole area (which up till then did not have one), which became the definitive map for a good many years. Of all the things he achieved, the way he did this must be quite the most outstanding. He attached a feather to a spoke of the front wheel of his bicycle and measured the distance the wheel covered between the departure of the feather and its return. He then pedalled off along bush paths, counting the clicks the feather made between two landmarks, say a bend in the path, an ant-hill, a palm-tree or a benighted hut. In this way he painstakingly measured and drew a remarkably accurate map.

Kenneth was married and I once met Elnor, his wife, on Red Cross business in London, but had never met Kenneth. He had gone on to be Governor General of Fiji and after retiring had worked as liaison officer between the governments of East Africa and commercial houses there. He and Elnor had bought a lovely old priest's house in the shadow of Cadbury Castle in Somerset, but she had died of cancer four years before I met Kenneth. Our lives had been so similar and we knew so many of the same people that it was not difficult to conclude that we should go on together.

As he was at this time seventy-four (and I was sixty-two) it seemed to some

Petra with a bronze replica of an Ife head and ebony original of the present Oba of Benin (both Nigerian).

people rather mad to get married; Julia interviewed him but came out the worst; another friend warned me that I would have to go through the trauma of bereavement all over again within five, at the most ten, years. However, we decided to be mad and managed to have twenty-one good years together. We travelled quite extensively, to Mexico for a start, on our honeymoon, where I was mugged and my bag with all my papers in it was taken. This was a good test of how we stood up to emergencies and we both passed to the other's satisfaction.

We escaped unscathed from a fascinating holiday in Peru, where we stayed at first with the New Zealand ambassador and his wife, old friends of mine from Nigeria, and so got one view of the country. Then we borrowed a car and drove along the coast to see the extraordinary Nazca Lines, colossal outlines of birds, fish, animals and geometric patterns, formed simply by clearing stones from the required area; they can only be seen from the air, and as they are thousands of years old the most likely theory is that they were made for the gods to see. Our happy career together was very nearly cut short here because another plane came down just as we were taking off and our plane had to veer to one side of the landing strip; our pilot said you had to keep a sharp eye out for other planes when flying around, as there is no airport control. Strange dolls were being sold which had been retrieved from some of the many ancient graves continually being found, but they smelt rather peculiar and I reckoned would disintegrate once they left the dry atmosphere of this desolate desert area. There was not a vestige of plant or animal life to be seen, though one day I drove inland (against all advice because it was 'dangerous') and did encounter people on horseback bringing herds of goats home from the hills – I saw a little girl jump from a high rock with her legs spread, to land on the back of her sister's horse.

We stayed in a charming, completely isolated, guest house by the sea, where I met Erik von Daniken, a writer who is convinced that the Nazca Lines and a number of other inexplicable things about the world, were made by beings from outer space. I had rather enjoyed his book but he was so awful in person that I had to think again.

One day we took a boat to sea to look at the sea lions which were so attractive, particularly at one spot where masses of them took off from a beach and came tearing out to see us, rearing up out of the water to get a better view, so that we felt the outing was beneficial to both parties. Some were huge, some wee, but none showed fear. It was lovely to see them get out of the water up the smooth rocks, waiting for a wave to give them a lift. Little islands were covered with boobies, Inca terns, three kinds of cormorant, condors and pelicans. We could see some of these birds from our veranda, and also some vile jellyfish which prevented our swimming: enormous, eighteen inches across, two inches thick, red-brown, which lay side by side flat along the shore, and we could see their horrid humps scattered thickly in the sea. Skuas diving for fish were a constant entertainment.

Of course we went to see the Inca town of Machu Picchu, perched on a hilltop, which is very exciting. At the top a little boy begged for money and was very charming, and he met our coach at the bottom, having descended straight through the bushes while we had zigzagged down the road. Lake Titicaca was beautiful and interesting but, the height being 16,000 feet, I suffered from altitude sickness and Kenneth had to go looking for help and oxygen in the middle of the night in a vast hotel in which the electricity had been switched off and there was only one rather elusive man on duty.

When Basil died in 1982 I was left with the responsibility of researching the family history, which we had both been interested in doing but had hardly done. We had two family trees, one English and one Sicilian, to start on, but our father was Irish and our mother half-Hungarian, so there was a lot of ground to cover. More than we thought. Kenneth and I had holidays in Ireland and Hungary, which produced nothing but were very interesting; we found joy in Wales and a little in Sicily, and I had good luck in Malta. Throughout my researches I met with wonderful luck in finding ancestors and stories about them, which is what I wanted. Trees are all very well but very dull – if a person has a title, military, naval or anything, one has a clue but on the English tree we have a succession of Joseph Coates all on the same farm for hundreds of years. I wanted to put flesh on the bones and in the end was able to do so in a book I entitled *Oh Yes We're British* in 1988. We began with one Cerdic, who came from Saxony in a longship in the fifth century and conquered all the land which came to be known as Wessex. The Normans and the Kings of Sicily were direct ancestors. I did not stick to the male line and people were not always legitimate; nevertheless the line is direct. And what fun I had tracing it. Another book had to be written called *Anything But British*, and then surprisingly Julia became interested and found out a lot more by following different lines, and made me a most wonderful framed tree of enormous size and great intricacy, showing the relationship to all the crowned heads of Europe, because, of course, once you get in among them, they are all related! The quest is unending and of constant interest. Even in 2004 I have discovered new facts (and mysteries) about the Norman forebears.

We went frequently to Menorca, twice to Italy, and also to Greece, Egypt and the Dalmatian coast, and I went to Eastern Turkey. In the Adriatic we visited the island of Kocula, its one town straddling the spine of the island. The museum sported a number of interesting objects, the best of which, nestling beside some blue willow-pattern plates, were several sketches by Leonardo da Vinci! There was also a picture of *The Last Supper* with a rather unusual dish of meat in front of Our Lord. I enquired of the guide what it was and he confirmed my worst suspicions: 'Why, it is dog!' he said brightly.

During our marriage we lost a great many members of our families: Kenneth lost his older brother and his stepmother, I lost my brother, both my sisters, and my beloved son, all of cancer. My son's death in 1994 was made worse by his wife disappearing with the three girls, cutting them off from the whole family and all their army friends, and we have not seen or heard from them since. But they say when one door closes, another opens, and I find this has been true in my life. When Basil died, we were able to give his children (by then grown-up) a place they could call home, and the girls spent quite a long time with us and have remained close ever since, despite the fact that both have married foreigners and live abroad. Charlotte was married from our house and two of her children were christened in Aldeburgh. When Pam died in 1996, her family not only missed her for herself, but missed having a granny-figure, and I have been able to fill that position to some extent. Julia has remained my constant, and her family feel very close to me indeed. Contact with all these young people has been very rewarding.

We saw each other through operations (Kenneth's serious heart ones and my two hip replacements). Latterly our annual holiday was a week in a Norfolk hotel, which I greatly looked forward to and Kenneth put up with for

My 85th birthday party when a lot of the family gathered, in December 2003.
What a wind!

my sake. We have had Burmese cats ever since Booby died, two at a time and all such characters and very different. At the word 'walkies' they leap to attention and accompany me round the block. They keep relentlessly to time and keep me amused, frantic, worried and interested. The garden is a joy.

I am still a little bit active in the town. I gave up my job with the Festival when we married but the work itself would not go away and it was only when I had to have hip replacements that I really gave up in 1991. Since then I have ricocheted from the PCC to the Town Council and back again; have been chairman of a Cruse committee; and, since I have had an electric buggy for shopping in the town, have organised a group of buggy-users to take part in the annual fancy dress parade in the Carnival – we were Red Arrows one year, 'Bell's Angels' another, and then Swan Lake, which really made the crowds laugh: me and three men in white tutus, with feathers in our hair and flippers on our feet.

I am alone now, because my dear Kenneth died three years ago at the age of ninety-four, upright and active and mentally very sound, until a stroke took him away from me. It has not been the utter devastation of my first widowhood because we both knew it could not be long, and at our ages death becomes a friend. And I am not often alone either: the young of my own and my brother's and sister's families come and go; I always hope my son's three

'Swan Lake' in the Aldeburgh Carnival, 2003.

girls will return; I have many friends and play mah-jong all day once a week; I occasionally have a group of musicians staying for perhaps a week; there are lectures and concerts and exhibitions; I swim in a private pool three times a week; I knit for a Mother Teresa group and visit friends in residential and nursing homes; and I still plan and make little sorties such as a week or two in Dubai or Saudi Arabia with nieces, in Oman with Arab friends, a trip to Rome to a goddaughter or to Menorca with my daughter, to Lanzarote with a friend, to the D-Day beaches in Normandy with a family party, or to London for a week catching up on various activities and lunches. I have yet to learn how to send e-mails and even how to use my new word processor. Life is never ever dull.

All the same, it is probably time I began to think about the Next World!

Index